Peter Adams has recently retired after battling with a terminal cancer diagnosis. He studied as a mechanical engineer, but his more recent career interests included IT development and digital marketing. His infectious, positive and inspiring attitude has helped him through life's challenges and he will continue to seek opportunities to share his learnings with others.

Peter is not someone who sits still and will always be thinking about new ideas and opportunities. He has become passionate about his photography, and likes sharing what he sees through his lens to encourage us to appreciate our surroundings.

This book is his first publication, but may well not be his last!

This book is dedicated to my Dad who recently lost his own battle with cancer after a hard fight…

Peter Adams

TELL ME WHY...

AUSTIN MACAULEY PUBLISHERS™

LONDON • CAMBRIDGE • NEW YORK • SHARJAH

A CIP catalogue record for this title is available from the British Library.

ISBN 9781398406544 (Paperback)
ISBN 9781398453890 (ePub e-book)

www.austinmacauley.com

First Published 2022
Austin Macauley Publishers Ltd®
1 Canada Square
Canary Wharf
London
E14 5AA

I would really like to thank my wife, Emma, for her tireless support throughout this emotional rollercoaster of a journey. She was always there for me and I felt like we became a formidable team together, standing up against the attack we were now facing. Ben and Katy have grown much more resilient and learnt much about this and themselves during this battle. They have seen the fragility of life and they appreciate more in their lives, seizing every opportunity that life has to offer. Thank you, team Adams!

I have been incredibly inspired by some key individuals as my life took this turn and they helped put sense and context to what I was experiencing and what I was learning. These include Gregg Braden, Joe Dispenza, Bruce Lipton and Aaron Doughty, to name just a few. They each have their area of expertise which complement each of them and they have used their own life experiences to tell their stories and learnings.

I read many books relating to subjects about nutrition, cancer, spirituality and personality. When you combine all of these subjects together, you can begin to see how they all relate to one another and work in harmony. Life is really about harmony within yourself, with others and with circumstances.

Please see the Appendix for suggested good reads!

Table of Contents

Preface

I have written this book to share my journey with you and to highlight all of the learnings and challenges that were experienced along the way. This journey was totally unexpected and this meant that I was then equally unprepared, as many are in these situations. You can quickly feel helpless and hopeless, becoming vulnerable to your own self. The purpose of this book is to give you the hope and empowerment that you need to deal with the journey ahead if you are faced with a life challenge like this, but to also take this opportunity to re-evaluate yourself, your life and how you live it.

I would encourage anyone to get to know your true self better—not the virtual mask you wear in your life or the competition you are having with others, the true you! Everyone will handle things in their own way, with their own knowledge and own levels of courage. Increasing your hope and empowerment in your own journey will be a result of building your own knowledge and confidence within yourself. It is my hope that this book will help you identify the areas you can focus upon and provide you with a head start that many do not have the opportunity or impetus to seek.

Many that I began my cancer journey with are sadly no longer with us and this makes me feel extremely grateful for a renewed opportunity that I now have in living my life with this increased knowledge and wisdom. If I am able to make a difference to anybody's life through this book, then this would make me very happy. I hope you enjoy the read and let's make a difference!

The Storm –
An Analogy of This Experience

I can liken this experience to suddenly going into a storm—unprepared and unaware, you find that you cannot avoid it and didn't even see it coming. You need to quickly understand your risks and dangers. You only have one path to travel so you just hope you have enough resilience and energy to weather the storm and you somehow manage to dodge the flying debris along the way. At this point, you lose touch with everything you knew—your family and friends, your hopes, your dreams, the material things you own. Nothing matters now except you and finding a way out!

In the middle of the storm, you weirdly seem to find a place of complete peace and tranquillity in the midst of all of the uncontrolled chaos. This place allows you to think with utmost clarity, rising above everything so you can see yourself within the storm with mind-blowing perspective. You find some reflective time to examine who you truly are and what you need to do to get out of this alive—you have no other objective at this stage! You can now begin to see new pathways out of the storm that you couldn't see before. At this point, your worrying begins to cease and it is replaced with immense courage and determination. You just know that you have worked out your exit strategy, so you buckle up and remain positive, focused and determined to get out of here!

You are unsure of which path to choose, so you now let your intuition choose the new appearing pathways that feel right for you—you feel drawn to them and you stick to your chosen path no matter what. Some of the pathways are a one-way ticket, so if you realise you have made the wrong turn, it's too late now! You are now more empowered, relieved and hopeful in reaching your point of safety. You begin to feel protected and guided somehow and you trust your intuitive judgements like never before.

You discover that there are signs and clues given to you as you progress these pathways which help you make good decision points at difficult crossroads and they seem to appear at precisely the right time, right in front of you! It feels like you have been in the storm for a long time now and you wonder what has happened to everyone and everything you knew whilst you have spent some significant time fighting it. Occasionally, the storm appeared to subside, but then rages once more, reminding you to not lower your guard just yet! You stay patient and committed to your path despite feeling very isolated and alone. You begin to doubt yourself in whether you have chosen the right path, because it feels so relentless, but your inner self reassures you and you continue to trust your judgements like never before.

Suddenly, you begin to feel the storm clearing—you feel it before you see it and this reinvigorates you. You begin to accelerate to what seems like a finish line in a race, yet there is nothing which defines the 'finish'. You now know you will make it out alive and you keep your head down, remembering you have been through the worst. You lift you head up briefly to check-in with yourself and to judge the progress of the storm. You are astonished to find that you are out of the storm already, but you were so focused you didn't even realise it! You check yourself over and look for any damage—you are cut and bruised, mentally exhausted and have clearly received a battering, but YOU survived the storm! Sadly, others did not. You were with them as the storm began, but they stayed on what seemed like the only path that was available to them. If only they had the courage and curiosity to seek alternatives.

I like this analogy, since the weather can be unpredictable, surprising and merciless. A storm will always clear, but it will destroy anything fragile or weak which I liken to your inner doubts or fears and aspects of you that are not strongly attached to who you truly are as a person. You become resilient to withstand the storm and learn how to survive within it. It will clear the decks and there is always calm after the storm. What is left after a severe storm is usually a levelled ground—a reversion back to nothing but bare bones.

However, there are foundations to build upon and you can rebuild with new wisdom and learning, so that the next storm does not affect you like that again. Others can also learn from you and adopt new strategies in their lives that you have inspired and awoken within them.

I am not the same person that I was entering into the storm and the storm has permanently changed me. I am now a person who truly respects life and appreciates every facet of it. I have let go of my ego and allowed my life to flow, as if I have an inner, intuitive guidance system which I have learnt to trust. I am grateful for every day and have learned how life works and how you can literally make even the most impossible desires become a reality. It is a miracle that I survived this storm, but maybe I was destined to? Maybe the storm was sent to teach me a lesson about myself and help me see life in a whole new perspective, appreciating aspects of it that I had not acknowledged!

I believe miracles are meant to happen in life and this one will hopefully inspire others to be strong and trust their intuition in life when challenges strike, and they will strike! There may be more storms ahead, but they will just be another challenge to overcome—you are more resilient than you will ever know so keep the faith.

The Beginning

My life started on Friday 28 July 1972 at 7 pm in Cheltenham, UK. I was my parents' first child and I kind of liked the fact that I was the eldest. Apparently, I didn't want to come into this world too easily and with all the pulling and tugging to extract me, I looked more like an alien with a cone-shaped head. Maybe I am an alien and this was my normal head shape! Being born when I was made me a Leo star sign in the world of astrology—I liked what this star sign represents and felt that my attributes were certainly aligned to them!

My parents met when they were teenagers and had made their life together in Cheltenham—a place that neither of them were from. They grew up in Grantham and lived only a few doors away from each other. However, they chose Cheltenham because they liked the area and the surrounding hills, which I can appreciate. However, my Dad was frequently changing what he was doing at the time and we soon moved to Melton Mowbray when I was pretty young, because of this.

By this time, my brother had appeared on the scene and we were both in tow now. The benefit of living in this location was that my grandparents were only half an hour away and we used to often see them at weekends, taking a bus from the town centre. My Mum didn't drive and my Dad was usually busy doing other things. I loved seeing both my grandparents and we would sometimes sleepover. It was tricky sharing time between them though.

My Grandma on my Mum's side was on her own—I never met my Grandad, since he sadly died not long before I was born. My Grandma used to manage the little local post-office and did so until she died at the age of 83. I think this is where I got my stationery fetish from—she had endless supplies of pens, pencils, paper and rubbers. I was forever drawing and designing things when I was young and that trait has stayed with me throughout my life. She inspired me a great deal looking back and it made me super determined to succeed in my life.

My grandparents on my Dad's side were your classic grandparents. Neither of them could drive, but they used to take us to all sorts of places on the train. I liked our little adventures with them and they were attentive to mine and my brother's needs, despite our devilish behaviour at times.

I started my first school in Melton Mowbray and have most of my early memories from here. We lived outside of the town and had access to walks that we used to do after lunch on Sundays. We had a good garden and my brother and I had a tree each at the bottom of the garden. They were great to climb, at least when I wasn't trying to cut mine down with my Dad's axe that I found in the shed! I used to catch the bus from the bottom of our road to school and felt quite responsible. Looking back on these times, I am not sure how anyone would know if I got there or not, but it was always ok. Funny how we so rely on phones and tracking each other nowadays! If you're offline for one minute now, you're considered in trouble!

I quite liked my school here, but only spent a couple of years there because my Dad was off again! Whilst I was at this school, I did manage to do all my gymnastics BAGA awards and found that I had an innate flexibility and considered it as one of my super-powers as a kid! I enjoyed doing this and it kept me motivated to continue doing things that would benefit from this later in my childhood, like martial arts.

I recall starting to feel like I was coming into my own from the age of about seven. I remember being able imagine and draw things that seemed beyond my years and was constantly making things with whatever I could find—cardboard, Sellotape, Lego, etc. At this age, I made a slide projector and my own slides to deliver a slideshow to my grandparents when they came over. I was ultra-curious as a young child and needed to know how everything worked so I could replicate and learn from them, like reverse engineering.

Unfortunately, this often meant taking things apart and not being able to reassemble everything completely again—who needs the leftover spare parts anyway! Well, people always say that those who keep trying and failing learn the most! I recall being very optimistic and had this inner confidence and knowing as a child, yet felt like I should hold myself back from learning too much too quickly, since I would alienate myself from the other kids my age.

On reflection, that was probably quite a mature thought process for a kid. I used to frequently question whether I was in fact 'normal' as a child, because I just wasn't your mainstream. I thrived on learning stuff and dreaming up my next inventions. I remember when anyone asked me what I want to be when I grow up, I would say an Inventor or a car designer. I was passionate about both and still am to be honest! I cannot explain this instinctive drive that I had within me from this early age—pushing me, motivating me and making me think outside of the box. I was definitely not your typical child and probably made it a rough ride for my parents, because they weren't prepared for my energy-bursting mind!

I can actually hear my Mum telling me not to be so ambitious as I am writing this now. That was a frequent piece of advice, but this only motivated me to be more ambitious, unfortunately for her—why should the stars be out of reach for me? This is where the title of this book reflects the questioning that so began everything in my life—well, in fact, life in general… Tell Me Why…? These simple three words inspire so many questions, which is why I like it. "Tell me why I cannot achieve my dreams?", "Tell me why we are on this Earth?"—it can get quite profound, can't it!

Mum and Dad had decided to move again, so we all had to leave what we ever really knew about our lives—where we lived, our friends and our garden with our own trees. It was a sad time, but there was a little sense of adventure because I am sure Mum and Dad had only half planned what they were doing next. The rest, well… let's just see!

We ended up in Cheltenham, back to where I was born, ironically. I think my parents were drawn to this area and wanted to find any excuse to move back there. There are great hills to walk and long views around all of this area. Mum and Dad had a few friends they had made here and one owned a shop on the outskirts of the town which had a sort of living space above it. My Dad was helping them renovate the shop and, in return, they let us occupy this living space until we found somewhere more permanent to live. Myself and my brother had to go to another local school and start making friends again, but we had no idea how much effort to put into this, since we may move again in a few months.

Anyway, it was for quite a while and I got settled into the new school, but found it hard to make friends through fear of losing them again. It's also not ideal joining a school part way through the typical five-year period because friendship groups are usually already established and you have to fit into one, rather be part of the forming process. I was quite a lonely child during this time and kept myself to myself. The kids were different to those I was used to and wasn't sure whether I resonated with them or not.

After about a year of this, we finally found a house, but not in Cheltenham. This meant another new area and hence, a new school…doh! The house was about half an hour drive away in Stroud and whilst it was exciting to have our own house again, you can imagine how I felt about this. We moved in when I was about 8 and I liked the aspect of the house. It had 3 levels and was built into the hillside. The front door entered into the first floor, where our lounge was, then you go downstairs to an open dining room and kitchen.

The house only had two bedrooms, so my brother and I would be sharing again. Having my own room was just a pipe-dream for me. The bedrooms were on top floor, but there was only one toilet in the bathroom, which was located on the ground floor. This was a long and scary walk at night if you needed the loo, I can tell you! The house had great views across the valleys and we could watch some amazing sunrises from this vantage point.

Looking out of the window felt like you were flying and I remember launching many paper airplanes from the upstairs window to see how far they could fly. I was probably the biggest litterbug in the area because of this and I remember trying to find the largest pieces of paper I could find to make bigger and bigger planes! Always testing the limits!

We hadn't been moved in long and had yet to have curtains in some of the living rooms. My dad was always up at the crack of dawn and one morning he woke us up at about 5:30am. I wondered what an earth was going on. He sounded both excited and slightly concerned in his voice and I was trying to imagine what he wanted us to know as I was slowly waking up. He said, "There's a big U shape in the sky—just hanging there!" I wasn't sure if I was dreaming, because it didn't sound very normal. My brother and I made our way down to the lounge where the back window overlooked the valley and the hill on the other side. I couldn't believe what I was seeing!

Dad was right, there was a big, black and bold 'U' shape sitting slightly tilted to one side above the hill opposite from our house. It was motionless and must have been enormous judging by how far away it was. We couldn't work it out. It wasn't like anything any of us had seen before. It was perfectly still and could not have been anything inflatable or powered by conventional propulsion. It appeared very solid and unwavering.

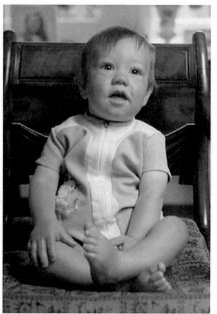

Baby me

Me and Dad in the car

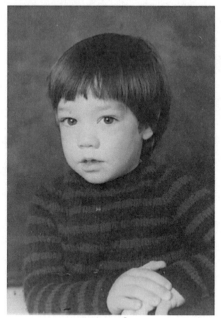

Age 3

Always wanting to go!

Me, Mum and my Grandma

Photographer — Age 10

Summer Job

First Car – Ford Escort

My dad had always made and flown radio-controlled models from a young age and had a very good set of eyes for the skies! My eyes were also pretty good and not much got past me in the sky! He knew what he was looking at and none of us could make sense of what we were witnessing. It was a clear, cloudless morning and the sun had not yet risen. We had no film in our camera and one of us went to get the binoculars and dropped them in the rush, damaging them.

Jeez, that is so typical, isn't it! Just think, nowadays, we would be live streaming it on our phones! Anyway, we accepted the situation and took in as much as we could about the position, size, orientation, etc., and sketched it out for future reference. My dad rang the local airbase to see if they had anything on their radar, but nothing was reported.

Wow, this is proper sci-fi stuff, I thought. We felt blessed to have been able to witness this unusual sight, yet we weren't sure what to do. We had nothing to benchmark it against other than planes and helicopters, of which this was certainly neither. There were often military planes flying over our house from this opposite hill direction, so plane profiles in this sky were pretty familiar to us. I recall feeling a little scared in thinking that it can probably see us looking at it and what might it do as a result. No sooner had that thought entered my mind, it began to right itself to an upright position and then slowly began to descend until it was out of sight behind the hill. It did this over about 5-10 minutes and there were no sounds, vapour trails, ropes or anything else visible—this was literally out of this world.

We chatted excitedly together afterwards and we were trying to think of some rational explanations for what we had just seen, but we had nothing to offer! As we gathered ourselves a little, the sky became noticeably cloudier and the clouds were moving a fair pace, so it must have been quite a windy morning. As we looked out at the hill wondering where the object may have landed, a bright orange light suddenly emerged and descended from a moving cloud that was closest to the hilltop and then disappeared out of sight behind the hill, just to one side of where the 'U' shape was seen. This light was bigger, brighter and more orange than any aircraft headlight we had witnessed and was not moving in a conventional aircraft manner.

Dad was straight on the phone with the local airbase again! No, nothing seen on radar and they didn't appear to be interested either. I know now that they have protocols when things like this happen and it is certainly not broadcasted! We were dumb struck. We just saw two UFOs in quick succession and had no idea what they were, where they went and what they were doing! They appeared to have landed somewhere too! The top of the hill opposite is a good few miles away, as the crow flies, and it is mainly covered in woodland. I sure as hell wasn't going up there to search!

Mum and Dad weren't sure what to do and they called the police. They weren't interested either and probably thought we were a bunch of loonies. They eventually found a UFO investigation society based in Bristol and they were very keen to come and take a look. They took this seriously and came to our house to interview us and then we all got in our vehicles and drove up to the hillside across the valley. It was very eerie! There was nobody about in that area and very few roads. We parked as far into the woodland as we could and just began looking and listening. They had some meters and stuff, but was not sure what they were measuring—radiation, most likely. There was a spooky silence that hung over the area, as if it was deliberate.

We wandered around for a couple of hours or so, it seemed, but nothing was found. We couldn't work out how far away the objects were from a vantage point of our house, so it was difficult to know where they landed. The investigators took lots of photos and documented everything and then left us, saying, "We will be in touch if we find anything out." We knew they wouldn't, but we couldn't do anymore ourselves! It was an amazing experience though and it was like living in a real sci-fi adventure on our back doorstep! I was eight years old at the time and from that day, I knew we were not alone in this universe and my interest into other worldly civilisations began! There were things that science we know certainly could not explain and that made me so, so curious.

Coming back to Earth, we managed to get into the local primary school, which was just over a mile walk from our new home. This was quite a walk there and back and Mum and Dad wouldn't let us bike there because it had the steepest final descent downhill that I had I seen to get to the school. Myself and my brother joined into existing classes and again got acquainted to new surroundings, new people, new friends and new teachers.

I tried hard at this school and put effort into my work. They even had a couple of BBC computers, which gave us a taste of what potentials these might provide in the future. We could not imagine at that time, how prolific and dependent we all are with computers now…it is like our life has been taken over by them! I got involved with the photography club at this school where we would go out and take photos on 35mm film, then develop the negatives and photos in a dark room that was created for us.

There were only a few of us in this 'club', but it started my fascination with photography and capturing moments on film that can be enjoyed later. I recall getting a flip camera for one of my birthdays so I could snap away when we went to various places. We had to conserve the film though and use it for 'special' days because it cost a fortune to buy film and process the photos. A huge contrast to today where our limits are usually how much our phones or memory cards will store!

From this age, I began to find myself being bullied by others in the school. I reckoned that this was because I wasn't your mainstream kid and my previous hunch about this had now become a reality. I was often punched, kicked and given verbal abuse. I just put this down to me being a little different with the interests I had, the effort and diligence I put into my school work and the fact I joined the school midway. However, I was not going to change for anybody and used my articulated vocabulary to respond back to them. I knew this would wind them up, but it also and importantly demonstrated that their actions will not affect me in anyway. Having said that, it did frequently worry me that they may gang up on me. I had simply been me, but that was enough for them to justify their abuse towards me. I didn't have many real friends during school and probably stuck close to only one or two.

After this school, I moved to a secondary school which was about 5 miles from home in the other direction. It was a long trek of a walk down to the bottom of the valley to catch the bus to school. The bus would wind through the valley picking the others up and then wind slowly up another steep hill to the school. I liked the equipment this school had in science labs, wood work shop and metal work room. They had drawing boards for design work and a computer room! It was like heaven for me and couldn't wait to get stuck in! It even had a heated outdoor pool so felt lucky to have this available for the next 5 years.

I worked a daily evening paper round during much of my schooling, which gave me a whopping £13 a week! That was pretty good back then and I liked the responsibility of collecting the monies and delivering it to the office once a week. The downside of this paper round was the fact that I would have to pick up the newspapers from the post office at the bottom of the hill and lug them all the way up to home and then distribute them.

Thursdays were the worst, because this was 'supplements' day and the bag was 3 times as heavy than normal! If I lived on an estate, the 30 or so papers could be done in 10 mins, but I lived in the hilly Cotswolds with a lot of long driveways and hills to navigate. This was another fitness opportunity for me though, so I embraced it and got on with it.

During my time at this school, I found I could further progress my creative side and learn more about new subjects I would resonate with. I loved the designing and making subjects of course, but also seemed to gel with French and English. I was fortunate enough to spend two weeks in two consecutive years doing French exchanges. Now, you would think that exchange means you share the responsibility of being with a French family and then reciprocate this by having the French guy over to stay in the UK in your house.

Well, my Dad didn't want any of that, so I was in an awkward position of wanting to go to stay with the French family, but not be able to entertain them in return. Anyway, somehow it was made possible and I managed to go on these trips without reciprocating! I really loved them and they really helped my language development at the time. I remember having my head buried in phrase books, looking for any opportunities to engage with real French people instead of listening to crappy, rehearsed voices on a tape in the classroom!

There was that time when I returned back to school from a recent exchange and everyone's parents were waiting for their kids. All of them, except mine… I stood lonely and patiently as I watched the family re-unions of everyone. Where were my parents? I felt embarrassed and neglected. I didn't need any more reasons to be picked on, did I! Eventually, one of caretakers managed to make contact with my parents at home and they eventually got on their way up to meet me.

I continued to be bullied at this school too, for reasons that I outlined before, I assume. My Dad wasn't working at this time and for this reason, I had to collect a free meal ticket from the front office every morning. This was embarrassing, because everyone knew what that queue meant! It was another label I didn't need in this new world of harassment. To this day, I don't truly know why I was picked on but, as before, I did not change for anyone!

Whilst I was at school, I started to do martial arts—Tae Kwon Do. I found really drawn to the discipline, the flexibility and the obvious defence moves that we learnt. I found that I was quite good at it and it felt pretty natural, like I was born to do this! I applied my flexibility I had discovered as a younger child and

I could kick higher than anyone and was very quick and agile. I was now practising this art like one of my idols, Bruce Lee. I took my training seriously and used to bike to and from my training for extra leg work! I progressed through a number of belts while with this club and felt like I could properly protect myself now.

Talking about my bike—I used to bike everywhere! One reason was that my Dad didn't ever give lifts and the other was that I was really into cycling—racing cycling mainly. When I was about 16, I ordered lots of components to make a racing bike—I had a catalogue and saved up £800 to buy a bespoke, customised frame, gears, brakes, wheels, etc. I built the bike myself and used to go out some Sundays with a racing club in Cheltenham. Cheltenham again! Why is everything there now I am here!

I used to cycle up and down the 15 hilly miles to Cheltenham to then a fast ride of 80 or so miles and then cycle another 15 miles home. I was very fit at this time and I felt pretty invincible on my bike! I remember the road down the hill into Cheltenham has a 30mph speed limit at the bottom and I was desperate to get caught speeding as I entered this limit. It must be a boy thing! I was a big risk taker in my younger years and I think I did well to survive my childhood to be honest! Anyway, the fastest entry speed I got at this 30mph limit was 56mph! I would overtake cars on way down and felt I had a seemingly endless supply of power and determination—my only restriction was how quickly my pedals could go around!

There was a time when I had stayed at a friend's house about 5 miles from home and biked back the next morning. It was a Sunday morning and it was about 10am. The roads were quiet and not many people around just yet. I had a good route back along a canal towpath, so avoided the roads for much of the journey. I was on my mountain bike and was feeling full of energy whilst biking along the towpath. It was a familiar route and I knew where all the little opportunities were to get some air off little ramps from rocks or curb stones. I was approaching one where there was a narrow access road going across the towpath and the raised tarmac had formed a great ramp.

Nobody usually drove down this access road, especially on a Sunday morning. I began accelerating hard and was approaching the little ramp section at about 35mph. I remember lifting off it into the air and then all I remember is seeing white and then nothing! I was out cold! I came around some hours later and found myself in a hospital in Gloucester. What the hell happened. I couldn't fathom it out and my body was hurting all over. I checked to see if I still had my limbs and everything seemed to be intact—that was a huge relief! My ribs hurt and my head was throbbing.

A nurse had seen me rouse and came over to see how I was. "Hello," she said. "You've been in the wars, haven't you?" she continued.

"What happened to me?" I asked. I had a missing block of time of about 5 hours and have no idea why. The nurse told me what she knew and I felt that I would need to ask a few more questions from others to find out the full extent of all of this. It turned out that I hit a white van! My bike had ploughed into the passenger door and my head smashed against the door mirror and then the side of the van as we both continued moving in different directions—me into it and the van still moving forwards.

I could only imagine the blood spatter on the white van as my head was cut open in the process. It would have looked pretty grim, since I must have got knocked out and lay unconscious on the floor, tangled with my bike in a pool of blood! I later discovered that a friend was doing work experience with the police at that time and he attended the scene, poor chap! I was lucky to be alive and it was before a time when everyone really wore helmets on their bikes. I had only fractured a rib and they had stitched the cut on my head.

I eventually managed to get out of my bed to go to the toilet and when I looked in the mirror, I didn't recognise myself! My head was all deformed and swollen on one side, I had black eyes and I could barely see out of one of them. I was re-assured that the swelling would go down over a week or so, so not to worry. I couldn't help but worry though—I looked terrible! Mum and Dad came into see me and they had a look of relief on their faces. I am not sure what they expected to find to be honest and didn't like the fact that I had put them through this trauma. After a few days, I was allowed home and many of my classmates even came in to see me before I was discharged—it was nice to feel their support, which was totally unexpected!

I finished school in 1988 and was the first wave of pupils to do GCSEs—a new UK-wide assessment scheme for certificate grading. Nobody seemed to really know what to do, even the teachers, but it worked out ok and I got enough decent grades to get into my next phase. I didn't fancy sixth form, which is the usual next phase at schools in UK. I knew I wanted to do something like engineering, where I could combine maths, science, design and project management. I felt that it was the right direction for me, given my interests and aptitude.

I decided to do a mechanical engineering diploma back in Cheltenham, so had to catch the bus there and back for a couple of years. It was great doing something specific now and honing in on what my career could entail in the future. The ride back home from Cheltenham on a slow double decker bus often sent me to sleep with the droning engine, crawling up the hills. There were regulars on the bus, so we soon got to know each other and share our stories from the day! The college treated us more like adults and the bullying stopped! It was around this time when Mum and Dad got divorced.

I was about sixteen at the time and it was sad to see my Dad have to leave the family house. He had found a flat in a converted roof of a big old building about half a mile down the lane. I was glad he wasn't far away, but he hadn't taken the divorce too well and it all seemed a surprise to him as much as myself. After he had left, I was constantly reminded by all the things he had done to the house and the garden that he had had to leave behind. Ironically though, I actually saw more of my Dad after this than I did when he was at home. I often visited him and chatted to him about all sorts of things.

During this period, I had 3 or 4 close friends and we used to do a lot together. One of them had a car by this time, so this opened up our options! We started going to nightclubs and got a taste for this night-life thing. Nothing happened in Stroud—it only had a pool, but no cinema, no nightclub, no McDonald's or anything for the teenagers! We used to go to different night clubs from Cheltenham to Swindon, but that became a bit boring after a while. It was the same thing every time and we couldn't chat! Between us, we had a few contacts and started going to house parties—they were all the rage in the early 90s and there was always someone having a party if you wanted it!

We started going to a few local parties as 'newbies' and found ourselves invited to lots more…we felt pretty popular and this was quite refreshing for me after having been a bit of a reject during my school years. I felt accepted for who I was and it was a turning point, in some respects, for my outer confidence. We found that most of our party invites were from the local girl's sixth form school pupils, so this was a bonus as teenage boys! We got to know lots of new people and this opened up a new world for us.

During this period, I was told I had a stalker following me. Apparently, this stalker would often follow me off the bus from college, into town and even delivered leaflets to my house! I felt both privileged and worried. Who was it? What did they want? I tried to remain vigilant, but wasn't aware of anything obvious. It wasn't until we found ourselves at another house party that I discovered my stalker was someone from the girl's school called Emma.

She belonged to another group of girls we had not yet connected with, but she had got to know about me through the others, I guess. Wow, I have never had a stalker before! Was she a crazy girl? I was intrigued to get to know more about her. We spent most of the party together after we were literally pushed together by our friends! Following this impromptu meeting at the party, we became inseparable. I knew in this moment, that I had met my soul mate, my forever friend and someone I wanted to spend the rest of my life with.

Emma was almost exactly one year younger than me with our birthdays only 3 days apart. She was another Leo star sign, so two fiery characters—we were a force to be reckoned with! Emma was still doing her A-Levels at school and wanted to pursue a career in nursing. Having now met Emma, I didn't want to zip off to university straight away so when I finished my diploma, I got a job at a local engineering firm who were an engine bearings supplier for the aerospace industry.

I worked as a jig and tool designer in their drawing office and received a decent income as a result. It helped develop my practical engineering skills and we were still using drawing boards and ink at that time. Computers were coming in for CAD, but these were for niche work only and you had to be pretty special to use them!

I had managed to pass my driving test during this time and get my first car— a Ford Escort! It was a new amazing feeling to have your own car and go anywhere you want at any time—your only limit was how much money you had for fuel! Emma and I used to drive to all sorts of places, finding our new freedom. We met in March and Emma was going to be on holiday with her family on the French coast in the Summer. We both felt like this was going to be a long time apart for us both, so we tried to work out how we could manage it!

I had spent quite a few summers cycling and camping around northern France with my mum and brother. We never had much money growing up, so these were great opportunities to see another country on a budget, see some sunshine and practise our French. Dad didn't ever come with us and just stayed at home. Not sure whether he wanted to or not—he didn't really seem to be involved in many of things we did looking back. He had his own hobbies, which he seemed to prioritise. So, coming back to the point of this—I was used to cycling in France and thought I could partly cycle and partly travel by train to meet Emma and her family on the West Coast of France.

Everyone seemed happy for me to do this and I got on and booked my ferry and trains. I arrived into France with my bike with panniers loaded up and cycled to the nearest main train station to travel the main chunk of distance down to mid-France. Not many seemed to speak much English and I found I had to properly use my French—it feels different when you have to use it versus can choose to use it and always fall back to English when you fail! I eventually found out that my bike would have to go on a different train to me and I would have to collect my bike from another main station in Rennes using a ticket they gave me.

Well, this was a bit of spoiler for my plans, but it was the only way and went with it. These were the days when we didn't have mobile phones, so I couldn't communicate with anyone I was meeting to let them know what I was now having to do. I was still on schedule for rendezvous, so I didn't worry myself about it. I waved goodbye to my bike, not expecting to see it again, and caught the train down. It was one of the fast TGV trains so was keen to see how it felt to go fast!

My expectations were soon slammed as we found most of the journey was having to made between 0-30mph due to fires in many of the fields adjacent to the train tracks. It must have been a hot period and many fires like this were around. Whilst we were still making some sort of progress on the journey, my bike was probably way ahead of schedule going a different route and I was becoming more and more delayed in getting to my destination. I couldn't call ahead or make any contact from the train! I was totally trapped and felt helpless in doing anything about my situation.

The train took most of the night to get to the final destination in the end, when I should have arrived late evening. I didn't want to delay myself any more when I finally got off the train in the early hours of the next day. Instead of trying to sort getting my bike, I jumped in a taxi and got to Emma's campsite as soon as I could. They were very relieved to see me I must say! They had been extremely worried and were already looking in ditches for me! I felt so awful about putting stress upon them like this, but was totally unable to communicate with them. If only we had mobile phones back then, hey!

The holiday was great and it was so refreshing doing a family holiday on the beach—I had never really experienced these types of holidays and Emma's family made me feel really welcome, despite them not knowing much about me at all! At the end of the holiday, the family gave me a lift to the station where my bike was so I can get my way back home again. Emma's dad then offered to stick my bike on their roof rack and join them back to the ferry terminal. How could I resist? It would mean I wouldn't have all the train and bike complications again—I was so grateful!

So, I squeezed into the back seats with Emma and her younger brother. It was good to experience the drive back on the seemingly empty French roads. I had really got to know Emma's family over the holiday and they learned more about me and I re-assured them that I was not some crazy person stealing their daughter from them. In fact, I think they quite liked me—I can be polite and charming sometimes, you know!

We soon got to the point in time where we had to enter our next phase of education—this learning business never seems to stop! I was off to a University in Hatfield and Emma was off to her Nursing College in Hillingdon. Emma and I made a pact that if we get through University and are still together, then this is a great test of our integrity and commitment to each other. I sold my car before I left because I was not going to have enough money to keep that going too. We did find a coach service that stopped almost at my door in Hatfield and at Emma's door in Hillingdon. We used this coach most weekends and took it in turns to see each other in our respective accommodation.

My first year accommodation was in some sort of prison block portacabin. You could hear everything through the thin walls which would flex a good couple of inches between rooms. My room was tiny and only room for bed and desk really! Emma had a larger room of solid brick walls, so it was always my preference to go there! I soon got a job at my local shopping centre at a Goldsmiths jewellers in Hatfield's Galleria. I worked part-time hours around my thirty-five hour degree curriculum and enjoyed the contrast of this to my coursework! It was funny that I worked part-time, yet used to sell more than the fulltime staff.

Christmases were great there because all the suppliers would offer incentives for highest sales. I used to sell anything from bespoke diamond rings to Rolex watches or posh pens! I often won watches, pens and vouchers for highest sales—it was easy work and rewarding too. I was earning quite a bit from this job now and managed to buy a car. Another Ford, but an Orion Ghia this time. It had electric everything and was quite the car back in the day! It looks pretty crap now though. No more buses and easier shopping trips here we come! I had found a University club that did martial arts. It wasn't Tae Kwon do, but another kung fu called 'Zu Wei'. I was keen to try it out and see what I thought. I enrolled and joined a group of about twenty of us, trained by some sixth Dan Iranian guy who used to train the army.

He was a black cab driver during the day! He was crazy and used to get us to do stupid things like run around a large circle in opposite directions and crash into each other head on as well as line us all up on the floor on our backs and he would run across our stomachs! It certainly toughened us up! We had crazy assault courses where we would have to jump over things, crawl under things, kick things, fight others with sticks and knifes! I enjoyed it though and it kept me fit and supple while I was at University.

During my 3rd year, I had a year in industry and got a great intern job at Millbrook Proving Ground in Bedfordshire. Myself and another chap both got a role there, so we rented a cheap house in Luton together. I had taken a massive pay cut though from my Goldsmiths job because Millbrook were only paying £50 a week—they were taking the micky out of us! However, the experience was well worth it! I worked on all sorts of projects involving prototype cars and new model launch videos. I was in heaven! It was a well renowned place in the automotive industry and I could see myself working there after my degree.

I went back to University to complete my final 4th year and dissertation, which tied in well with Emma's course finish time too. It was a tough University year with a heavy workload. We had a huge computer centre at this University, but I had managed to get a cheap PC built and was able to sit in my room and work. I only needed to go to the computer centre when I needed to print things, so batched this up. I would have to log on to one of their PCs and join the long, long print queue with everyone else. I soon found that they hadn't got any protection over this queue and was able to pause everyone above me so I jump to top of the queue—that was a handy secret I kept to myself! I can't say I always remembered to un-pause everyone afterwards—they are probably still waiting!

Before we had finished University, Emma and I talked about where we could work and live. I had often driven past a large BP office building in Uxbridge and dreamt of working for a big, global corporation like that one day. It looked intriguing and was fascinated in what engineering opportunities could be available. However, I really liked the work I did at Millbrook and they actually offered me a conditional position upon graduating. This was great and gave us some stability of income if nothing else.

Emma looked at local hospitals and managed to get a job in Milton Keynes Hospital. Millbrook was only 30 mins drive from Milton Keynes so we decided to look for a place to live here. Before either of us had finished our courses, we were house shopping—this was even more exciting than getting a car. I couldn't believe we were in a position to buy a house already. We found a new-build on the far west side of Milton Keynes—a two bed semi with a garage and driveway at the end of a cul-de-sac.

We were so lucky to find this and we put a small deposit down to secure it. I managed to arrange the mortgage in advance after a bit of negotiating with the bank—I had the job in the pipeline, but hadn't started yet! Wow, we suddenly got a brand-new house and brand-new jobs—we were living the dream!

We moved into the house in 1995 after spending a bit of time in some dodgy nursing accommodation near the Hospital. That was an experience for sure and would frequently have a face appear at our upstairs window where someone would be climbing the adjacent street lamp! We were now engaged too, so planning a wedding for the following year. Things had moved quickly for us all of a sudden and we settled into our new lives with excitement and anticipation for our future together.

The first year in our house went quickly with our new jobs, new life and discovering the area we now called home. I was enjoying my new job and found I had much to offer already. I had my University thesis published as a paper and journal article and I was off to Florence, Italy, to present it to a science and engineering conference. This was my first business trip and had only just started my job—I was pretty excited! My thesis was about a mathematical model for turbocharger matching, which enabled you to find the optimum turbocharger design size for your engine for a desired power and torque output, for those who were curious (not many I reckon!).

We were planning our wedding for 1996 and this was another exciting chapter in our lives. Unfortunately, my Grandma, who was still working, died suddenly and then so did my Grandad on my Dad's side. I couldn't believe this happened so suddenly and at the same time! They won't see us on our wedding day now and I was gutted that I hadn't seen them before they passed—it all happened unexpectedly. I so wanted them to see our day and to enjoy meeting all our friends and families.

I had always looked up to my Grandma in admiration—she had lived alone for some time and still worked, still drove, still travelled internationally and had a great ethic about her. She inspired me a lot and I still often think of her when I meet challenging times or achieve something she would have been proud of and understood! My Grandad made me laugh and I enjoyed spending time with him either on his allotment, watching the wrestling or out walking in the hills—he was quite an outdoors person and had worked hard all his life. My Grandma was never the same after he died and soon got dementia and eventually forgot who we were over time. A sad time, which too many families face.

I had got our car washed and waxed a few days before the wedding, so it was ready for post wedding travels. I was a bit OCD about my cars and keeping them clean—they always seemed to drive better when they were clean and I looked after them impeccably. During my last day at work before the wedding, I found that my mates at work had managed to completely fill the inside of my newly clean car with shredded paper through the sunroof! It was jam packed right to the top and it took an age to empty—the stuff seemed to triple in size once it was out and I was creating a huge mountain of paper next to my car! It was pretty funny, but I was a bit miffed because I had spent some time getting car clean for our big day!

Our big day had finally arrived—it was 24 August 1996 at last! We were married at our local church and as we exited for photographs, the heavens opened and down came the rain. Well, that's probably about right for a summer's August day in UK. It was impossible to do our photos in the church grounds, so we did them inside and then waited as long as we could for the rain to die down. We then clambered into our vintage Rolls Royce wedding car and pootled along the narrow lanes to our reception venue. The rain had stopped by this time, so there was time to capture some outdoors photos of everyone now in the grounds!

It was mind-blowing seeing so many friends and families together in one place—we felt very humbled that all these people were here because of us! It was a fantastic day and one we will remember forever. We feel like we haven't changed much since then, but many of the children at our wedding are now grown adults and have children of their own! We honeymooned in Barbados and this was such an indulgence for us. Neither of us had been anywhere tropical before, so we felt really fortunate and were excited about the experience.

We had a lovely corner balcony room, overlooking the beach and the pool. They had spread rose petals on the bed and gave us a nice bottle of champagne.

It was such a relaxing holiday and we rented a Mini Moke to get us around. We managed to do a full circuit of the island in one day—each coastline in the North, East, South and West is so different! We caught the edges of a passing hurricane, which was an experience! The level of the rain and wind was just something we had never seen before—not sure how those trees stayed standing. We got caught in an absolute downpour whilst driving the Moke and by the time we stopped and put the hood up, the rain had stopped! We made some good memories on this holiday and it was a great start to our new life together.

Our first child, Ben, arrived in 1998—he is quite proud of the fact he is a 90s baby and born in the previous century. Ben's arrival certainly put everything in life in perspective for me. No matter what problems you had at work, what tasks you were stacking up and what money worries you had—nothing, but nothing can be as important as your own flesh and blood family. I felt immensely proud to now have a son and we were one of the first in our friendship group to get married and have a child.

This was brand new territory and we felt ready for it—everything was seemingly slotting into place and our lives had some kind of flow to it. However, Ben was not a good sleeper at night and this was a particular challenge I will also never forget. It took about 18 months before he went through the night—he was some kind of night owl!

Not long after Ben was born, we decided to move. We loved our house, but the housing market was moving quickly and house prices kept going up and up. We found a nice 3-bed detached house just in the next estate and it was another new build, so we could choose our décor. It had a big, flat and sunny garden which would be great in the summer. It was here that Katy arrived into the world in 2000. She was funny, feisty and determined—not a lot has changed in this respect! She was sleeping through the night by 5 weeks and running before she was one and seemed to skip the walking bit.

We were now a complete family… Emma had always wanted more children, but that was before she had experienced having them! We were a great family unit and supported each other through any difficult times. I had joined a local Tae-Kwon Do club to resume my martial arts again. It wasn't far away and trained at least twice a week with some great people. I progressed up to black level here and we did a few competitions within the UK. As the kids got older, demands increased and we had to adjust ourselves accordingly.

As a result, I decided to quit Tae-Kwon Do as I was also finding that work trips were disrupting my training. This was an era when mobile phones were introduced and I had a work phone—Nokia brick with a battery that lasted almost a week! The kids soon wanted phones as they got to about 8 years old. It didn't seem long until Ben and Katy were at school and discovering what they liked or, more importantly, didn't like about it all.

Ben was fully into BMX, skating, skateboarding, snowboarding and scooters as he grew up and had a good balance of this with his PlayStation. He was about age 14 when he got his first job was at our local, indoor ski centre where he used to work in the café and help with parties. He was too young to be paid, so they gave him free slope time for his snowboarding—he absolutely loved this.

Katy spent much of her childhood doing gymnastics and competing nationally and later, becoming a trainer too at age 13—she enjoyed the challenge. We seemed to spend much of their childhood as taxi drivers for all the activities they were into, which I am sure is the same for anyone with kids these days. There is so much opportunity for kids nowadays and it was a stark contrast to my era when I was just glad to have my bike to keep me satisfied!

We only lived in our new house for a couple of years and found that if we didn't make our next move now, we wouldn't actually be able to afford the next jump in our house evolution! The housing market was moving fast out of everyone's reach. We found a new area being developed next to woods and fields on the far west of Milton Keynes. We kept moving west as the edge of the city kept moving! It was very quiet and had a nice character to it. The houses were larger and more spaced out.

Yes, it was another new build and we watched the stages of it being built with the kids. It was exciting for them and this had an even bigger garden than our current house. It was a detached house with double garage and on a tree lined avenue. We had fields opposite and it felt like this would be our last move for a long time, because we had everything we needed. We felt very privileged to be able to own a house like this! We moved in Dec 2001, just a few days before Christmas, so you can imagine the chaos!

It felt so spacious and the kids seemed very happy here. We still live in the house now and the kids have lived most of their lives here. The house has evolved and adapted as our needs changed and we added bits on and converted other sections. It is a bespoke house now and we feel very safe and at home here.

Needless to say, the fields we looked onto were soon sold and built on, which was a bit disappointing as we didn't expect it.

I was still working at Millbrook and found that I wasn't able to progress as quickly as I wanted to, career wise. I had commissioned their brand new engine test lab and was managing the operations and big client programs. This was a whole new business for Millbrook and it was exciting to be responsible in its creation and subsequent marketing. I really enjoyed this work, but I couldn't move upwards until someone else moved—it was like one of those puzzles. I remember having a frank conversation with the MD and he wasn't able to change anything soon—it was a tough period in the auto industry.

I walked back to my desk feeling a little disheartened, pondering what I could do next. I didn't fancy moving areas for a new job, I liked where we lived and wouldn't want to move the kids like I had been moved about when I was their age. When I got to my desk, I noticed I had a missed call and voicemail left. I listened to it thinking it was a customer with questions about some data or something, but it was a recruitment agency!

They had been given my name for a potential new role in Shell Oil Company. Wow, this is good timing—I will discuss timings and coincidences later in this book! What could Shell possibly be interested in me for, I asked myself. I didn't hesitate to find out more and promptly replied to the voicemail. The job was similar to what I was doing, but at Shell's research facility. The only problem was that it was up near Chester, about a 3-hour drive from home! Oh well, I thought—nice idea, but can't see that happening!

They were offering a decent package with relocation and much better progression opportunities than my present role had to offer. I went for the interviews anyway out of curiosity about my potential desirability to other companies. After several interviews, I did actually get the job offer and it seemed too good to turn down. I have always followed my intuition and things happening for a reason! Following a lot of considering and thinking, I decided to take the leap and if it didn't work out, look for another job.

If I got this one, then I am sure I could get other roles in other companies. I managed to buy a new flat up near the office and stay there three nights a week. I was lucky to be able to have this place to live whilst there—it was a spacious 2-bed apartment on the top floor of the 3-storey building. This was 2006 and the kids were still kids. I missed them and Emma terribly, but felt like I had to do this to move to the next chapter of our lives and look out for more signs of opportunities once there.

There was a reason I got this job—it came out of nowhere and my name was on it—we had to make it work! I would be lying if I said it wasn't a painful time, but I was looking for every opportunity to get to our London office, where I could commute a 30-minute train journey instead! To cut a long story short, I managed to develop a new software concept for fleet management and sold the idea to the management team. I then joined a team in London to build a business case for senior Shell management teams to consider as a brand-new commercial offering across Europe. This was a big step out of my comfort zone, but I had created this opportunity and a lot was at stake.

Three of us were now based in London, formulating a plan and developing the business case for kick-starting this and sourcing suppliers to help us deliver it. I was now travelling all over Europe acting as primary liaison for all technical sales and marketing across this region for this new product and service. I managed to create a few patents for Shell through this work, which are still valid now. It certainly raised my profile and I soon became embedded as part of a key new IT and Innovation team based in London.

My plan had worked like clockwork—everything seemed to fall into place without me really pushing anything. I was now London based for 3 days a week and worked from home for the remainder. What a transformation to my previous experience! I loved the work, loved the people I worked with and my network was growing quickly. I later moved into a new business marketing team and was then focusing upon introducing mobile to Shell's consumer and business-to-business offerings, but now globally.

It wasn't long until Ben was doing his GCSEs at school and considering his next learning or career path. He was an avid drummer and was Grade 8 level by this time. We had many noisy practice sessions in our house and soon band rehearsals too, as he become more involved in that scene. It was so nice to see him enjoying this and he felt like music would be a career path for him going forward. We were worried that he wouldn't earn much of a living from this, unless he became the next big rock star!

However, I soon learned that there are many facets to the music industry and I wasn't going to deter his passions at this stage. He started sixth form in school, but didn't like it and quit after the first year. He had had a conversation with one of his music teachers about a music academy in Guildford and he quite fancied that. I am sure he did, but we weren't ready for him to leave home just yet and live down there. Anyway, he did eventually start there and we all adjusted to both the sudden absence of Ben and to the fortune it was costing to keep him down there! He completed his first two-year diploma and proceeded to the degree.

However, we found that he wasn't attending much of his lessons and he decided to leave his degree before completing it. We were fuming—all that cost and upheaval for what! However, he had begun to form his own business whilst doing the degree where he would produce and edit videos for music artists for cash! Well, if he wanted to pursue this angle for his career then at least he found his niche and we would continue to support him, so Ben began this new path.

Katy then began her GCSEs and had no idea what she wanted to do with her career life. We used to throw all kinds of suggestions at her and at one point, she was considering becoming a midwife. A what! She was not that caring, ha-ha…I think she said it to shut us up. Katy had achieved Grade 6 in singing during school and we thought that this might be an angle she may pursue.

However, she was more of a business woman, directing people, or hair and make-up artist. We explored many avenues with her and she decided to see how she felt about this later, so we backed off and gave her space to think this through. She finally chose 'fashion' which we should have guessed judging by her love of clothes! She got into an academy in London to study fashion retail marketing and successfully completed it two years later. The degree seemed an obvious next step, but she was hesitant about this now.

Wow, this sounded like Ben's viewpoint on his degree. Katy really then surprised us by announcing her intent to do a three-year nursing degree at Northampton's university which she could commute to. We weren't expecting that and the jokes about becoming a midwife weren't far off in the end!

The Diagnosis

It was during this busy time, when I was finding that I was getting indigestion a lot when I was eating and it felt like my food was not going down very easily. I dismissed it for a while, since I thought I was eating too quickly and not chewing my food enough. You think of all sorts of reasons to avoid anything more seriously affecting you! I eventually went to the doctors, because I thought there may be some medication I could take or maybe I have a stomach ulcer? My doctor appeared suspicious about my symptoms and fast-tracked an endoscopy for me.

She didn't show any outwardly concern, but she wanted to use the symptoms as an opportunity for me to jump the queue. I thought she was being kind, but concerned was probably a more relevant thought. I went for the assessment—it wasn't a nice experience that's for sure, having a big tube stuck down your throat with lots of pushing and shoving. I expected a more delicate approach and the sedation I had elected did not seem to have done anything whatsoever! Nothing was said during the assessment and I was waiting for some confirmation of a stomach ulcer or similar. I waited on the bed whilst the consultant cleaned himself up and he wandered over to me and just came out with it. "It looks like you have cancer, chap! So sorry about that!" he said. He tapped me on the knee and walked away.

My world just disappeared from underneath me at this point and my biggest concern now was how to tell Emma who was in the waiting room, totally unaware of what I now knew. I wish I could have wound the clock back an hour and take more time to experience life without knowing you had cancer. Only I knew this right now! This would crush her—how could I be so cruel! I had to tell her though because I was in a state of shock and felt like nothing mattered in the world now apart from my little family. I sent a text to Emma and told her— not the best method I know, but I had to break this somehow.

She was obviously in shock like I was and tears started to fall from her eyes—neither of us had expected this outcome. I could not reassure her either—I had no idea what was going on! Our next biggest fear was how to tell our kids. Ben was living away and Katy was doing her GCSEs. This would ruin them—nothing prepares you for the cruelness of having to tell your close one's bad news! We had yet to learn more about the cancer—how bad was it? So many questions and needed answers.

Emma came through to see me and we hugged and cried for what seemed like forever. We felt that all we lived for, dreamt about, hoped for and worked for had gone in that instant. We had nothing now, so it seemed. Nothing, but each other that is. A nurse took us into a small room—it looked like a 'bad news' room where you got told your fate! Just seats and a table with a tissue box on it. She explained about the next steps and a bit about process.

Wow, this was unchartered territory and one we had not prepared for. We had to wait for the histology report from the biopsy to be done and I would need scans and further tests to determine the extent of the cancer. From this point in time, my life seemed to be spent in hospitals. I had never been ill in my life, always fit and healthy and rarely took medication or drank much alcohol. What just happened—I was only 44 years old, still had my hair and not even grey yet!

Having tests and waiting for results was the new emotional roller coaster we found ourselves on. I say 'we', because your family is now on this journey with you and being affected by it too! I was so grateful that I had a supportive wife and she's nurse too! Emma was as determined as I was to find a way through all of this, but we never spoke about the ultimate consequences. It was like we had an unspoken understanding between us that was focused only on surviving this horrible disease.

I had my first CT scan, which was an interesting experience for my medical inexperience—here you have to consume a fizzy powder which inflates your stomach and then they put what is called a contrast into your bloodstream via a canula. I just went with it—whatever! I lay on the bed and it passed me backwards and forwards through this measuring ring with a voice telling me to hold my breath and then breathe normally! I can hear it now! They wanted this scan to check for any spread of the cancer, so we waited for the results and scheduled an appointment with the oncologist to discuss them.

I was still trying to get my head around the cancerous tumour in my oesophagus, let alone anywhere else! This is one hell of a mind-bending experience and began to appreciate all those others out there that are also, unwittingly, being introduced to this new world of cancer! The CT scan was pretty straight-forward and it was now a waiting game until the result came through!

We finally went to our oncologist meeting to learn more about my fate. This is like waiting for a death sentence in a court room! We were called to the oncologist's room and we both walked in and sat down in complete silence. It felt like the world around us was on pause while we learned more about our future. The oncologist was pretty frank and to the point—I guess they have to be and not get tied up with everyone's emotions. We waited for him to speak, which seemed like forever. He didn't look at us much, which didn't fill us with much confidence. He appeared to be more interested in looking for files and information on his computer screen than engaging with us. However, we later realised this was his style!

Eventually, he did look up and inform us of the cancer staging. He confirmed that there is a cancerous tumour measuring 5.7cm in the lower section of my oesophagus and it had penetrated the walls of the oesophagus and protruded into my stomach. It was very active and quite aggressive according to him. There was an additional concern following a review of the scan, because they found some suspicious shadows on my liver. OMG! WTF!

I would need an MRI scan to better determine what this is and so it was duly scheduled, along with my other library of mounting appointments! The oncologist was already considering whether it could be cut out and removed, but I was not up for surgery because we had already read about so many others that had their cancer surgically removed, only for it to return much more aggressively with the majority of people not surviving. I wasn't going to consider surgery as my first option at this stage and was prepared to do battle with it first to test its resilience! The oncologist requested a PET scan in Oxford so they could further verify the extent of the cancer before they could consider any surgery and didn't see this to be a problem because I would have a second opinion from a scan point of view.

PET scans are the ultimate scan for cancerous growth and activity checks, so was curious to see if there was anything else to learn before we embarked on the treatment journey.

My PET scan day was here and I wasn't allowed to eat during the morning, which I find so difficult—I get so hungry in the mornings! We drove to Oxford and wondered what the PET scan involved and what it might reveal. We were still taking stock of the initial prognosis. We had not told the kids too much about that—they already knew I had cancer and that I was starting treatment soon after a few more tests. We didn't want them to truly know how serious this actually was, which was hard for us both because we had to hold onto that truth and protect them as much as we practically could!

The PET scan was much like the CT scan, except you had a radioactive glucose injected into you and then you have to sit for about an hour before they scan you. I sat alone in a little cubicle trying to remain occupied, but I couldn't concentrate on anything right now. Emma waited patiently in the waiting room, but there was no signal on each of our phones, so we couldn't share our feelings with each other. Eventually, it was time and I was again passed back and forth through a ring and it was done quite quickly considering the prep time. The scans are the easy bit, it is the waiting which is painful and we were now becoming familiar with the anguish that this waiting time inflicts upon you!

You learn what people mean when they say that they live scan to scan. Although, you don't really do much living in between with the hope, worry and overall anxiety that is generated in this continuous cycle of emotional events.

We got home and just sat down, feeling exhausted with the mental strain. Emma was lucky that her work had been flexible with her time so that she could support me like this. I was so grateful and we formed quite a team bond in working out a plan to beat this horrible disease. We were well and truly on the cancer journey now and it felt we had been for many, many months when in fact it was only weeks. We felt like we had climbed a huge mountain already and I felt like we need to keep climbing, because the higher we got, the more we could see and the more we would learn, if that makes sense.

Seeing more of not just my disease, but the whole landscape of cancer—the medical segment, the patient segment, the alternative segment, what works and doesn't work… You never stop learning and wanting to learn. I felt that if we didn't, then we would not survive this for one minute! We kept climbing and helped each other over the difficult obstacles that were put in our way! Team Adams! This cancer chose the wrong people to mess with and I wasn't going down without a fight, that I was sure about!

It was soon appointment time with my oncologist again. We were becoming familiar with the medical staff now and felt like regulars already. We had to go through this mental torture of scan results again and we arrived early in eagerness to hear of any new findings or confirmations. Unfortunately, and as per usual, our oncologist was running late on his appointments and we waited a further hour beyond our appointment time. During this time of anguish, we watched many others go in for their appointments with their respective oncologists and wondered what news they were also facing today. You feel so helpless in these situations and it's difficult to know what to say to people. We kept ourselves to ourselves, apart from the polite "hellos" to the newly familiar staff—who would have thought I would be seeing them for the next 3 to 4 years!

"Peter Adams," my oncologist called into the waiting area and up we got and followed him to his office. He never said much and hid any thoughts in his body language well—he must have learned to do this from much of his bad news sharing with patients. What a job, really? We sat in our familiar seats and waited patiently for scan news. Once he had fiddled with his computer and finally gotten access into the system, he had a quick read of the notes as if to remind himself of who I was and what I had—it didn't fill me with confidence and I think he felt that mental thought I had.

He turned to face us and told us that the liver spots were benign, so he wasn't worried that these were anything serious and that gave us a sigh of relief—at last a bit of 'good' news! He then continued to inform us that there was evidence of a metastatic spread to my lymph system, with quite a few nodes affected in both my lower and upper body. Why hadn't the damn CT scan picked this up—I lost faith in CT scans at this stage and thought what is the point of them if they miss vital information like this.

Imagine if we had relied on this and had surgery and then spread my cancer around my body like wild fire! This was Stage 4 cancer! I had always associated Stage 4 with being terminal, so knew the prognosis was not going to be good. The oncologist did not dwell on the prognosis and instead took the conversation towards treatment options. Now, this was going to be a quick conversation, because when you have Stage 4 cancer, you have very few options I have learned. Emma reached out for my hand, as if to console me, but I think it was to console her! I held it tightly as if I wasn't ever going to let go. It was a good job that I didn't want surgery, because I expected anything in this area of my body to be a major operation with big risks and life changing impacts.

I was sort of relieved when he said surgery is not an option, but nor was anything else though, including radiotherapy. You quickly realise that the oncologists only have 3 cards to play in the cancer game—chemotherapy, radiotherapy and surgery. I was already against the odds, since I was only eligible for one out of three, so chemotherapy was considered my only option. It was considered palliative care, which basically meant we cannot ever cure you, but we can attempt to control the cancer and reduce the speed at which it takes over your body. This might buy you a little bit of time, but not much!

We were completely numb during much of this consultation and information overload was beginning to manifest. I had to sign a form to accept chemotherapy treatment, not really knowing what this was or what I was signing for to be honest. I was even given an appointment at a wig specialist in a near-by town—I couldn't even think about that right now! This was a new world we, unwillingly, found ourselves in. We left the consulting room and just hugged each other. How the hell do we tell our kids and rest of the family about this? We felt like we were both in this battle, and we were fighting different battles for the same cause! It could not have been a much worse prognosis and the gravity of it all began to hit us!

We sat down with the oncology nurse and she dictated the proposed chemotherapy regimen to us. Not much empathy there then! I guess these teams are dealing with this every day and it becomes more of a process, than a people task. I was due to have a combination of both intravenous and tablet drugs, none of which meant anything to me. We searched for the side-effects and they all pretty much said the same things—covering almost every possible symptom to cover their arses I suspect! I wasn't sure if I would lose my hair or my mind! This just seemed like some crazy dream, or rather nightmare, and I couldn't wake up from it! My date was set for May 2017 for my first chemotherapy treatment and dreaded what might be in store—this was so alien to me.

See Learning Focus in Appendix: 1.1 Impact of Diagnosis

We headed home and didn't talk much with each other on the journey back. We had to tell everyone more bad news. We had to tell the kids about this new prognosis, without worrying them, yet finding a way to ensure they understood it was pretty serious. We had already crushed them with the cancer diagnosis. Why the hell are we in all of this mess—why did it target us! So many questions! What do I do about work? Our complete and entire world we knew was gone and turned upside down in a flash! The 'tell me whys?' were starting to build in our minds as we tried to take stock of the new crisis situation we found ourselves in. So many questions about why I had got this damn disease, what happens with my treatment, how will I respond, will I survive—this list is practically endless as you can begin to imagine.

We arrived home and we just felt so numb about this whole, surreal situation. Home already felt different somehow. I remember Katy arriving home from school and she could immediately see the torment on our faces. We didn't have to tell her it was bad news—she already sensed that! We began to explain what we had learned about the cancer, but didn't say much about the prognosis bit! She was already in absolute floods of tears and sobbing quite uncontrollably. Great—we had just turned Katy's world upside down too now! We found little left to console her with, or ourselves—it looked bad whichever way you wanted to look at it now. We hugged for what seemed like forever, none of us wanting to let go of each other as if it was the last time we would do this.

Such a sad, sad feeling that we will never ever forget, unfortunately. I think Emma called Ben and told him about the latest findings and kept it more matter of fact and focused more on the treatment planned for me. Ben was away from home in Guildford, so he couldn't see our faces fortunately. I was never sure how Ben felt about all of this—he showed a strong exterior, but had no idea what was going on in his head. Ben was not a fan of the planned treatment they called 'chemotherapy'—he didn't like anything medical though and I was with him on that one, but felt I had no choice, or time for choice, as we jumped onto this conveyor belt of cancer treatment!

I had to inform my employer, Shell, about this and was apprehensive about dropping this bombshell on them. I didn't have anything to say other than I have pretty bad cancer diagnosis and prognosis and I was to undergo some treatment to see how I respond. I had no idea how I would feel, how long it would last, whether I could work or couldn't work—too many unknowns and my head was going in all directions. However, I had to inform them of this because I knew I was going to be seriously compromised. They already knew I was having various tests and were probably as curious as I was to learn more about what the problem was.

I needed to let many people know and it would have been impractical to inform people on one-to-one basis. I began to write an email to my global network and to those who I work with in the head office. I felt immensely sad updating everyone about my condition—I loved my job and loved the people I worked with. I had some great aspirations for my future career and it was all crumbling in front of me as I wrote this email. I finished writing the email and pressed the send button—it felt like I was lighting a fuse to a bomb and I waited for the blast to occur!

It didn't take long for my network to begin responding and there were some actually heartfelt, supportive messages. I was getting love and support from people I didn't even really know and also from those who I didn't think had much heart! I was touched and this made me feel more compelled to beat this, yet I was incredibly sad having to take a step back from my role while I focused upon the necessary steps in my treatment. The email responses continued over several days and I hadn't realised how much I was liked and appreciated—they say it takes a crisis to learn these types of things. A bit extreme way of learning though!

It felt like forever, waiting for my first treatment day. We were curious about how it would all work and what I would be subjected to. I was obviously anxious too, but hopeful that this treatment would kick the ass of this cancer in some way. Ahead of treatment, I did a quick bit of research on one of the main IV drugs I was to take, Cisplatin, and found that it was discovered in 1845 and licensed for medical use in 1978. What the hell! Why are they giving me a drug from the dark ages? What the hell had all this cancer charity and research funding been spent on? I was losing faith fast about my treatment already and I hadn't even started it.

This was the beginning of some doubt in the medical domain and felt somewhat misled and cheated by being prescribed such an old medication! This is 2017—surely a more up to date approach or drug has been found in the last 172 years? You would tend to think so with all the advertising the cancer charity marketing does in promoting themselves. I was surprised that nobody had really questioned this, but you probably know me by now—I am curious and would like to know 'why'!

My treatment day had finally arrived and I couldn't wait to see how well the dark ages drugs were going to work! It was a full day scheduled from 8am until 6pm. I was still working at this time, since I wasn't sure how long I would be having treatment or needing any other interventions that would require me to use all of my sick leave entitlement. I just didn't know what to expect, so chose to try and work through this, like others have done, and preserve my sick leave for later when I may need it—who knows!

Emma joined me and we parked the car and headed to the oncology unit in the hospital. We checked ourselves in at the desk and were shown to a couple of chairs—a comfy one and not so comfy one! I was sat in the comfy, tilting chair and began looking around at all of the other chairs—most of them occupied already. Everyone seemed quite a lot older than me and I felt really out of place like I didn't belong in this environment—I didn't belong in it! How did I end up here? We got chatting to the older couples who were adjacent to us and it was their first time too! This put my mind at a rest a little, since we were all in the same boat and learning about this together—a subtle kind of unity and bond seemed to form between us that helped us all.

We were all assigned a nurse who would be our focal point for the day and we waited to be seen and have our measurements taken—weight, blood pressure, temperature, etc. The nurse then complimented me on the size of my veins and she couldn't wait to stick a needle in them—I bet you couldn't, I thought! They proceeded to put a canula into my hand and had trouble getting any blood out— my veins were having none of it, as if they were refusing to play this game! They tried in another location and managed to outwit my vein on this occasion, so I was primed and ready to go.

Before they started the treatment, they discussed all the possible side effects and what drugs they had to deal with them—there seems to be drugs for anything and everything, but not really sure what they all actually did! The side effects list may as well have said 'anything is possible', because it was literally covering every possible reaction you could think of!

I don't get ill very often and believe that I am quite resilient to most things, so thought that I may only get a mild side effect of some description and remained hopeful as I felt the drugs starting to enter into my bloodstream. They gave me some steroids and said this would help with the side effects later. I didn't think I needed them—I never even take tablets for headaches usually. Well, that is me plugged in for 7 or 8 hours! Once everything was set up, it was quite a social event where we got to know our neighbours more and take our minds off what was actually happening. This helped us all and it was refreshing to compare notes with others going through a similar life changing event.

It wasn't long until the lunch trolley appeared, offering sandwiches, crisps and fruit—they didn't look too bad, so took the offer to at least try something! One thing you quickly realise is that with all that fluids being put into you, you need to pee very frequently! I pee frequently anyway, so this was just ridiculous! To top it off, you had to pee into a cardboard bottle every time and write your name on it! What weird world have I just entered into—let's just leave our dignity at the door, shall we?

By lunchtime, I was already winning with the highest number of bottles filled on the rack! Apparently, they have to measure your fluid intake and output to ensure you are drinking enough to dilute the drugs—more drink? It wouldn't have been so bad, but when you are connected to a drip stand with pumps and stuff on it, you find it a bit of a job navigating through the maze of chairs to the toilet and every time you unplug the drip stand, it beeps continuously, highlighting the fact you're on the move…again!

As the afternoon progressed, many patients were leaving and going home. When you have these drugs for first time, you have to stay an extra couple of hours to ensure you had no reactions. It got to about 5:30 pm and we were practically the only ones left on the ward. Finally, we were allowed to go home, but we were armed with all sorts of tablets to take until the next chemotherapy session. There were more steroids, anti-sickness tablets, strong painkillers, mouthwash to help with sores, more chemotherapy tablets to take daily—I think these were four a day and they were massive and wasn't even sure how I was going to swallow them.

What did all these tablets do and did I really need them—another 'tell me why' moment. What if they all interact—my body will not like them, I told myself. My body works fine without pumping drugs into it! Anyway, I was disconnected from everything and we put everything into a big bag. We now had a book to track our treatment and they scheduled the next blood test and chemotherapy session. I was put on a standard 'every 3 weeks' schedule and had to have blood tests prior to each treatment so they could keep check on my immune system.

The chemotherapy really hammers your immune system apparently, so that was something else to look forward to! What had I just signed up for! I was feeling good as we left the hospital and was optimistic about the side effects that had been described to us. I didn't feel anything and was feeling quite proud of myself!

When we got home, we had so much to take in and to read and understand. This was an alien world we just entered into and had so much to learn about the disease, the treatment and its effectiveness, the prognosis, the side-effects. The list went on and on—there are so many angles that this affects and it's one massive physical and emotional nightmare. I was still getting my head around the sudden change to our lives and we just couldn't think beyond each day, each hour.

I was feeling quite tired from the day's events, despite doing no more than sitting in a chair all day. The mental impacts of everything weighed heavy on my mind and we opted for a relatively early night. I checked over the tablets and collated the ones I have to take into a container. What a concoction! I took my time getting everything down and waited for any adverse reactions. Nope, nothing felt, so hugged Emma for a while as we lay there in total silence. I could feel Emma's thoughts and they were matching mine—we were both scared of what lies ahead on this journey, but at least we have started the journey. The oncologist made it clear to us that they will not ever be able to cure this, but are seeking to control it so that it does not get worse. What was our life going to be like for the next year or the next 'anything'—I just didn't want to think about that and our focus on the day in hand was a good practice for us to adopt.

I seemed to sleep ok, but as I awoke, I was very aware that I was not in a good place. I could hardly move and my head felt like it was on a very rough sea and was feeling extremely nauseous. I couldn't even lift my head off the pillow. I needed the loo and wasn't quite sure how I was going to get there. What has this stuff done to me! I felt poisoned and as if I was trapped on a small boat in a huge rough sea—the sickness feeling was like nothing I had ever experienced, even from really bad hangovers! I could not escape myself—I was trapped in my body feeling like I was a warmed-up corpse!

I gritted my teeth and eased myself slightly upright in bed with help from Emma. I had no strength! She helped me to the toilet and I was sick almost straightaway. I felt no better afterwards and how the hell was I going to take more massive tablets feeling like this? Emma was keen for me to have some anti-sickness tablets or the liquid stuff we were also given. I tried to take them and just vomited it all back up again. Nothing was staying down—not even water!

Oh my god, I thought. I could not see a way out of this feeling and felt a very dark cloud hanging above me. I reflected on how well I was feeling after my treatment and thought I was going to get away with the side-effects. On the contrary, I had almost all of the side effects they listed and all were bad cases of each of them! This treatment is going to kill me before the cancer, I thought to myself. Is this what it is like to die from this horrible disease? I could see the same realisation coming over Emma's face as she was frantically trying to help me, but knowing she couldn't do anything to stop this horrible experience.

I thought this might wear off after an hour or so and tried to keep my mind occupied somehow. I couldn't listen to music, watch tv or anything like that—

everything made me feel worse and my head was swaying, spinning and my whole body was aching with indescribable ill feelings. I felt hopeless and helpless. Time seemed to drag, probably because I was willing every minute to go by quickly so I could reach some point of safety soon. That 'soon' never happened. As the day went on, I felt the same and the tablets that were given to me for all these side-effects did absolutely nothing and I was feeling pretty hopeless. This was one of the lowest points of my life. I had been reduced from what I was to this—a curled up, weak and shaking wreck on the bed.

Poor Emma—I can't imagine how disheartened and hopeless she was feeling as she was unable to do anything to make me feel any better. I could not eat anything at all and could barely drink any liquids either. How am I going to do the planned six sessions of this? I can't even endure this first one! I was hoping to work from home on these days and keep occupied and employed whilst on my treatment. I believed that work would be a welcome distraction right now, if I was able to concentrate and remain focused. I had seen others not feeling hardly any side-effect from their treatment and this made me feel quite resentful. How come I feel like this and they don't—tell me why?

I stayed in bed all day and Emma kept popping up to see me, but I was in some kind of comatose state and had totally lost touch with reality. I just wanted to sleep this off and feel ok again. What was this chemotherapy doing to my healthy body? I was dreading the next treatment session already. Night time had finally arrived and I had eaten nothing and drank only sips of water. I tried to find a new way in which to lie that could make me feel better, but after trying most combinations all day, I was still feeling dreadful and kept fidgeting to help my body deal with this chemical abuse!

This went on for most of the week and I remember Ben coming home to see me. I didn't want him to see me in this awful state. I couldn't seem to be able to properly communicate with anyone at the moment, but was desperate to see him again. We hadn't seen much of Ben since he moved out and the times we do get together are sacred. I remember him entering our bedroom and I was laying on the bed in some kind of foetal position. I could see his face trying to take in what he was seeing of me—I should be his strong, father figure, not some curled up, chemically induced mess on the bed!

He kept a face of positivity and optimism, which I found welcoming and appreciated it. God knows what was going through his mind! I tried to prop my head up on a pillow and we stuck the tv on so we could share this moment together. I just couldn't communicate—my head was a mess! I held his hand as we both gazed at the tv and we exchanged our feelings in this way as we watched something on Nat Geo about survival, ironically! Ben and I share the same interests in many respects and we always like watching extreme, real-life stuff on the tv. We had extreme, real-life stuff going on in our house, but this wasn't a show I wanted to watch!

It wasn't long before I had to put my head level again and close my eyes. Ben stayed with me for a little longer and I felt him get up and quietly leave the room. I wish I could be different, feel different and not put my poor family through this 'in your face' experience!

This feeling went on for at least a week with this intensity. It takes a strong mind not to go crazy with this feeling inside! I finally managed to get into the shower, but every time I was upright, it felt 10 times worse! I quickly showered, gritting my teeth with the relentless feeling of sickness and dizziness. I couldn't wait to lie down again for some relief. I managed to start nibbling dry crackers, but only tiny amounts over a long time. I was losing weight already, but didn't have much fat on me anyway. It was my muscle that I began to notice fading away. All that effort over years of going to the gym was fading in front of my eyes at a rapid rate! I felt fragile and hopeless. I was losing myself and who I was and how people knew me—my identity. You just want to hide from everyone and you certainly don't feel like seeing anybody!

As the second week progressed, I began to feel some easing of the sickness and dizziness and this gave me such a sense of appreciation. I never thought I would ever not feel any sense of wellness ever again! That was some dose they must have given me in my chemotherapy session! I had to live with the side-effects because nothing they gave me to combat it was working! I was starting to look ill and haggard and began hating who I saw in the mirror. Who was I becoming? Would I ever feel normal again? Would I ever be able to do anything again? The questioning crops up continuously—tell me why?

Home had become my sanctuary and it was a place I could safely hide. I wasn't able to get into London to the office much at all and did not want to risk catching something from the other commuters on the tubes and trains. I had to be really careful now, because the treatment depletes your immune system and if you get an infection, it can be life threatening—oh yes, that's the other risk you're told about during information overload! There aren't many positives about this treatment are there! It better bloody work or do something, I thought.

Whilst I was having a rough time since the first treatment, Emma had been frantically researching and finding out how others have coped with the treatment or found themselves cured from a variety of other means. She had found some useful and relevant Facebook forums. You can soon gain some good insights into a wide spectrum of people going through similar experiences and others trying non-conventional treatment strategies. There is a lot of information on the internet and it's hard to validate it and know what to believe and what not to believe.

It is also hard to consider anything other than what is being proposed by the medical professionals, since they are always discrediting anything that does not fall into their three-card trick offering—chemotherapy, radiotherapy or surgery. I had already been disheartened about the poor hand I was dealt with in my 172-year-old chemotherapy medicine! Doesn't the museum want it back? Hearing stories from others helps datum yourself and it provides a gauge in which to begin to judge how well, or not, you are doing. I was not doing well at all and the chemotherapy had already made a massive impact on me!

As I entered into the third week after my first treatment, I began to regain some of my normal function and was more able and more active. I felt very damaged and weak from just one treatment and could not stop thinking about how I was going to get through this, if this was my only option! In my mind, I knew that there must be more options and I was determined to find some. It is in my nature to look for solutions, so this almost became a project for me—for both of us! I began to feel grateful for the time I now had feeling a bit better and waited with baited breath for the next treatment!

The second chemotherapy session was fast approaching by now and I went to the hospital for my scheduled blood test. That wasn't too bad an experience and pretty quick and I was soon home again. They have to check your blood to make sure you are not unwell and to pass certain limits that allow you to have chemotherapy. I found it ironic that the chemotherapy destroys your blood, yet they want it looking good so they can bash it down again!

The day had finally arrived for my second chemotherapy session. We arrived at the hospital early again and got checked in. My blood counts were noticeably dropping, but still within limits for treatment. If they are not within limits, they defer the treatment until they recover again. This just prolongs the agony really, doesn't it! We got sat down in our chairs again and met the others who we started with three weeks ago—we were in sync with our treatment regime and it was actually nice to see familiar faces in this environment. I was not feeling at all optimistic about this treatment this time and was reluctant to start this horrible process once more.

I had literally just recovered from my last treatment and, BANG, it is starting all over again! Our new chemotherapy friends were asking how it was going and we explained how bad it has been and the dread of doing more of the same. We were shocked to learn that none of the others had hardly any side-effects and could continue their lives pretty much as they did before! I was both jealous and confused. How come I am getting these awful side-effects and they are not? Tell me why! I always remember the saying, "No pain, no gain!" and I kept this constantly in my mind. If the chemotherapy was not doing anything, I wouldn't feel anything and vice versa.

My previous jealousy for the others not getting side effects was soon replaced with concern and worry for them. How could the treatment be working if they could not feel any of its effects? I was weirdly reassured by this fact and was willing to take the hit on these side-effects if it meant living a little longer! I was more worried about any lasting impacts from the treatment. I already had rashes on my face and my nails were becoming brittle and thin. I just had to forget what I used to look like from now on and focus on the task in hand!

The format of the second chemotherapy was not surprisingly any different from the first one. At least now we knew what to expect and we watched with compassion as new patients were going through what we had done only three weeks ago. The worry and confusion on their faces and similar questions we had. I just hoped that some of these older folks don't get to feel like I did after treatment—it would destroy them, I'm sure.

Patients were coming and going all day long. Some only came for 30 mins and some for only the afternoon. Some were already plumbed in with what are known as 'PICC' lines, so they didn't need to stick needles in each time. This was a strange world for sure, yet fascinating. The nurses just got on with their jobs and seemed to be immune to emotional effects—was this a skill they have learned or an attribute they have built-in? However, some were more compassionate than others I learned and I already had my favourites, and least favourites! We were eventually signed out by the nurse and she asked about the medication.

We told her about the sickness and she suggested trying a different anti-sickness tablet and a liquid-based pain relief. I welcomed a change and this was the start of the trial and error stages you go through in this treatment regimen. I was hopeful that this might get some control over my sickness and dizziness this time! We took another big bag of medication and headed home.

Emma and I had already completed quite a bit of research and were finding that there are avenues to pursue other than the just the medical one. They range from things that can run in parallel to some which are exclusively based on a particular diet, for example. There are a lot of opinions on the internet and you have to first take stock of everything that is being published and then look for the common themes within the 'haystack' of it all. I actually enjoyed this though, since I could apply some logic and analysis to it. You never stop reading and learning whilst you are in this situation—you don't want to miss out on any opportunity. It can become quite exhausting because it is on your mind constantly and you are playing 'what if' scenarios in your mind continuously.

Unsurprisingly, I awoke the next day feeling absolutely beaten up and had the same sickness and dizziness feelings as before. The change of side-effect medication had not done anything and I was half disappointed and half expected this. I concluded to myself that I must be having quite some chemotherapy dosage and nothing is going to abate these side effects. It is was it is and I will just need to find the strength and will power to endure it! We now began to write off the first two weeks after every treatment and didn't plan to do anything during these periods.

This had cut our 'good living' time one week out of every three and it felt very frustrating and unfair! I had more of the same symptoms as before—the only difference with this time is that it was familiar! What a life this has become, I kept thinking to myself! I could see no escape route from this at the moment, let alone having the energy and ability to escape. I couldn't even physically escape through an open door right now, feeling like this! I was glad in some respects that Ben was not seeing me in this condition, but really felt for Emma and Katy where it was really in their faces. What must be going through Katy's head—I wish I could reassure her, but had nothing to reassure her with except my love and determination.

Katy knew I was determined in everything I put my mind too, so maybe this reassured her. She had inherited my determination and was very sure of herself. Emma had somewhat learned to cope by being my busy researcher. She was accumulating quite some knowledge. Emma is a nurse practitioner, so knows the medical side pretty well. We were both unfamiliar with anything like this, as most people would be I guess, if they had not experienced it.

See Learning Focus in Appendix: 1.2 Personality Analysis

One of the interesting, recent learnings was the broad healing power of cannabis extracts. There are two strains of cannabis, the hallucinogenic and non-hallucinogenic ones, known as THC and CBD, respectively. Both had unique abilities that had reportedly shown to address cancer symptoms as well as evidence in halting cancer in its tracks! Both were a welcoming find for sure and we knew others which had been using both for the treatment of their conditions. Unfortunately, the THC strain is illegal to possess and use in the UK and it was the one providing the 'killing' power that I was keen to leverage. The UK had no sign of legalising THC, even for medical use at this stage and so it was a risk to integrate it into your medical regimen.

Emma and I deliberated this topic for quite some time, looking at the pros and cons of using it, for obvious reasons. We finally plucked up the courage to try it—my life was on the line here and I was more than willing to accept the risk and consequences of it given this situation. My life was more important to me than anything else! We found a source of medical grade THC oil and pursued our enquiries to obtain some to try it out. Our provider was down on the coast, so we took little time in organising a trip down there and decided to make a day of it.

Our provider has been helping many individuals in a whole range of medical conditions and started doing so after curing her own cancer with the same regimen! This medical grade THC is expensive stuff and we calculated that it would cost us about £2,000 a month! However, money was not as important as my life was at this stage, so this wasn't a barrier to prevent us trying this out.

We arranged to meet at their house so jumped in the car and headed down. We were both excited and apprehensive about this—we didn't want to get caught with all this stuff in our possession! We felt like we were in a movie and heading to a rendezvous to do an exchange! It was a nice sunny day on the drive down and this put us in a good mood. This was our first pursuit outside the medical world and it felt somehow empowering and refreshing. This was something we were in control of and it was first move of many to come.

We parked up outside the 'rendezvous' house and knocked on the door. She opened the door and was very welcoming and her house was a definite reflection of her more natural healing practices. There was a nice joss stick aroma in the air and it felt very calm and peaceful. We sat down and talked through everything. She wasn't sure if I was the one who was 'ill' because she said I looked pretty well. I said, she should have seen me before! I quietly liked this compliment and it gave me a welcome little boost! She explained everything to us and other things we should do and shouldn't do to give this cancer a run for its money. Her words were, "You need to throw the kitchen sink at it!"

From that day, that is what we did! She empowered us with a wealth of tangible knowledge and confidence to run a parallel path of our own 'treatments' with a more natural and back to basics approach. Our eyes were opened and this world of cancer was just starting to become clearer—you cannot see the wood for the trees initially and you are simply overloaded with information, emotions and have no ability to take a step back and really think things through rationally! This visit had given us confidence to take that step back and look at the bigger picture—it was poignant moment in our cancer journey and one which certainly gave us the impetus to begin our own parallel treatment regimen! We paid for our 'natural medicine' and she had put it in an inconspicuous Disney bag with Mickey Mouse on it! Nobody would suspect anything!

We hugged our goodbyes and she wished us all the luck! She was helping so many others with cancer and it was quite humbling to be part of this little underground network that the medical world could not help! We decided to drive down to the beach seeing as we had come all this way. We drove the short drive and got parked up. It was a lovely sunny day and we felt a renewed energy and enthusiasm about this cancer as we looked across the bay. We both felt it and it boosted us a lot!

We believed we had just started to carve out our own pathway through this and we already felt like we had an edge on the others who were going through this cancer treatment. If anybody knows me, they know that I do not give up easily and have courage to take calculated risks! This certainly felt more like my way of dealing with things—I was not happy with a single path approach to this cancer. It needs a multi-prong attack from all sides to find its weak points. It must have weak points. Emma and I walked down the hill and decided to have some fish and chips from the renowned chip shop on the shoreline. We couldn't resist and we knew it was a bit of a deviation from the nutritional advice, but we felt like treating ourselves! At this stage, we didn't know how much longer I had on this planet and wanted to enjoy my time with Emma as much as I could!

We sat on the steps and looked across the shoreline into the endless sea view. It was such a calming feeling and we wanted to press the pause button on this precious time so we could enjoy it for longer! When you find yourself in situations like this, you quickly realise how important those little things are and you appreciate every damn thing! We loved each other a lot and had been through some tough times together in our lives, so whilst we knew this was the biggest challenge we now faced, we did believe that our combined strength will make a dent on this cancer and hopefully catch it off-guard! We had an enormous enthusiasm building between us to conquer this and to show the world that miracles can indeed happen!

We finished our fish and chips and let the hungry seagulls finish the scraps. We headed back to the car holding each other's hand and feeling each thought that was going through each of our minds. We were in 'full on positive' mode and found ourselves smiling with a new hope. As I am writing this, I am recalling these emotions and little tears are falling from my eyes onto my desk! God, having a life is just the most wonderful thing!

We drove home before the traffic started to build and as soon as we arrived home, we got out our new THC cannabis medicine and pondered on the potential of this new wonder drug! I couldn't wait to start it, but was clearly apprehensive about it from many perspectives! It wasn't legal and how would I feel after taking it? When should I take it? Emma was paranoid that we were going to get a visit from the authorities, but she is a bit of a worrier when it comes to rule breaking! Hell, I am not giving up my life just yet! I had to start with a very low dose and build it up over the course of 30 days as my body became more tolerant to the effects! I felt like a right druggie!

We decided that taking it late evening would be best and it could work on me overnight. We prepared it all and waited for the evening to arrive so we could begin. I purchased some clear, digestible capsules to put the oil in and put a couple of drops in one of them. The time finally arrived when I could take my first capsule. I popped it in my mouth and swilled it down with water, filtered water, of course! We both waited for a reaction, neither of us knowing what that reaction might feel like! Nothing yet! After about 20-30mins, I began to feel a warm sensation building from within me—it is almost impossible to describe and it was such a relaxing feeling and you could almost feel every part of your body begin to lightly tingle.

I was excited about this and felt that it was already working on me. If this is just a couple of drops, what is a whole capsule going to feel like, I thought to myself. Boy, I was going to sleep well tonight and I did just that. It sure helped me sleep and I soon fell into a deep and calm sleep!

I awoke the next morning feeling a little drowsy, but not like a hangover. I still felt pretty calm and pleased that I had achieved my first dose of THC without any major consequences. I knew that I was going to able to handle this new daily introduction of THC and was keen to ramp up to full dose. The full dose required to hurt the cancer was 1ml per day which was quite a lot considering the potency. Emma had found another Facebook forum where they help you set the optimum dosage for THC based upon you and your cancer type.

I was never sure how they determined this, but just went with it for now because I had no other means to judge it—it wasn't going to do any damage that was certain! I also acquired medical strength CBD oil—this was to be used in combination with THC to help with its effectiveness and also helps address some of the chemotherapy symptoms apparently. This is not the CBD strength you generally find on the high street with a typical CBD content of only 5%.

My source was producing around 35-40%, which meant it was going to be more effective by the same volume. My armoury against this cancer was growing and felt that I had only just begun! I was feeling empowered and was keen to learn what the cancer thought of all of this—I bet it wasn't expecting it!

It was already time for more blood tests and off I went to my hospital appointment. I wonder how my blood is doing. I felt I wanted to begin tracking the various blood counts so I could see what was going on and curious whether anything correlated with these changes. I was all done in not time and headed home again, back to my safe house! The bloods are analysed before your scheduled chemotherapy and there was usually a two-day gap between my blood test and treatment. The next day I received a phone call to inform me that my blood counts are too low to have my next chemotherapy session. What? I had only had two sessions and needed six!

My heart immediately sank and my body was already not tolerating the treatment at this early stage. I had to wait another week to see if my blood had shown any recovery, which meant delaying my next treatment and having to have another blood test. I would now be out of sync with the others I was sharing my chemotherapy journey with, so felt somewhat alone again. I cannot begin to describe what a frustrating and worrying time this is. What will happen to my cancer if I cannot have any more treatment? What can I do to restore my immune system? More "tell me whys!"

We focused our attention to our immediate, new problem which was to regain an immune system. I had to be so careful now and felt very vulnerable to catching infections—I had to avoid being in public as much as I could. I had to become a recluse in reality. We looked at how to increase your immunity through diet and found that the following natural nutrition helps, amongst other things:

Blueberries	Spinach
Turmeric	Sweet potatoes
Sunflower seeds and almonds	Ginger and garlic
Broccoli	Green tea
Oranges and kiwi	Peppers

Many of these were becoming familiar to us as cancer fighting foods and we started to integrate them more and more into our diet. Getting regular exercise and stress management was also recommended and I began to explore meditation as a method to reduce my stress and keep my mind intact. We started to learn how powerful diet and nutrition is on maintaining good 'whole body' health and how a bias towards certain foods can even help fight the cancer itself.

Healthy eating isn't anything new, is it, but knowing what to eat to help target cancer was something new to us. It is not discussed by the oncology team at all and the dietician's advice was laughable in light of what we had already learned in a matter of weeks! Dietetic advice for cancer patients was biased and single-minded towards maintaining weight—they called it 'treatment for undernutrition'. It was all about high calorie intake and the drinks side was recommending high fat milk shakes, milky drinks, ice-cream smoothies and even cider, beer and sherry (you can tell the age group this was aimed at!).

For snack ideas, how about Cornish pasty, cheese, sausage rolls, pork pies, samosas and croissants—a very random selection. There was generally a lot of high fat, high sugar, meat and dairy suggestions which were going directly against my new learnings about cancer and what it thrives upon. The advice appeared to be general advice for any patient and was not seemingly tailored to cancer patients, who should be avoiding high sugar, for one thing. We had been reading many sources of literature and got a few books from Amazon to help arm us with information. They tell you nothing about things like this in the medical world and I was seeing massive flaws and gaps in this industry of cancer already. I was fast becoming more vegan as time went by, simply through what I was learning about nutritional links to cancer.

I could not seem to resist my urge to be more vegan—it felt an obvious and natural transition! Ben was a vegan already and his initial reason was because of the animal cruelty, but he was finding real benefits of this way of eating too. So much of the truly, cancer fighting foods were natural or plant-based. I could not ignore what I was learning and became more and more disillusioned with the medical staff who appeared ignorant and unaware of so many important factors about cancer links to diet and lifestyle. How was a vegan meant to operate within such guidelines?

My veganism and parallel approach were becoming a talking point in the oncology unit. They used to mock my veganism initially, but as I told them more about it, it was changing their understanding too. I was feeling quietly empowered by my new learnings and became increasingly uninspired by anything the rigid medical approach to treating cancer in its broadest sense. I am an analytical, scientific and logically thinking person and I was making my own sense now amongst the contrasting advice and guidelines within the medical environment.

I took what I needed from the hospital and continued on my own broadening journey along the cancer treatment road. I had to be selfish about this and the medical side was becoming the minority in my treatment regimen now, since I was introducing many other factors into my own personalised, self-taught regimen. I felt like the tide was turning and I was keen to get my immune system back on track for starters.

I attended another blood test appointment and waited for the dreaded call to tell me that I am unable to receive chemotherapy due to my immune system again. The day of treatment soon arrived and I had no call! Was I ok for treatment or had nobody remembered to call me? We got ready anyway and headed to the hospital ward. They were expecting me and this was a relief, since it meant that my blood was recovering. Emma was keen to see my blood test results, since she knows about these types of things! I let her analyse them and give me her opinion.

She was able to compare my previous results with these recent ones and she noticed a small recovery across a number of measurements, but they were still very borderline. I'll take that! I just wanted to get this over with so I can see what the outcome is. I had found out that from my biopsy that I was what is termed 'HER2+' which is usually more common with breast cancer patients! Interesting, I thought! So, what's it mean? Well basically, this relates to a protein which promotes the growth of cancer cells. Unfortunately, this meant that my cancer was more aggressive, but there was an additional drug called 'Herceptin' that I can have to deal with this and help counter this effect. There are few side-effects, apparently, but it can affect your heart so this meant more tests—this time it is heart echo appointments every 3 months.

So, they added this to my portfolio of drugs and it was just another bag on the drip stand that needed to work its way into my bloodstream. I had not discussed anything I was doing in parallel with any of the hospital staff—it was my little secret for now. We had an appointment with my oncologist soon, so thought we would make him aware then and see what he had to say. We weren't sure how well he would welcome our own intervention with treatment, but it was my body at the end of the day and it belongs to me!

We got used to passing the time during my treatment and Emma took the opportunity to pop into town to run some errands whilst I was plugged in. I had actually brought my work laptop, so while Emma was away, I decided to log in and see what was going on my work world! I had quite some emails to catch up on and had begun to delegate some of my 'day to day' work to my colleagues— that was very nice of them! I felt that I was disrupting things at work with all my appointments and treatments, and I am sure I was!

Emma and I started talking about getting away for a week, just the four of us, in the summer during a week when I 'should' be feeling ok. I was still feeling pretty awful after treatment, but by the second week was starting to recover, so that's progress. I was feeling like I was getting back on track and this invigorated me.

First Photo After Diagnosis

Began My Photography Passion

Contemplating the Future

Invigorating Sunrise in Bergen

Drone Time!

Our Devon Family Holiday

Drone Lighthouse Photo

I had my usually sickness and dizziness again—it was becoming very familiar and predictable now. I dreaded treatments now, because the aftermath was just horrible. It was like a roller coaster, where you are feeling better each day after the first week of chemotherapy and then you drop right down to the bottom as the next treatment is administered! After I was feeling a little better after this 3rd treatment cycle, we started to look at some UK holiday destinations—we could not travel abroad with all this going on and who was going to insure me anyway!

We knew the UK weather is unpredictable, so we didn't have high expectations. We found a nice Airbnb near the south coast in Devon. We liked it down that way and being near the sea is quite rejuvenating. We booked just a week in August to fit in with my potential treatment regime, if I was to stay on track. I should technically have finished my six chemotherapy sessions by then…fingers crossed! It was something for us to look forward to and we didn't tend to get together fully as a family much these days with Ben living away. I had recently bought a drone, so was keen to try that out in a new environment. They were pretty new in the market back then and people weren't quite sure about them!

A week after my treatment, I began to feel unwell and didn't think much about it—I had felt worse, but this was different. I wondered what might be happening because I hadn't done anything different to attribute it to. I was feeling quite weak and lacked energy. I began to feel like I had hot flushes and just thought it was because it was particularly warm at the moment—25-30 degrees °C, which is really something for UK! Emma came back from work and checked my temperature and it was sky high!

This isn't good when you are on chemotherapy and it was one of the watch outs—you can catch serious infections when you have very little immune system and it can be life threatening. OMG, as if this isn't bad enough—you can die of an infection! Emma got me into the car and we headed to A&E at the hospital and we got a bit of priority call because of being a cancer patient. All sorts of things were going around in my mind—how did I get this, where did I get it from? More whys!

We were soon seen by a doctor and they confirmed that I had contracted sepsis. Sepsis can kill you in 12 hours if it gets out of control so this was a pretty serious situation and I soon found myself quarantined on a hospital ward. I was feeling quite delirious and just remember the room having very squeaky door hinges and every time anyone came into the room, the hinges would squeak and then the door would slam itself shut. This sound was driving me crazy since nurses were constantly in and out doing things or asking questions about this, that and the other! I just want to be left alone and I just want to feel well were my only thoughts at the time—how on earth did I end up like this?

Anyone who came to see me, including the nurses, needed to be gloved, masked, etc.—I felt like I was in a movie where I was the casualty of biological warfare! I was worried by the severity that was being taken with me, but grateful I was in the hospital receiving antibiotic treatment. The room I was in was very warm, like 25 degree °C—it was 30 degree °C outside and this room had no air con! I needed to cool down, not warm up! The heat made me feel even more nauseous and the sickness and diarrhoea was now in full force. I felt absolute crap again and could not find any way of alleviating these horrible feelings.

This was another one of the lowest points in my life and I couldn't believe how infirm and dependent I had become. I was the one my family turned to when they needed help and I was now a wreck of a man lying in a hospital bed, no use to anybody! Emma's mum had come over to help out and give Emma some company and support. I appreciated that, because Emma wasn't getting much support and she was going through this as much as I was! I recall us all being in the room and I was trying to socialise, but I was totally out of it and was feeling so nauseous! They were all in their rubber gloves and aprons and it was over 25 degree °C in the room—we were all sweating and feeling really uncomfortable. I was not allowed to be out of the room and if we opened the windows, it would let hotter air in.

I was thinking how utterly crazy this is and why the hell is there no air con in these rooms—this temperature would not be allowed in an office environment, so why does it not matter in this, more serious environment? I would feel a whole lot better being cool. I kept getting a cold flannel to put on my face to offer some brief cooling, but it soon became warm and useless. I was trapped in this dire place and while I was here, one of our twin cats died. She was quite old at around 14 years old, but felt sad because these cats had grown up with the kids and were really part of our family.

What else can go wrong, I kept thinking, but kept not wanting to think that at the same time! I was kept in for a few days and was eventually starting to feel more human again and was keeping fluids and some food down by now. My temperature had stabilised and they were happy for me to go home at last. I really felt like I was dragging my whole family through all this crap and I just couldn't see any way out of it. I could only focus on each day at a time and my energy levels were rock bottom. I couldn't yet imagine ever getting better, but had to push those thoughts away as much as possible because there were not positive thoughts and I needed to remain optimistic! This was difficult to do when I was feeling so low, so lifeless and so defeated.

Emma brought me back home and it was so nice to smell our home, feels its peace and to feel safe. Home had very much become my sanctuary now and I was really appreciating this space on a level I hadn't ever before. Emma's mum had managed to cut our grass and the garden was looking nice. I was grateful for the help—you don't realise how much you cannot now do in these compromised situations and it was hard for me to handle because I did most things garden and housing fixing wise. I had to just let it go and let others pick up those tasks.

I was feeling strangely redundant in my own house, which is a difficult transition after previously being so dependable. I realised that I had to put who I used to be in a box and forget about him—I was constantly comparing myself to who I was and it was not helping with my sanity. I mentally packaged the old me up and hid it away in my mind. I focused on a new me from then on—one who was going to beat this disease and one which had begun to learn about the power of the human mind and body and how we can literally eat our way to health. This was making me feel empowered and I started to reconstruct who I was in my mind.

It wasn't long until another blood test appointment appeared again. These appointments are relentless and there is always something to attend to be prodded, pricked and poked. This new way of life was already becoming familiar and I had accepted that I had to just go through with it all. It did make me feel like I was some kind of 80 year old though and I was definitely a contrasting age to many of the other cancer patients at the hospital. They got my blood and I was off home again to wait for the call. The next day, I got the call—I was kind of expecting it, to be honest!

I don't think my body was liking the chemotherapy much and it was responding as if to say, I am going to put you out of limits so that you don't have any more of it! The nurse confirmed that my blood was showing very low immune system and also signs of anaemia! I had also begun to get pain in my left calf muscle—it felt like cramp, but didn't think much about it at the time. Is there anything else I can suffer from! This really is a crap experience!

We had an appointment coming up with the oncologist so were looking forward to hearing what he thought of my progress, or lack of it! I was becoming quite ill and not from the cancer. The pain in my calf kept returning and I told Emma about it—she was immediately concerned, since she knew this was a sign of a blood clot. OMG—this chemotherapy is going to kill me before the cancer does! We added it to our list for the oncologist because our appointment was only the next day. We arrived at the hospital in good time for the appointment and checked-in at the reception desk—I didn't have to give my name now, they knew me and it was like a second home in a funny sort of way. Not that I wanted to live there!

We sat and waited for my name to be called. He was usually running late, so expected a 40 min delay. It's a long time to sit in a waiting room full of cancer patients waiting for news of their fate too. Such a strange world we have found ourselves in. I heard my name called and we jumped up and followed the oncologist to his office again. He sat us down and asked me how I was doing. I gave him the headlines on what has been going on and he looked shocked. He didn't always know the full ins and outs of everything, so he listened to all the crap I had been going through since our last appointment.

He didn't have a choice though—I was determined for him to know the full extent of it all. Emma helped with the details as I talked him through the headlines—we had become quite a double act in these appointments. I could see the oncologist look at Emma with a wry smile because he knew she was a nurse and probably had some very valid questions and queries which kept him on the back foot! He reviewed my blood results and he confirmed how poor they looked, which we knew already. He said that I need a blood transfusion to help with my anaemia, which I didn't mind if it gave my blood a booster. I told him about the pain in my calf, but he dismissed it, much to our surprise.

Emma attempted to reinforce the severity of this, but he thought it wasn't a blood clot and probably just a chemotherapy symptom. Neither of us were convinced, but we didn't wish to argue. Emma and I looked at each other and exchanged similar thoughts without saying a word. We would have to keep our own eyes on this. I had a CT scan coming up very soon, so let's see what that reveals. My calf pain wasn't there all the time, so I convinced myself it wasn't too serious.

There was not much else to discuss with the oncologist—I was basically not doing well on the chemotherapy as my body was struggling to endure it! I did begin to wonder what else I could do though, because if I cannot tolerate this treatment, there isn't anything else to offer! This fact did make me begin to worry a little and was suddenly feeling quite vulnerable after previously feeling quite upbeat about the little learnings and adjustments we had made already.

We set our next appointment with the oncologist and a time I could have my blood transfusion. You really go through emotional ups and downs with all of this and we felt like we were on a down again! We just felt rock bottom with everything and thought that it can only get better from here, surely! This thought weirdly kept our heads up and we continued with our own, evolving regimen. Let's focus on what we can control, we thought!

It wasn't many days before I had my blood transfusion and CT scan appointments. I had been trying to focus on work for a period—I was finding this a good distraction amongst the chaos in the other world of being the poorly person! It helped pass the time, but I was still trying to shuffle meetings around constantly around my mounting appointments. In between, the researching and reading continued. You never actually never stop doing this—it is like you are looking for gold, hoping to find that nugget which will liberate you from this situation. You never stop the looking and the hoping to find! My mind was constantly reminding me, "If you stop looking, you will not have a chance of survival!"

I checked into the hospital ward for my blood transfusion and they sat me down in a chair in the oncology unit. I didn't know how they would do this, but it was much like when I have my chemotherapy. They put a canula into my vein and then hooked up a big bag of blood and basically pumped it into me! It sounded much worse than it was, so was relieved about this. It was soon over and they were happy for me to go home. On the way home, I was thinking that I must have experienced all the scans, checks and problems by now. I just hope so!

I found myself living around my appointments now, which meant it was controlling me and I just had to accept this—I couldn't change anything, could I? Talking of appointments, I needed to go for my CT scan now. Another familiar drive to the hospital and another department to check into. I sat and waited for the scan—I knew what was entailed now. The most impacting thing about these scans is not being able to eat! I was starving, as ever! I took some snack food with me this time so I could eat it after the scan. I recall how the first CT scan I had didn't show the cancer in my lymph system, so wasn't filled with confidence in doing this scan. I felt it a waste of time and money.

However, I wasn't going to argue at this stage and just got on with it. They called me in and I did the usual consumption of the fizzy powder and they got me on the sliding table. Breathe in and hold, breathe normally… blah—the scanner was talking to me again! About 20 mins later, we are all done. I got dressed and drove home again. I was getting quite slick at these appointments—it was becoming quite a challenge to handle them all and I was trying to schedule them more strategically by now so I can make them fit my schedule a little more! It was the usual waiting game for the scan results now.

Since having this cancer, I had begun to reflect upon my life and mentally thought about what I want to do with the rest of it. I wasn't thinking of what I wanted to do before I die, because I wasn't even entertaining that ever occurring. I was beating this damn thing and no matter how crap things become, nothing was going to deter me from this objective. It had become a major project and I was doing the research and risk assessment—this was a familiar process for me and why should I not treat this cancer as I would a new business proposition.

The only problem was with this 'project' is that I didn't have many mitigation options to all of the risks! Too many red flags—this project would never fly! I still felt mentally strong and was taking things one day at a time—your brain cannot seem to cope with any more than that. I had only completed three chemotherapy sessions and still needed three more. Haven't I endured enough already? How the hell will I ever complete this—it seems a never-ending endurance.

It was scan results day and we both were feeling quietly optimistic. I was thinking about the 'no pain, no gain' approach again and this was the first scan since starting this treatment. I hope it has done something, because it has seriously taken its toll on me. It has to give me something back! We found ourselves in the office with the oncologist soon enough and we sat in the same old chairs again. The oncologist began informing us that the CT scan showed that the tumour had begun to reduce in size a bit, but it was a 'measurable' bit.

I was really pleased to hear this, but I was worried whether the scan was any good given the misses it made on my first scan! Emma was already smiling a glimmer of hope with these results and it is just what we needed to hear right now after the recent events we had experienced. Whilst Emma and I shared a smile, the oncologist then continued to point out that the scan had also found two blood clots on my lungs.

He mentioned them rather casually, but we both immediately stopped feeling relief as it was now replaced with fear! What! Two blood clots on my lungs that could kill me at any time! OMG! Emma instantly reminded the oncologist about my complaints of calf pain in our last meeting, but he didn't have much to say about that. I felt vulnerable once more and felt like I was in a game trying to dodge the bullets that were trying to kill me. Every time I had thought I had mastered a level, a new challenge was introduced. This was insane! So now I have another life-threatening situation to deal with both physically and mentally. He got me a direct appointment with another team who would have to help me out with this. I now learned that I will need to have daily injections of blood thinning drug to help dissipate the clots. Really? Daily injections now!

How could I get these done every day?—Emma could do them, but this was becoming quite impractical! I thought that I might only need these for a short period to alleviate the clots, but I was told, "No, these are for life!" Oh great! I could see my future not quite shaping how I had imagined it and dependencies like this were starting to creep in, destroying the vision I had hoped for.

I could not rely on others having to inject this into me every day, so I quickly learned how to do it myself and this made me feel less of a dependency! Just something else to add to the tally of things I now need to do to stay alive, I thought. In addition to the injections, I would need to wear stockings for a period of time too. These stockings were like the flight socks you can wear, but these were a nice tan colour! It was summer in the UK and these won't look cool with my shorts, I was thinking—trying to find a funny side to this situation!

We eventually got home again and I really felt beaten up! Armed with more medication and requirements, we were emotionally exhausted with the roller coaster we found ourselves on. This was one hell of a ride—plenty of twists and turns and you cannot get off it because it never stops! One-way ticket to where, I thought! I was losing my trust in some of the hospitals antics and this motivated me to become more reliant on our own path we had begun carving for ourselves. Our own learnings were starting to make more sense and empower us in a variety of areas.

We had begun to see themes amongst the vast information out there about cancer and cancer treatment. We had also noticed how different regimes were even between areas within the UK, let alone the rest of the world! This didn't fill us with much confidence because how do you know which is right or wrong, best of worst! This is certainly a trial and error game, but trial and error needs time for mistakes to be made.

I was still becoming more and more vegan and cutting out the stuff I shouldn't be eating and consuming more of the stuff I should be eating! I had totally gone off coffee, which I used to love and drank far too much of, upon reflection. I had another blood test soon and hoped that my blood transfusion had done the trick to bring me back up to speed—enough for me to receive another beating from the dreaded chemotherapy. I needed some good news for a change!

I was getting a dab hand injecting myself every morning—one less dependency on others is a big deal when you are in this dire situation. I was experimenting with different sites and stabbing myself with the needle quickly and also going in slowly. It felt pretty weird injecting yourself, but what the hell—I treated it like a new skill I was learning. It was one of those stinging injections—as you pushed the liquid in, it would feel like a bee sting and sometimes I found I had to push really hard to get the stuff into me. I think I was using the same sites too often and there were hardened lumps under my skin.

Every morning, I would do my injection first before I forgot and then start wading through all my medication and supplements. I would stagger the supplements throughout the day because at first I was downing them all at once and it was making me feel a bit nauseous and this was something I was definitely keen to avoid. In between the scan to scan living, you live treatment session to treatment session. You cannot stop yourself revolving around them because they are so impactful and you are both dreading the after-effects whilst hoping they are doing something beneficial!

This journey was one to challenge your mind, that was for sure! I read and was told about how coffee enemas helped boost your immune system and can detox your body which sounded right up my alley—literally. I was not a fan of the concept of enemas and if you don't know what they are, then it is basically an 'up your bum' thing! I was more focused upon the benefits and hear some people swear by them in their treatment regimen. I didn't have anything to lose, so ordered a kit online. It soon arrived and I had read the procedure several times, so I knew what I should be doing. It sounded a bit messy, but here goes anyway! You have to lay on your side and get your coffee solution, which is basically a strong Americano, in a small container bag.

Skipping ahead, I was done and I was waiting patiently for the reaction. I lay down for a bit and massaged my tummy, as was suggested. Nothing was happening…oops, spoke too soon! I was off and it certainly did its job! I felt drained and exhausted afterwards though, but half expected this because of the detoxing effects. However, I was feeling more and more exhausted and not very well at all after this. Well, this is just typical! I try one thing to help me out and it makes me feel like absolute crap! Maybe the coffee was too strong—who knows! Outside of the hospital treatment, you are really on your own and there isn't any proper support for anything more holistic.

The doctors aren't interested in anything that is not medically based—they are really under tight reigns with the protocols and so on. I was fast learning how cancer was an industry that is primarily controlled by the pharmaceutical industry. Imagine if everyone was curing themselves of cancer through more natural means—they would not have a business! It is predicted that the cancer drug market will reach $176.50 Billion by 2025! (Site: prnewswire.com, 14 Oct 2019) You also see headlines like this one from the Independent, UK: "Pharmaceutical giant plotted to destroy cancer drugs to drive prices up by 4,000%"—you cannot seem to trust the intentions of these giant businesses and they seem to manipulate and monopolise the industry to favour themselves.

In England alone, the NHS estimated that this would have cost them $380 million per year—this is a massive industry! More and more of us are getting this horrible disease and this means more and more revenue for the pharmaceuticals. We need to wake up and change our lifestyles so that we don't need cancer treatment, because we can remain healthy by simply being more in tune with our bodies! I have certainly learnt that we can avoid many serious illnesses by listening to our bodies more and living healthier lifestyles—it sounds simple and obvious doesn't it, so why don't we! Tell me why!

My blood test was finally done for my 4th chemotherapy session and it was that waiting game again for the results. I had my fingers crossed that the transfusion had helped me out, but on the other hand I didn't want the chemotherapy to destroy it again. You can tear yourself in half with these emotions—it was a double-edged sword because you wanted to treat the cancer, but at such a detriment! Your mind and body are going crazy and not knowing which way to turn—it feels like you are having to endure ten rounds with Tyson in the boxing ring! You get hit and fall down, but manage to get up again somehow and no sooner you have got on your feet, BANG! you are hit again and down you go!

But each time you fall, you become scarred and begin to experience permanent damage from all of the falls! I was still determined not to be beaten and would need to use my head to win this fight—I already knew this and I believed that if I kept my head focused, then I would find a way to win this battle! It was brains and not brawn that was going to triumph…

Guess what? No phone call to tell me I cannot have my chemotherapy, so felt pleased to be back on track. I had lost touch with my 'cancer buddies' now, since I was totally out of sync with their treatments. I headed to the hospital for my treatment and realised I was now passing the half-way point in my treatment. I was seeing new faces in the ward and again felt on my own. In fact, I had been feeling more and more on my own as I was doing more of my own treatment alongside the hospital visits! However, I turned this loneliness feeling into one of empowerment, believing that I was ahead of the game against all of the others on this ward. I was on a different path to them and had gained so much knowledge in the process—even more than the staff working on the ward in terms of 'how to treat cancer'.

People would ask me how I am doing and I would explain how I am battling the cancer and they seemed surprised by how I am having the courage to do so much else in parallel to the intermittent chemotherapy sessions. I was already making people think about their own journeys and inspiring some to try additional things—I was giving them hope, focus and empowerment. So many of the cancer patients are solely trusting the medical path and put all of their faith into it, having no courage to think outside of the box. I felt sorry for these ones because I felt they were not learning about the true cause of the cancer and weren't being motivated enough to give something else to their own body which may help it restore itself!

I quickly understood that everyone has a different mindset about cancer and you certainly cannot force anyone to do anything they are not comfortable with. I, however, am a risk taker and will also push every boundary to see if it moves! Somebody has to or we will all continue to function within a boundary which has been defined by somebody else—who says it is always right? Nobody made new discoveries by staying within a boundary. When you reflect upon this some more, you will find that you have defined so many boundaries within your own life without realising it and often find it difficult to operate or explore beyond that boundary. It could be a boundary within your workplace where you feel a lack of confidence in moving to a more senior role or in in your personal life where you won't pursue a passion because you are afraid of failing or what others may think. This is YOUR life and YOU can do whatever you want with it—whilst staying lawful, of course! Don't let YOU restrict yourself in following a dream! You live once—make it count and make an impression!

Anyway, back to reality! My fourth chemotherapy session was about to start. The nurse was trying to put the canula into my veins and already had made two attempts. Oh, here we go, I thought. You could get my veins with a barge pole! The nurse asked a colleague to try, so let's hope we can find a vein this time. Well, three further attempts later and I was starting to look like a pin cushion! Still no success! I think my body was telling them that I am not to have any more of this toxic poison called chemotherapy! My body was right, of course, but this wasn't the objective of my 'hospital' treatment plan!

Another nurse came along and I had become a new challenge for the nursing team. First one to get into my vein wins a prize! Whilst I could see the funny side of this, I wasn't happy with the damage that was being done to my body. It finally took eight attempts to get a vein willing enough to surrender itself to the treatment! They had found a weak link! I was covered in plasters on the other 7 holes in my hands and forearms!

It had now become a standing joke about my veins' unwillingness to cooperate and the nurses were fearing doing the job from now on! Emma hadn't joined me today and I glad she wasn't wasting her time sitting around here in this depressing world! I had taken my work laptop and managed to catch up on a few things whilst I was stuck in a chair. This helped pass the time and I got a little more up to date with my work—win-win!

I was still managing to function at work, but continued to disrupt them with my more predictable 'bad days' and relentless appointments. I was somehow maintaining a level head despite what was being thrown at me throughout this treatment regimen! I had no idea how all of this was going to end up, but decided not to focus upon that and concentrate on the here and now. Nothing could prepare you for this experience and you have to learn and adapt quickly and keep ahead of the game. If you don't, you will end up not being in control of your treatment and rely totally upon the medical environment and the decisions that they make for you. I was not going to this place…ever!

Today went pretty quickly and Emma picked me up from the hospital. It was nice to see her again and we headed back home to our familiar and safe sanctuary called home. I didn't really want to see people I knew at the moment—I didn't know what to say about everything, because I would have to reflect on everything which meant looking back. I wasn't doing any looking back right now and considered the past, the past—my focus was forwards and much of my conversation about my status and progress was in the present tense, which I conveyed in an optimistic manner.

I was optimistic though and never drifted from this approach, even through really bad times. It was so important that my mind knew what my intentions were and I maintained this train of thought throughout everything I did. I told myself that I may look like crap whilst I am going through this, but it would be a temporary thing and I can, and will, recover from this. When I do fully recover, I will be stronger, wiser and healthier than I have ever been, so watch out future! I couldn't stop reading books about how others had beaten cancer and there were many methodologies and experiences. I was liking the breadth of these, since it meant that there are many options!

I had choices in my regimen and considered everything carefully and concisely, continuing to apply a mental analysis of more popular and evidence-based themes—a histogram approach for those with a more mathematical mind! I was enjoying learning more and more about these emerging themes and how I could adopt or transition to them. It was a continuous learning process and you seem to have this energy inside of you that will not stop wanting to learn. I liked this energy and used it to my advantage. I was starting to feel quite a really powerful ability developing inside of me—it is hard to describe. This had become a project for both Emma and I where we compared notes with each other after each independent learning episode.

This was helpful, since it helped us validate what we had just learnt, because we had to recite this back to each other. This process continued throughout the entire treatment and it was like we formed our own judge and jury for new pieces of a jigsaw puzzle that we wanted to introduce. We were a formidable force and we had doubled our learning pace with both of us contributing to the process! Team Adams!

My enthusiasm was soon hampered by the side-effects of the chemotherapy, which had kicked in again with its usual full force! I was getting tired of this continuous onslaught of feeling ok and full of energy to suddenly becoming like some comatose wreck again! I just longed for more stability in myself so I could be more dependable at work and at home, as well as be more consistent with my own treatment regimen, which was now becoming disrupted by the medical treatment! I was feeling like my own treatment regime was stabilising and it was more of a case of consistency and focus.

I had recently added juicing to the plan, which consisted of fresh lemon segments, spinach or kale and beetroot. Each of them had been shown to provide great benefits in what I was trying to achieve, so created my own cocktail, which I consumed every morning as a smoothie with ice. Not something you would probably think would taste nice? Well, you're right, it didn't taste nice and you had to almost chew it down. Heck—this was valuable medicine, so I was all in! I had lost my care for what my palate thought! Here are some of the benefits that I was focused upon, so you can see why I chose them:

Fresh Lemon:

- Cancer preventing
- Reduces infections—vitamin C
- Improves liver function
- Strengthens nails—mine had become brittle and weak
- Helps balance PH levels—I was on plant-based diet and the more alkaline, the better for cancer

Spinach/Kale:

- Packed with vitamins A, C and K
- Spinach helps as an antacid, which was beneficial for my cancer and its location

Beetroot:

- Improves blood flow—this means more oxygen distribution which cancer doesn't like
- Boosts stamina—I needed this with the chemotherapy impacts
- Detoxifies the liver
- Helps reduce risk of cancer—vitamin C and red cell regeneration to help prevent anaemia

I was feeling super-charged after this each day and it just became a routine in no time!

After my fourth chemotherapy session, I found I was bouncing back a bit more quickly. Well, bouncing might not be the best word, but it certainly felt that way in contrast to how I used to respond. I knew my body was becoming more tolerant to the treatment, even though it was still hurting me. I felt I was doing everything I could possibly do to not only try to counter the nasty effects of chemotherapy, but to also fight this damn disease with my own armoury! I was really fighting two battles simultaneously, it seemed!

I was due another meeting with my oncologist, but didn't really feel there was any benefit in these meetings. I was feeling like I knew quite a bit now about cancer, the cancer industry, the medical approach and was really struggling to believe in any of them! In my view, they were limiting, narrow minded and lacked any holistic or integrated approach to treating this disease. It was out-dated and seemed somehow constrained by something. I was continuing to transition to my own treatment regimen more and more and felt in control at last in where it was heading.

We had our meeting with the oncologist despite my reservations and sat somewhat despondently in the chair nearest his desk. He began fiddling with his computer as he always did and was focused upon this more than he was with us, his patients! This didn't amuse me and only fuelled my reservation in having these meetings. Always login issues and then it would be printer problems—either he needs training or someone needs to fix this stuff, I thought quietly to myself.

Emma was thinking the same and we would often smirk at each other when he wasn't looking at us, which was most of the time! Eventually, we were all connected and we could continue. He asked how I was feeling as per usual and it was pretty much the same in respect of the chemotherapy side effects. I was still angry about the blood clots not getting enough attention beforehand and the resulting blood clots in my lungs. I decided it was time to tell him what I was doing that was not within his treatment control. I presented a prepared list of all of the supplements I was taking and discussed my use of cannabis oil, diet and nutritional regimen. He looked surprised—it was an impressive list!

I was waiting for a reaction, but he didn't say much other than a mixture of facial expressions which I had to interpret for myself. I wasn't actually bothered what he thought—I wasn't seeking any approval. I thought he might learn something from it! Before I shared the list, I outlined the approach I was taking with supplements and nutrition and he said, "Oh yes, I have heard that this root thing is good for treating cancer…oh, what was it called…I can't remember…!" Well, you can imagine how I was feeling about this half-hearted attempt to bring some non-medical, yet relevant, content into discussion.

I replied, partly interrupting him, by saying, "It's turmeric!" I knew all along what he was trying to recall and it amused me to watch him dig into his brain to find this buried piece of information. That was all he could offer for alternatives! Anyway, we pushed him for a PET scan to see how things were progressing. It is always difficult to request PET scans because there are not many of them around and our closest was in Oxford, just over an hour away. He did always manage to justify it somehow, which we were grateful for.

Still lacking in faith of the CT scans, we were keen to gain some more reliable information about the activity of the tumours as well as the sizes. Me, being logical, felt that the tumour could be large, but inactive so the net threat is low. Conversely, it could small and very active and therefore present more of a threat. It was the context I was seeking and was of course hoping that the tumour was becoming less active, i.e., dying!

We set our next meeting with the oncologist and returned home. This new world of appointments was becoming quite familiar and I was getting used to their disruption—I had simply accepted that they need to happen and I would just need to work around them. I didn't mind the scans, but they came with a physical and emotional impact. On one hand, you are seeing what it going on inside of you, which you can only see by scanning really, and on the other hand, you don't want to know if it is bad news and this was the emotional roller coaster in action! The double-edged sword! The scan date came through just before our holiday which was perfect timing really. It meant our minds would be occupied whilst waiting for the results. All these scans and checks were so familiar to us now and we took them in our stride as if they had always been part of our lives. They were certainly part of our lives and we reluctantly had to fit around them!

I was getting into more of a routine with everything now, partly through familiarity and partly because of the cyclic nature to appointments and treatments, unless they were disrupted by something. Our holiday that we had planned in Devon was fast approaching and as it became closer, it became more exciting. I was really looking forward to this break, as was Emma. We felt we needed it big time and it would be nice to see Ben too and catch up with him. I was really missing him not being home. I miss the chats we used to have about the common interests we had with cars, science stuff and conspiracies!

This weekend, we were off down to south coast again to get some more cannabis oil supplies. The weather forecast was good so we planned a bit of a walk along the coastal path whilst we were down there. Ben was over for the weekend and he was keen to come down with us and see what all this was about! We awoke to a bright sunny morning—this always put me in a good mood. I just love being out in the sunshine—I feel like I can recharge from it. We got our essentials and jumped in the car. I was keen to drive down and felt good. We didn't experience hardly any traffic on the two-hour drive and everything seemed to flow. You know when you get days when the traffic lights are always green for you, the slow trucks are behind you, the junctions have convenient gaps for your arrival! You are in a flow state when it is like this and it is like something is arranging the timings of everything just for you!

We picked up our supplies and didn't need to chat so much this time. We discussed my progress a little with our supply lady—she was always keen to learn how I was getting on and offered her advice on some of the alternatives. There was so much to try and do, it was practically impossible to do everything, so we made our own judgments about which of the alternatives we believed made sense for us. We said our goodbyes and headed for the beach. It was pretty busy because it was a weekend and the sun was out! Those two things don't always happen in the UK! We were in a good place we felt with everything and I was feeling quite well considering. I didn't look too bad either, but maybe that was just my opinion. I held my head up high and pretended I was normal and had none of this crap going on in our lives.

We found our favourite fish and chip shop again. I was mainly vegan by now, but I fancied some fish. I wasn't an ethical vegan, although I don't like the thought of us eating animals. Today, however, I was treating myself. I still wanted to enjoy food and this was indeed a treat for me! We sat on the sand and looked out at the sea as we ate and chatted about normal stuff for a change. We watched the surfers trying to catch the larger waves and watched the families on the beach playing and probably not having to deal with the things we were going through. I wasn't envious, because I wouldn't wish this on anyone—it was more of a reflection on our lives before this happened.

My mind was replaying all of the great holidays we had together as the kids were growing up and how grateful I felt for being able to experience these precious times! We had certainly got some lovely memories which we will all cherish forever. If I am to leave this world, then at least we have created memories, I quietly thought to myself! As we were finishing eating, the cheeky seagulls were already waiting for the left-overs. They won't find any from me! They do come very close to you just in the hope of something. They are pretty big birds up close and some seem to have about a 4 to 5 feet wingspan!

We decided to walk up along the beach barefoot for a bit—it felt so nice to feel warm sand under my feet. It seemed to soothe everything and I felt like I was reconnecting with the earth again. Such simple things in life had become everything to me these days and I was super appreciative for every day, for every experience. I was definitely living for the moment, living in the 'now'! I had recently bought a drone and was keen to try it out further down the beach where it was more hilly. We headed back to the car and drove further along the beach where there were less people. I unpacked the drone and soon got it in the air.

Drones were just starting to becoming more popular and you find you attract quite an audience once airborne! I was starting to get into my photography at this time and the drone was a decent camera in the air, so could capture those angles you would never normally achieve. I flew it out to sea and spun it around to see ourselves in the camera. I was loving the flying experience as well as the camera angles. It can go completely out of sight so have to rely on the GPS map on my phone display to see where it is and which direction it is facing—a bit unnerving to begin with!

I took some photos and video of the surroundings and flew it back—a successful flight with no damage! Ben was getting into videography at the time and producing videos for people. I could see he had his eye on the drone and was already thinking what he could do with it! We packed up our things and got back on the road. We were keen to beat the rush hour traffic on the motorways and we were hoping for another 'flow' state trip home. We weren't disappointed—we had a real smooth drive home and we all felt like we had been away for a two-day break. I had more of my cannabis stock now, so could continue with my dosing!

My PET scan appointment day was here. Emma had taken some time off to take me to Oxford. We had done this before, so we knew the format now and how long things take. You aren't able to eat before the scan, so took some food with me for afterwards. We had a fairly early appointment which was good, but it meant we had to drive in rush hour and this can add 20-30 mins to the journey!

Anyway, we arrived in good time and checked-in at the reception. We sat in the waiting room and we began to think what the results could be from this scan.

We so wanted some good news, which meant the treatment regime was working and we could continue on this trajectory for a better outcome. I was called into another waiting area and got sat down in my isolated cubicle. The nurse came over and put the canula in my arm and began injecting the radio-active glucose into me. It felt cold as it worked its way through my veins. I could see why the cubicles are isolated with these radio-active substances around. I felt like I was in some bio-warfare movie with the level of protection the staff were taking!

Now I had to wait for an hour for the solution to work its way around my body before the scan. There were some crappy old magazines to read and an old looking DVD player with some outdated films to watch. I was prepared this time, I had taken my iPad in and downloaded something to watch. It really helped pass the time! I hope Emma had something to pass the time in her waiting room! Our phone signals didn't work here, so we couldn't communicate during this period. We were both quite anxious about the outcome of this scan, so it was probably best that we distracted ourselves for a while.

I headed into the scan room and lay on the bed. They buzzed me forwards and backwards for a while to set their datums as they do in the CT scans. Right, off we go and about 20 mins later, I was done! The results waiting game clock can be started now. This clock starts whether you like it or not and the more you try not to think about it, the more it will pester your mind! We got back in the car and began our drive back home. We were optimistic about this scan—we both felt like it should show progress. I hope so and we clung onto that thought as long as we could. We were going to be on holiday whilst we wait for the results, which was annoying timing—not what you want to be thinking about then! Anyway, we weren't going to let it ruin our holiday.

The long-awaited day had arrived—our holiday! Ben was home already and we got the car packed up pretty quickly. It reminded me of beach holidays we used to do with the kids when they were younger and trying to fit all of the stuff they wanted to take into the car! The forecast wasn't looking great which was a bit frustrating, but we're going anyway so let's make the best of it. We had to pack a mix of clothes from swim stuff to winter coats to cater for the un-predictable UK weather! We had the dog too, so she needed a seat! She sat in the back with the kids—she is a Westie, so not a big dog, although she likes to spread herself out!

We got on the road and it felt liberating. It was like we were leaving all of the troubles behind and giving ourselves some freedom for a week. We usually holiday abroad in the summer where the weather is more guaranteed, but we simply couldn't really do that at the moment. It felt too soon to be trying to do that with everything as it was right now. We were officially on holiday and we had some time together as a family again. Hell, these were precious times now and I so wanted a bit of normality for a while—we all did! We finally arrived at the house we had rented. It had three levels and was built into the hillside, where it looked across a tree-filled valley. The main living area was on the mid-floor and it had a balcony across the full width of the property. The bi-fold doors would open up the entire back of the house, so it felt like you were outside. It was perfect!

We had a great bedroom at the top with a fantastic view across the valley from the massive bed that positioned right in the middle of the room. We thought that was a bit strange at first until we lay on the bed and could see an amazing out of the bank of windows built into the eaves. It was cloudy and a little breezy, but dry and we were going to make the most of this short break. We looked at the map to see where we were in relation to our surroundings and had a quick think about what we could do. I don't think we are going to be swimming in the sea though!

We unpacked our things and made ourselves at home. We had like an outdoor eating area with a couple of fire-pits which we were keen to use. It was about 3 pm and we decided to chill here for the afternoon and go out somewhere tomorrow. We had brought some provisions with us, so didn't need to go shopping just yet. It was so relaxing being in a different environment and chilling out. We all appreciated that moment for a while. This was a cruel thing that was happening to us, but it had chosen us, so we had better just deal with it! I was feeling like I was putting so much strain on my family—I know I couldn't help what was going on, but you just cannot stop that feeling hitting you, constantly!

Despite all these emotions, we continued to try and relax and catch-up with each other. As the evening approached, Ben was keen to light the fire pits, so we found some stuff to burn and got them both roaring! We needed them because it was damn cold, even on this August evening in the summer! We had brought some marshmallows with us and I probably shouldn't be eating them because of their sugar content, but did allow a few in.

They did taste very sweet though—you really find sweet things ultra-sweet when you have cut out sugar from much of your diet. We were all quite tired that evening—I think it was the whole cancer situation making our minds work overtime and exhausting us. We were mentally tired! This was our first night here, so we were all keen to try out our beds and our new rooms.

We awoke to a sunny morning and we all slept well. It was pretty quiet where we were staying and it was nice not waking up to alarms. I got up and made a cuppa for us both—I was loving my green tea at the moment. I hated the taste at first, but treated it like medicine until a couple of months later and I was craving it. Not like an addict, but it was definitely my 'go to' hot drink if I had a choice. I would always carry green tea bags with me when I was out in case I needed them in a café or something. Green tea is everywhere now, but even just three years ago, it was barely available in cafes and restaurants.

I think Earl Grey was as close as they could get back then. I checked the weather forecast and it looked like it was going to better in the first half of our week and then become more and more cloudy and, most likely, wet. Typical for an English summer, I thought. I was keen to get on to the coastline and check that out. Our dog loved the beach and the sea, but so many beaches do not allow dogs in the summer time. We searched for 'dog-friendly' beaches, which was a short list. We found a couple to explore and we gathered our winter and summer clothes because you just don't know how the weather will be for sure!

We huddled into the car and began our adventure. The beach was only about 25 mins away and we found a little grassy car park on the top of a hillside. There was an ice-cream van parked up so we hoped it would be there when we got back—a special treat for me! The beach was not easily accessible and you had to walk down quite a few wonky, make-shift steps built into the cliff to get onto it. The dog found these steps a bit too much for her, so she was carried for most of them which she liked, I think. There was quite a breeze along the beach which made it feel chilly, but the sun was shining and we had our shorts and t-shirts on.

Being on the beach felt like it was recharging me. I love the feel of looking out to sea and watching the continuous stream of gentle, rhythmic waves flowing towards us—it was mesmerising. I could sit and watch this spectacle of nature all day long, but we had exploring to do! There were quite a few people that had got down to the beach with their dogs too and our dog was wasting no time in getting acquainted and checking out the water temperature. Ben and I decided to go for a short walk around the cove into a hidden bay. The tide was coming in, so it was now or never. We found a route across some slippery rocks and we went to see what we could find.

We loved doing simple things like this together and it was a chance for us to catch up with nobody else around. We tend to enjoy the same types of experiences and I realised how much I had missed his company now that he had moved out. We didn't talk about my illness and just focused upon enjoying the time together in nature! Ben was an avid vegan and he had inspired me to become mostly vegan by now—he had researched all the benefits and it made total sense to me. Ben always did some in-depth research before buying something or embarking on a new path and I trusted his judgements in this respect. It was nice to talk about boy's stuff and how the universe works with him! We eventually found our way to a hidden cove and sat on some huge rocks to take in the tranquillity and absence of other people. We looked out across a very still sea, as if the world had stopped for a while—it looked more like a lake and the sun was reflecting on the small ripples in an incredibly hypnotising manner.

It felt like our beach for a brief time, but the tide hadn't stopped moving and our hidden cove was soon filling with water! We kept ourselves high and found a higher, more precarious, route back around to the main bay. This is what we had missed doing and I was forgetting that I was ill with this horrible disease. In that moment, so many memories of our previous holidays with the kids were flooding back and it felt quite over-whelming. We have had some brilliant holidays and made so many memories which we all cherished individually. Memories had become so important now and I was clinging to all of them!

Emma and Katy were playing with the dog in the puddles on the beach. Our dog loved water and chasing, so she was in her element here! There were many tide-made puddles around the rocks and they glistened as the sun shone on them, highlighting their presence. We had bought a little picnic to the beach to snack on. It was so nice to get away from everything and have this simple family time on the sand. We found a sheltered spot and sat and chatted about the anything and everything. Emma and I spoke positively about my outlook and what additional actions I was now taking as well as the medical path of chemotherapy.

This reassured the kids and it gave them a sense of hope in the midst of this crazy situation. It still didn't feel real to me and I almost wanted to keep that feeling—it kept the disease at a distance, as if I wasn't letting it in! it was damn right about that though! I was not letting it in—into my mind at least! It may have infested my body, but not my mind and it was my mind, I decided, that would need to win this battle and support my body through this.

I have a mindset where I love to find solutions and will take on almost any challenge to find a solution. While this mindset can drive Emma mad sometimes, it was vitally needed now! At a basic level, I knew this challenge wasn't any different, other than I would need to make and maintain radical changes to overcome it. This didn't faze me and I was willing to endure anything that led me to this winning outcome!

We finished up our snacks and gave the dog a few treats so she didn't feel left out. The sea looked inviting, but was way too cold for a swim. It would have been ok for an endurance, but this was a holiday! I was already losing weight and was beginning to look a little gaunt in my face. I always took pride in my appearance, but knew it was going to be taking a hit from all of this cancer treatment. I just accepted it for now and focused on getting over this, rather than worrying too much about what I looked like! I just didn't want to look ill—I wanted to disguise this as much as I could because I hated the thought of people knowing you are not very well and trying to awkwardly sympathise.

I wanted to quietly just get on with it and almost hide in plain sight—being as normal as possible! I had spent years going to the gym and building up my strength and stamina. All I could do now, is watch it all fade away in a matter of a few months. Whilst I was trying to maintain my positive mind, there are constant reminders and nudges from your mind. It says things like, "This might be your last family holiday!" or "How will Emma and the kids cope when you're gone?"

I hated this barrage of thoughts that you seemed to have no control over. I ignored them all, but they fester away at you and try to bring you down! This was one hell of a physical and mental battle—I may keep saying this, but it was the conclusion I kept coming back to! I had only two more chemotherapy sessions to do to complete the six planned. It was like a finish line, but not sure it will result in any finishing in reality other than just an ending of a phase. I couldn't see beyond this point at the moment. I had no idea what state I would be in or what happens to any other treatment. This was all they could offer, so I was going to be screwed if the totality of what I am doing is not working! My mind returned back to our holiday and found myself still sitting on the beach. My mind had wondered somewhat as it tends to do now and then these days.

The days together on our holiday were going by quicker than I wanted them to. I wished I could press the pause button on life sometimes and have a little longer to enjoy those precious moments. We spent the next few days doing pretty much the same things and taking each day as it came, deciding what we felt like doing. The weather was holding out so far, which I was grateful for. Emma's brother and family were not going to be far from us later in the week, so we arranged for them to come over for a catch-up. They had young children who kept them pretty busy!

I recalled how busy we used to be when our kids were their ages—it was a constant taxi service to gyms, football training, skate parks and parties. Always a party for the kids to go to! Our kids seemed to have grown up overnight and become adults. Where had that time gone! It's a familiar question that I always remember my mum and grandparents saying and now I find myself saying it!

We found a place with a lighthouse on the peninsula of a rocky coastline. I was keen to check it out and thought it may be a good place to fly my drone. It had become pretty overcast today, but we weren't letting that stop us doing things. Katy wasn't too keen though and would probably have preferred to stay in bed! It wasn't too far from us and we thought it was worth having a look whilst we were down this way. We had a late, lazy breakfast. Not as enthusiastic as we would have been if it had been a bright, sunny day, but we can't let this damn weather dictate our holiday, I thought.

We packed a few snacks and began our journey. I was liking the distraction this holiday was providing and hadn't thought once about my scan results, until now! It was that mind again—knocking on your door to remind you about all that stuff! I quickly pushed it away and focused on the drive to the light-house. We found a little layby to park in and we got our bits out the car. It was looking like it was going to rain, but we thought we would risk the short walk down a narrow lane to the light-house. We hadn't seen it yet so didn't know what to expect.

We headed down this single-track lane—there were not many people about considering it was middle of summer holidays in UK. It winded slowly downwards towards the coastline and I was liking the anticipation of what may be around the next corner. The dog was enjoying the new smells, but need to be frequently dragged away from them so we could actually make progress down this lane. We turned a sharp corner where this lane became steeper down the hillside. We could now see the light-house. It looked quite impressive at the end of this rocky coastline and was immediately filled with enthusiasm to get my drone into the air to check it out from all angles!

I quickly unpacked it and attached the propellers. A quick calibration check and it was quickly high in the air. It was such a buzz flying this drone and watching the 'bird's-eye' view from my phone's screen. Ben was keen to try it and although he had only flown it once, he was a dab hand with it and managing to maintain a constant camera angle as he manoeuvred it around the sky! It must be a boy thing—Emma and Katy weren't so excited about it all ha-ha... I got up close to the light-house and flew around it like a helicopter filming an action film. It was really cool to fly over the sea and catch some camera angles you would never normally have access to. This was a time when I had begun to get into photography and this was fast becoming one of my favourite pastimes!

I had captured some decent images and video and the battery was getting low, so started to bring it back into view and away from the sea. I was still really nervous about flying it over the water—one false move and it's game over! I had joined some Facebook drone flyer forums and there were some trying to modify their drones so they could fly up to 30,000 feet and up to 10 km away! That was before they enforced the drone code a bit more rigorously!

I got nervous when mine had just gone out of sight, let alone flying above the clouds! I packed up the drone and we headed down further to see more of the lighthouse close-up. The sea was a turquoise colour around the lighthouse rocky coastline and it looked almost tropical. We couldn't go into the lighthouse—it looked like someone actually lived there. Wow, talk about room with a view! We headed back up the lane to the car and decided to check another bay out on the way back to our house. It wasn't very warm today, so no t-shirt and shorts this time!

I was always a little disappointed with the UK's weather—it is never consistent enough to rely or depend upon it! The weather could be almost anything between March and September—it was like a lottery really and in most cases, you lose! We often used to holiday in the UK when the kids were young, so we were used to this uncertainty. We soon learnt to holiday in places like South of France, where there was more guarantee in the weather. As the kids grew up, we also used to ski in the winter, usually in the French Alps. This was a nice contrast to summer and a nice adrenaline type holiday where you expect the cold!

We found a little cove on the way home, after a little diversion. There was hardly anyone around and there was a narrow footpath that led towards the sea. We didn't know what to expect, but the path was leading somewhere! It was staying dry and the wind had dropped a little. We could hear the sea in the distance, so knew we would find it soon. Our dog was getting excited about another new adventure route and was leading the way for us, as her anticipation also grew.

Finally, we reached a ridge from where we could see the sea. The tide was almost all the way in and the waves were crashing against the rocky coastline. They call this the Jurassic coastline for a reason and much of it is rocky, yet provides some stunning scenery. There wasn't much beach left, but we clambered down to a section of sand still not yet covered. I was still savouring every simple moment of this holiday, but it felt strange reflecting on the circumstances surrounding the holiday.

Nothing was normal now and however much you pretend that everything is ok, it wasn't. I could sense this feeling in Emma and the kids, but didn't say anything. I felt their emotions and wished I could change things. I continued to focus on what I can change and this was finding an exit route out of this thing! I was realising how emotionally strong you need to be to beat these diseases—it is so vital that you are able to remain focused and disciplined. Nobody discusses this or teaches you about this in the medical world and you have to rely on your intuition and own fact finding. Some big gaps noted here and I will share my learnings with you later in this book.

We continued our holiday with lazy mornings, short excursions and cosy evenings! Emma's brother was coming over later today and it was our last night before heading back home. We needed a few provisions so Ben and I drove down to a little local store we had found on the map. We parked and took a little bag with us as we went inside. A little bag would hopefully restrain us from buying stuff we wouldn't really need, which is often the case. As we walked around the isles, Ben bumped into a friend from home. It was like a double take. Wow, all this way away and they found themselves in this small convenience store at the same time! His friend was staying not too far away with his family. That made Ben's day!

God, this break had zipped by and wasn't looking forward to facing the medical environments again. I was just getting used to a bit of normal life as a family again. This also meant Ben going back to Guildford and us not seeing him again for a while. I felt an anger build inside of me because of the impact this disease was having on all of our lives. I had to put a stop to it! Anyway, I had to again tell my mind to stop these unhelpful thoughts and let's just focus upon going forwards. I was talking to myself a lot recently, but found that it was helpful to put things in perspective. I don't mean talking out loud like some psycho, but just that mind talking thing—I am sure we have all done it!

We checked our cupboards to see what other food we had left for our last day and evening. Luckily, we now had enough to cook up something for all of us, when Emma's brother arrived with his family. It was a really foggy and damp day. We had no view today and couldn't see much of the garden, let alone the view over the forest. We had hoped we could all go for a walk later, but the weather put a stop to that. Emma's brother has three kids—the eldest a boy and two younger girls. The eldest girl loved Katy, so that would keep her occupied.

I thought we could fly the drone with the eldest boy who was about six—he would love that, but the weather was pretty dire. Let's see how it looks when they get here! The brother and family arrived after finally finding us. It was good to see them—we hadn't seen much of anyone since my diagnosis as if we were in hibernation, at least that's what it felt like! I had a lot to discuss about my new found vegan cuisine and felt I had become somewhat a Jamie Oliver of the vegan world! I was intrigued by the creative aspect of Veganism and finding novel ways to make, bake and fry.

Emma's brother had been vegan for many years and found it difficult in the early days—nobody really knew what it meant and there was nothing with 'Vegan' labels on any produce back then. Ben was keen on discovering new vegan cuisine too, so between us, we had a lot to share with each other. The weather was still crap, so we chose to stay put and chill and chat! We liked our house we were staying in and it had plenty of space for us all. It had become quite a sanctuary for us for a short time and it had allowed us to distance ourselves from our current reality.

Emma's nephew was still keen to fly the drone, of course, but it was so foggy. I guessed we could have a quick balcony fly so he can get a feel for it! I launched it and by the time it was about 20 feet away, we couldn't see it, but we could hear it! I took it up high, hoping that it might break through the fog above us, but even that was too dense. We tracked the drone on the phone's map so we knew where it was and eventually brought it back to us. We heard its buzzing sound getting louder and louder above us and I was slightly relieved it was finally back in view.

I am not a fan on not seeing where I am flying. The drone was saturated with water like it had been submerged. I hadn't appreciated how much moisture the foggy clouds were holding. I was just glad it hadn't stop functioning! Anyway, the fly had done its job in satisfying curiosities! I soon began preparing our 'last supper'. I was enjoying cooking at this time and decided a stir fry type meal would work for most of us. I got chopping and quickly knocked up a tasty meal. Emma and Katy had begun to become vegan as much as they could in support of my transition, which I really appreciated. They still loved to eat meat, so this was a big decision for them. I was trying to become more alkaline, so acidic meat was far from my desires!

We said our goodbyes to Emma's brother and family that evening and began thinking about packing our stuff up the next day. We had to be out by midday, so we could have a pretty easy-going morning. Ironically, it was a bright sunny morning and I enjoyed an early green tea in bed looking out across the forested valley. Emma was still sleeping, so tried not to disturb her as I did some reading—more learning about cancer and less conventional options. I was hungry to learn and there seemed so much to learn. I was still wading through many angles of opinion and evidence, trying to find these common themes.

Some people had devoted much of their lives to researching and had become very passionate about their angle. Others had just done things like juicing and became cured. I was more sceptical about these because cancer isn't that simple and it adapts once you stop one of its life lines! There must be more at play and I was quickly learning how much the mind had to do with healing yourself.

Emma soon woke and we chatted about my new learnings for a short while, without being too heavy on her sleepy head. We enjoyed a late breakfast looking out over the valley. It had been a lovely break and I had really liked us all being together at this trying time. I hadn't felt bad all week and this had given the kids some confidence that I was doing 'ok' and much better than I was previously. We gathered our belongings and put the house back to how we found it. It felt like we were closing a brief chapter of our lives as we left the house and headed home. It had been an important and necessary part of our journey and another memory for Emma and the kids if this all went bad for me!

A Lovely Trip to 'The Grove'

Sunset Silhouettes Appreciation

Trying Some Arty Shots

Beautiful Lake in Norway

Looking for Hope and Inspiration

When yo u arise in the morning, think of what a privilege is it to be alive – to think, to enjoy, to love

You never know how strong you are, until being strong is the only choice you have

We arrived back home in good time and had enough day left to sort ourselves out; the kids caught up with their friends. Emma and I had needed that break and now we were home, thoughts quickly moved to the anticipation of my scan results. We had no idea of what to expect and our appointment was only a couple of days away. We felt like we couldn't get on with anything until we knew what was going on inside of me. I had been doing so many things in parallel to my chemotherapy, I was both excited and scared about how it was going.

This was our first scan since commencing treatment, so you can imagine how pivotal this was for us. It was either going to better, worse or the same. It sounds simple when listing it like that, but that is the crux of it. We were hoping for same or better—we just wanted it under control so we had more time. We had work to distract us for a couple of days, so focused upon that for the time being.

First post-treatment scan day had arrived! This was a big deal. We had a morning appointment and was grateful for that. Emma and I didn't talk much that morning and did more hugging than talking. We just felt so sick inside about what the results may show. We just wanted to know whatever the outcome. It's a horrible feeling. It was soon our turn for our appointment and it wasn't long until my name was called. My oncologist had a poker face and didn't give anything away whether good or bad news. I bet they learn that face somehow!

We followed him again to his room and sat down. He did his usual fumbling with his computer and asked how I was whilst doing this. I felt like he asked these types of questions to buy him time in sorting his computer out, rather than being genuinely concerned about my welfare! Anyway, I replied about how I was feeling and how much better I had been recently. I was certainly not looking forward to more chemotherapy, that was for sure!

He finally got access to my notes and began reading as if it was new news, like before. We prompted him about the scan results to get him along a little. We were becoming increasingly impatient by this time! He looked up and recited some of the scan report. The tumour had significantly reduced in size by about half and the activity rating term they use was showing a 70% reduction! There was no more spread to the lymph system either, so my metastases had ceased as well. In that moment, I felt almost cured—well, certainly on the right road towards it! My oncologist couldn't help but smile as Emma and I hugged it out in front of him!

This was better news than we could have ever expected at this stage. We were winning this battle of terminal cancer. The pain had been so worth the gain and I was immediately empowered to kick the ass of this cancer even further down the road. He asked us if we had any questions, but I think we were feeling too elated to think about that. The oncologist then mentioned having surgery to cut the tumour out, since the spread was no longer visible and the tumour was only in one place now. There was no way I wanted surgery, so declined instantly. Could they not consider radiotherapy first if they believed that could help target the tumour too? Less intervention, I thought.

Anyway, my oncologist got the message from me and I could see he was curious about what an earth I was doing to turn this cancer around like this! I kept that my little secret at this stage and said I would complete the final two chemotherapy sessions and go from there. I would keep postponing any surgery discussions! We agreed our next appointment date in about six weeks and left the room. We could not stop smiling and it felt like we had won the lottery! We had technically, life is a precious thing and it is priceless! You learn that quickly when something is trying to take it away from you! We couldn't wait to tell the kids and they were blown away with the results. We were feeling like we were in control and had the upper hand now. Our renewed confidence would keep us really motivated and disciplined over the coming months.

I was now back to hospital appointment routines again and had another blood test ahead of my fifth chemotherapy session. I soon received 'that' call from the hospital telling me that my blood had not recovered enough for chemotherapy. I still had very little immunity and this had become an ongoing struggle to try and replenish it. It had taken a real hit from the chemotherapy and had stayed extremely low as a result. I was trying everything to try and improve it, but must still have a lot of toxicity in my body! I waited for my next blood test and it was still out of range for chemotherapy and the next one too! I could not carry on like this.

By this time, our next appointment with my oncologist had arrived so we discussed this with him. He didn't have any suggestions really and we concluded that we would take a permanent break from chemotherapy. You can imagine that this came with mixed emotions. No chemotherapy means no more sickness and no more toxicity, but on the other hand, it means that they will push me down the surgery route, but my blood will have to recover in any case.

I considered my position and told my oncologist I will carry on running with this on my own for a while. The recent results and given me hope and courage to battle this with my own nonmedical regime. Surprisingly, he agreed and this was new territory for him too. I bet he doesn't meet many people like me who decide to run it alone. Well, you know by now that I take risks and I am not your usual person. Right, this is 'our' battle to fight now!

We spent the rest of 2017 being as disciplined as we could and stayed focused. We looked forward to a Christmas and New Year with the family! Wow, we were looking forward again! Christmas quickly arrived and I could not seem to remember much of the latter months of 2017. I must have been so focused and I hadn't dared look up in case I missed something in my regimen! I was ultra-determined now after knowing the improvements in my condition.

We spent Christmas at Emma's parents' house in Gloucestershire. It was our old stomping ground for both of us and it did always feel like home going back there. We always spent Christmas day with Emma's parents and then saw my parents and brother on Boxing day. It seemed to work out ok that way! It was still tricky trying to see Mum and Dad with them being divorced, so always expected some kind of juggling act. Before knowing my scan results, I was always wondering how many more Christmases I would see before my cancer took proper hold of me. It was a sad thought, but a realistic one at the time.

The emotional rollercoaster was well and truly running and I was on a high right now and wanted it to stay that way. The Christmas holidays were quite chilled and I didn't want to over-do anything to upset my own treatment plan! I had to be so rigid on this because I didn't want to look back and think, "I wish I didn't eat all those cakes or drink all that wine!"—you just never know what is going to trigger anything inside! Whilst this discipline was good, it was also a constant reminder of why I was doing it. You can never not worry about this!

No sooner than we were home from the Christmas festivities, we were off again to Dorset on the south coast of England. It wasn't too far from where we stayed in the summer! Emma's family on her mum's side always get together over New Year—this stems back from her Scottish grandma and the tradition continues still now! The family has become too big to celebrate together at anybody's house now, so we generally rent a large property to house about twenty of us. This year was a farmhouse with converted outbuildings. It was about a 3-4 hour drive down, so intended to stay for a few days to make the most of it. It was a great catch-up opportunity for everyone because it has been getting harder and harder to all meet up with everyone's busy, independent lives.

We arrived in the dark the day before New Year's eve so we had chance to settle in. We drove along the longest single track lane to get to the farmhouse. It was pitch black and the night sky was filled with stars, which we could plainly see without the pollution of light. The air was still and as we parked and got out the car, it already felt calm and tranquil. We emptied everything from the car and said our hellos to everyone.

Emma and I were looking forward to having a bit of a chill over next few days—we had already felt like we had done battle and come out on top. It is as if our relief was now exhausting us, as we re-adjusted to a new path on our journey. We did a bit of walking while we were here and got down to the spectacular coastline with the dog in tow. At this time of year, she was allowed on any beach so she was having a lovely time in the cold, wavy sea. The weather was pretty good for this time of year—cold, but dry! I was taking my camera to most places these days and was loving landscape photography. I used to feel selfish wanting to stop and take photographs all the time, but not anymore. It was my passion and hobby. I was going to enjoy every day I had now!

I was certainly living each day and taking time to appreciate its beauty from even the smallest things. We do live in a beautiful world and I had become quite angry with so many people not taking enough notice of Earth's wonderful nature and seem more interested in their phone screens! However, another side of me was grateful that so few were appreciating it, so it was like I had exclusive access to seeing things others didn't even know were there! I had begun to believe that I had become ill as part of my life's journey and to learn some lessons.

I had never listened to my body telling me to slow down and my head was always in charge—at least that's how it felt. I appeared to handle stress well, but I was probably just used to it and not realising the damage that stress was doing to me—more on that later! In these quieter times, I began to reflect much more on absolutely everything. I was really getting myself back to the core basics of my existence and started to take everything in my stride, rather than resist or repel things I feared or wasn't comfortable with.

Everything happens for a reason, I would tell myself and I found that once I had this mindset, life flowed much more easily. When I say 'flowed', I mean that everything seemed to happen at the right time, barriers to certain progressions appeared to dissolve and I would appear to discover something or someone exactly when I needed to. It is hard to explain, but I was noticing this more and more in my life. It was like I was, incrementally, being given clues to a puzzle and solving each part, then moving onto the next.

I was enjoying this and it made life more fun and mysterious, anticipating the next clue or discovery! I know I have digressed somewhat, but these are the constant thoughts that were now occupying my mind. I had felt a transition from fear to freedom, where I was finding a new path of hope and empowerment. This transition never ceased after this point and from this time forward, I knew in my heart I would survive this. This is all the news my mind was told from now on!

We had enjoyed our break on the coast and were now home and back into the usual pattern of life. Ben was back in Guildford and I was still working and enjoying my work and the contact with the great colleagues I engaged with. They were very supportive and appreciated any time I could provide to my role. I could not have asked for anything more and it made everything much easier to cope with, like I had a safety net with them. Since I was feeling much better from not doing chemotherapy, we had planned many small trips away during this year.

We had spent the early part of January making all of our bookings and we had a full year of travel to look forward to. We felt it would break the year up a little and help us focus. I had a few business trips coming up too within Europe so was looking forward to getting stuck in. My first work trip in mid-January was already upon us and I was off to Bergen in Norway for a few days. We were developing an app in conjunction with an EU consortium and it was to help improve driver safety for private and professional drivers. I was working with a truck haulage company, whose drivers were helping us validate the app and its functionality.

It was my second time in Bergen and knew what I was doing this time. It was snowy and the landscapes are breath-taking. I was going to be spending a whole shift with one of the drivers and I was fortunate to see some amazing scenery as we navigated all the fjords and steep landscapes. I had made good friends with the driver and I am still in touch with him and others now. He was an ex-school headteacher and decided he wanted to do something less stressful! That resonated with me, since I was now very focused and aware of stress impacts. I had captured all the information I needed and then headed back home. I liked travelling and seeing new places and meeting new people. I found it very rewarding and motivating.

I had some great travel opportunities with my work and I valued these immensely and was a nice contrast to being sat at a desk behind a computer screen. The following week, I was working at a conference in London and was fortunate enough to meet the explorer, Robert Swan, who was the first explorer to walk to both poles. He acknowledged my own journey and battles and wished me all the strength to beat it! I remember how piercing his eyes were when he spoke and I felt like they were looking right into my soul.

I admired the courage he had endured during his exploration expeditions and was greatly inspired by this. I would have loved to join them on one of their pole expeditions, but my health would not currently allow this—I was invited! I noted that Robert Swan shares the same birthday as me, so that was a nice bit of coincidence for me to savour.

1.3 Stress Management—how to recognise and moderate?

A couple of days later, I awoke from my sleep early. I was aware it was still dark outside and I just found myself crying and sobbing my heart out. I felt so many emotions just surfacing and releasing in floods of tears. I couldn't resist this as my body seemed to want to purge itself. As these emotions began to diminish, the sadness was replaced by emotions of joy and love for everything and I have never ever felt such strong emotions. I couldn't stop smiling and was almost laughing. Suddenly, my body felt as if it was raising up from the bed towards the ceiling. From this vantage point, my mind could see anything and everything. Everything was visible to me and it was like I was looking down on the earth.

Whilst in this position, I felt huge energy surges ripple through my body like electrical charges, reaching every nerve and every cell within my body. This whole experience lasted for about 20 minutes and I finally came back to earth, literally! Once my emotions had settled and I composed myself, I felt like I had a massive upgrade. My body felt different, my mind felt stronger, my senses seemed heightened and I was feeling so content with life. I was not the same person after this experience and noticed that I thought differently about everything—I felt much more tolerant and compassionate than I had ever been before.

I was soon Googling to see what the hell just happened to me. I was trying to explain it to Emma who was wondering what the hell was going on with me. It was a pretty scary experience, but somehow felt that I shouldn't fear it and just let it happen! I concluded that I had just experienced a spiritual awakening. What an earth was that, I thought! I was not a religious person at all and always believed that we are in control of our destiny and things like religion are for those who aren't strong in their own beliefs and stature.

However, I quickly learned a whole side of our existence which had never been visible to me, until now. I found I had actually had a 'Kundalini' awakening, which is a strong and intense physical reaction where your nervous system is unable to handle the amount of energy that is wanting to move and this can show up in a number of ways. This process was intended to clear out the energetic blocks and stimulate your own healing potential. A whole range of circumstances can trigger this and I discovered that many people can spend much of their life trying to achieve it. Trauma is one of those triggers and it may have been a related reason why I had received the awakening, although I did not feel at all traumatised.

Something inside me had initiated this and it is reported to represent a new chapter in your life! I felt like I was in a totally new world and one in which I was in control of and extremely appreciative of! I have shared the signs of the 'Kundalini' awakening below, so you can understand the areas of impact:

1. Things are falling apart, you have a nervous breakdown or your old life isn't working
2. Physical, emotional and energetic symptoms
3. Courage, willingness and desperation to try new things
4. Miracles and synchronicities appear and you receive support from unexpected places
5. Increased sensitivity to external things (food, media, people and places)
6. Awareness of internal energies, intuition and inner truth
7. Increased compassion, desire to be of service and recognition of oneness
8. Sense of purpose and destiny

(Ref: https://www.gaia.com/article/kundalini-awakening-signs)

This was a definite sign for me to change my life and I was enjoying the new experiences that I was now noticing within my life. I could relate to all of the signs in the list above. They really resonated and I was now living with a new excitement for life and my awareness radar was on full alert from this point forwards. I reflected on my life and realised that some of these were already happening around me, but I was not taking notice or learning from them, which is the overall purpose and objective of this in our lives.

Life is full of lessons and if we don't learn certain things as they show up, they will keep occurring and occurring until we break or we learn! It sounds really stupid writing this down, but I felt like I had been re-born and with that came new awareness, wisdom, healing and contentment. It was as if I had lived the first half of my life in a certain way and now 'boom', a major disruption had occurred and changed everything. In that moment, I seemed to have lost my ego and wasn't bothered by the competition in life. In fact, nothing really phased me anymore and felt like I was in a really good and powerful place now. I was ready to live my second life—that's what I called it!

I was living from a totally new place now and it was wonderful! I felt I could achieve anything that I put my mind to and my first challenge was to beat this cancer! I wasn't going to stop beating it until it got the hint and left me alone. I had something to prove here and I was certainly prepared to do battle with my new found superpowers! My arsenal against my cancer was growing evermore powerful and I thought that my cancer won't know what hit it from now on! Guess who's in charge now…ME!

See Learning Focus in Appendix: 1.4 Spiritual Enlightenment

I continued for weeks researching more into spirituality and the history behind it all, which stems from many thousands of years ago. I could not help myself and found so much motivation to find out why we are here on this earth and what our purpose is! Spirituality is not a religion in itself per se, it is that which relates to our human spirit or soul as opposed to material and physical things. It also acknowledges various levels of existence beyond the physical realm. There is an additional relationship with 'life-force' energy which exists within us and all around us—other cultures call this energy 'Chi' or 'Prana', but all describes the same thing.

I felt like I had unlocked a whole new and mysterious world and I was fascinated by the potential it was presenting. I believed that I had some sort of a guardian angel at my side and I was being protected and guided throughout the twists and turns in my life. I would often wake in the mornings to find different lamps being switched on in the house and interpreted these as some kind of sign of reassurance from a higher existence we have yet to fully comprehend. I did not discuss this with anyone because I thought they may think I have gone crazy.

It is hard for many to understand, since it is not generally something we are taught or engaged with in our lives and it is not generally visible to us. I was discovering many correlations about our bodies and effects from nutrition and stress, but now there was this angle too and everything was connected in some way. This had now become a puzzle for me to solve and I was beginning to find the pieces and create my own puzzle of knowledge. I didn't yet know what I didn't know! My rate of learning since being diagnosed was ridiculous and I had so much energy and desire to learn.

I was researching many perspectives now and was starting to see a much bigger aspect of us as human beings and was only scratching the surface of 'how life works.' I knew there was knowledge out there which under-pinned fundamental questions like, 'why are we here', 'what is our purpose' and 'what can we do with this life-force energy'. My 'tell me whys' had gone off the scale by this point in time! I don't even know where to begin in describing it all here in this book!

As my learning continued into my newfound world of our existence, I was finding insightful information about how our bodies can heal themselves. It is not just about what you eat, drink and your general lifestyle, your mind and body can be affected by your own thoughts and emotions too! Ok, this is getting quite a subject now, but I was determined to learn and apply this new found knowledge. I had no idea how this all worked or what an earth I was doing at this stage!

My first discovery that I began to apply was meditation. I had preconceptions about meditation, yet didn't know much about it in all fairness. It was one of those things you hear mentioned, but have no idea what it really is and what it does. I just thought it was something that Buddhist monks did all day long and I didn't have time like that to devote to it. I was wrong, of course!

There are many aspects to meditation and reasons for doing meditation and I realised the best way to learn about it was to try it out. You only need to do 10 minutes a day to make a difference apparently. I didn't know what to expect at all and was finding all sorts of meditation styles on YouTube—I didn't know where to start at the beginning and found a 10 minute guided meditation that talked about unblocking your chakras. What are my chakras, I asked myself?

I felt like I needed to learn a bit more before I got the grasp of meditation. I found out that your chakras are your main energy centres within your body and you have 7 of these within you. They all serve different purposes and they can become blocked over time. Ok, this was beginning to make sense so far. I wonder what blocks them, I thought. After a little more digging, I discovered that lack and excess of things can create blockages, emotions can cause blockages and negative energies too, amongst many other reasons. There was much more to this than I first thought and knew that this was going to need some progressive learning. Let's just give this a go and see what happens, I thought.

I found a quiet place in the house and put on my headphones. I got comfortable and started the guided meditation. I felt a bit silly at first and kept peeking through one eye to see if anyone was looking at me. I stuck with it and tried to remain focused and not distracted. I listened to the instructions and was trying to move my energy focus within my body to different parts of my body, as the guide was navigating each chakra in turn.

I couldn't seem to keep up with the guide at first and I was realising you needed to use your imagination a lot to get your mind and body to work together. I remember getting towards the end of the meditation and had become quite tuned into myself. At this point, I heard heavy footsteps bounding into the room. It was Katy and she was laughing at me in my meditation state. I felt stupid and this is what I thought people would think of me whilst doing this. She didn't mean anything by it, but I was already conscious of what others may think. They were probably thinking I was turning into a monk and I would be shaving my hair off next!

Anyway, I didn't let it faze me and I resumed my composure and completed my meditation. Afterwards, I reflected on it a bit and actually felt pretty good, like it had done something good to me inside. I decided that I would need to learn more about meditation and these chakras, which prevent the energy flow within your body if they are blocked. I had also found out that this energy flow can help heal your body, so this had definitely grabbed my full attention and this became the initial angle I pursued with my meditation practise.

My learning rate was forever increasing and as I dug deeper and deeper, I would find other connected avenues of learning to pursue. This 'spider's web' was becoming a full-time job with all this research and I was finding a persistent desire and impetus to learn more and more—I had become hungry for it! This had progressed into a very purposeful study that would directly benefit me in the short and longer term. These were life lessons that I was learning and the more I dug, the more I wanted to dig! There was so much to learn and I love to learn, so I was actually in my element during this time! I was certainly feeling like I was solving a puzzle of life and it was going to put me in good stead to win this battle.

I continued with meditations from this point in time and incorporated them into my daily routine, doing them in the morning and before bed. They became really important to me and felt that they had an extremely essential part to play in my healing and keeping me sane—they were making me feel really good. I was beginning to see different perspectives of the society we live in. Well, we call it live, but it's more like work, stress and survival. I was recognising how little time we actually spend reflecting upon ourselves and taking in the 'now' moments within our lives.

We have become too busy, preoccupied and distracted. We seem to cram so many things into our daily routines and live a repetitive lifestyle that we often operate on auto-pilot. Most of you know that feeling when you have driven for the last 10 mins and cannot even recall driving! This is our auto-pilot, or rather our subconscious, doing it for us because it is so familiar to us. Whilst this sounds pretty cool, it really means that we are not aware of our 'now' and we are living and thinking either in the past or the future. When our lives become so repetitive, we tend to find that we don't consciously remember much of what we have done because it is so routine or we are constantly focusing on achieving future goals, for example.

In addition to this, we are likely to develop stress as our bodies are trying to continually respond to the relentless, triggered demands. When we overdo something in sport, for example, we could pull a muscle and we would know about it and have to rest it until it recovers. We don't seem to do that with things we don't readily recognise, like stress. Our bodies can become used to the feeling of stress and this becomes the new normal and so you can be consistently stressed without even noticing it. This applied to me and used to think that it just meant I can handle stress, but I had actually just gotten used to it.

I don't think any of our bodies are designed to handle it over sustained periods and our primitive stress responses were designed to react to sudden danger and produce a dose of cortisol, or adrenaline, into our blood stream. The long-term activation of the stress-response system and the over-exposure to cortisol and other stress hormones that follows can disrupt almost all your body's processes.

Living with It

We had many trips planned for 2018 with almost something to look forward to each month. Looking back now, 2018 was our year of distraction! We wanted to live as normal as we could for a while and enjoy exploring new places, do things we hadn't done before and put ourselves first, which neither of us really did in our lives. I felt like I was in the driving seat now and had control of this vehicle called 'life'. I could control the pace and direction of this vehicle and which passengers I wanted to share the ride with!

We fitted the appointments and everything around us, instead of the other way around, which really allowed the mind to relax a little. We had created an intricate weave of work, scans, treatments and check-ups around our life and we found a place of harmony with everything—a flow state! I had become skinny and bony by now, which chemotherapy had initiated, but I was not restoring my weight by consuming sugars and fat—I had accepted how I looked and I actually felt quite well on the inside. I would still tire easily and had done since chemotherapy—it had already done its damage and my toes and finger tips were still numb too. Anyway, I was alive and I was taking what I had and running with it and not dwelling on the past.

We had always considered moving house at some point, but could never find what we wanted in the right location. We also wanted Ben and Katy to settle somewhere first, since their living locations would influence our own living location. We had held off doing much to the house as a result and things were starting to look dated and old—this is because they were old and dated, especially the kitchen. We decided that we won't plan to move just yet and agreed to invest in the house and bring it up to speed. I was now spending more time at home and I would certainly appreciate that. We got some builders lined up and planned an upgrade of our kitchen, sunroom and lounge.

We were going to knock out the utility room and integrate the space into the new kitchen so we can have the all-important island! We were really pleased with the plans and it included bi-fold doors across the back of the house and making a fireplace in the lounge for a wood burner. We decided to widen the drive too so we could get cars onto it more easily. The work was planned from the summer onwards, so we could go and enjoy ourselves knowing this was all in hand.

Our next trip was in April and this was skiing in Austria. We hadn't skied in Austria yet and usually go to the French Alps, so was curious to see what it was like. I can get to try some of my German again, which had got a bit rusty over the years. Our ski trip was with much of Emma's family that we tend to spend New Year with, so a big group! I found two great adjacent chalets which could house all of us and they looked fantastic. Before this holiday though, I had to endure some more scan results.

We had managed to convince our oncologist to provide a PET scan, instead of the standard CT scan, which we were grateful for because they cost a fortune. It was that familiar scan result time feeling and I was pretty anxious about this one, since the last scan showed a really good improvement in tumour size and activity. It could only go downhill from here couldn't it? We found ourselves in the waiting room again, listening for my name to be called. After the usual 40-minute overrun on the appointment time, I heard my name called and we both followed the oncologist to his room once again!

Emma and I held each other's hand and I could feel Emma's anxiousness too as we entered the room. We got sat down and waited patiently for my results to be shared. However, the oncologist forgot about the results and then became a bit flustered in front of his computer as we caught him on the back foot. He never seemed that prepared at the best of times, but we were disappointed that he hadn't remembered the importance of this meeting. The waiting and not knowing is the most gut wrenching feeling you could imagine.

Eventually, he got access to the files and started looking at the results and reading the notes. He was totally silent and you could have heard a pin drop in the room. Please just tell us, I thought! The longer he took, the more anxious we grew. "Right," he said and turned to look at us. He left the images on the screen as if he was about to present them to us. He explained that there was no further increase in size of the tumour and it had remained the same size. Phew, we both thought and Emma and I exchanged a brief and positive glance at each other before he continued. "However," he continued…

Our initial high was now dampened by the apprehension of what he was about to say next and we both leaned forward, as if to brace ourselves for the next bit of news! He continued to inform us that there was a slight increase in tumour activity, moving from the previous activity rating of 5.2 to 8.7. Whilst these measurements are still relatively small, this was a 40% increase judging by my maths and we felt this was quite a big jump. Conversely, I couldn't help thinking how the activity might fluctuate, so these instantaneous measurements are snapshots of what may be going on day to day! I still wasn't familiar with this rating scale and it was difficult to judge what was good or bad on an absolute basis and we could only make relative comparisons.

The oncologist didn't appear to be too concerned about this increase and we agreed to continue doing what we were doing, which is predominantly my own regimen plus my Herceptin infusion every 3 weeks. This infusion only takes about 1-1.5 hrs end to end now, so much less impactful than chemotherapy was and I wasn't getting any side-effects from it! My oncologist then asked us if we had any questions, but I was only keen to let him know what I was doing in addition to this Herceptin treatment. I could read the curiosity in his eyes during each of our meetings, so decided to be upfront with him and put him out of his misery.

I had prepared a list of everything I was doing, or taking, in my own fight against this cancer. He was aware that I was doing my own things, but he probably thought it was just taking something like turmeric supplement! I introduced my list to him and presented a sheet of paper with everything on a single page. I just watched his eyes become wider and wider as he looked at the comprehensiveness in my regimen. He remained silent as he scanned each element—I am sure he didn't know half of what was listed, so I felt a little more empowered and in control. I could justify and explain the benefit of everything that was listed and after a long silence, he turned to us both and just said, "That's quite a list, isn't it?"

He didn't elaborate on this and made no further comment about it, other than a request for an electronic version which he could integrate into his notes. *Well, that's flummoxed him*, I thought quietly to myself. I am not sure whether he was allowed to comment or had any reasonable background for any meaningful discussion. He simply thanked me for the information and that was that! At least he didn't push back on anything! He was still wanting me to consider surgery and we kept stringing him along a little with this one, since it was justifying the insightful PET scans for now.

My next scan was due in June and we set the date for our next meeting and said our goodbyes. I didn't feel that we had anything else to discuss right now—it was business as usual for now. I would continue my regimen and also continue researching other aspects to consider. We felt a bit disheartened that the scan showed more activity, but it was still under control, so we focused on carrying on for now.

We could focus on our ski trip now and got our skis, boards and boots packed. We have our own ski gear which is nice, but you have to lug it about whenever you go skiing! We were flying out of Stansted in UK and agreed to meet all the family in the main terminal building. We all set off from our various locations and headed to the airport. Ben and I had all of our gear in one of our cars and we set off earlier so that we could have time to park car and get all of the gear onto trolleys ready for check-in.

Emma's parents were passing our house on their route, so Emma and Katy travelled with them a little time later. Ben and I were first to arrive and we parked up without any problems and eventually got two laden trolleys into the terminal building. We checked with the others on their whereabouts and some were also parking and others not too far away. We hadn't all skied together for quite some years, so it was going to be a nice get-together in a new environment.

As Ben and I were waiting for sight of the others in the terminal building, I pointed out to Ben that it looked like a bus was on fire just outside the terminal building. I thought I had seen a reflection of those free-standing gas fired flame lights in the window which made it look like the bus was on fire. Well, I realised very quickly that it was not a reflection and the bus was actually on fire. It had broken out behind the driver and the driver had not even noticed at this point. I called to the airport staff and told them what I was seeing and they got onto their walkie-talkies. We were closest to the bus and the passengers had not long gotten off.

The driver suddenly became aware and he just looked at the fire and got off the bus. He could have attempted to put out the relatively small fire, couldn't he? I felt angered by his lack of duty of care and thought I could have got onto the bus and put it out myself, but I had believed that the airport would properly handle this. Well, the airport didn't handle this well and the bus was soon engulfed in a fireball of flames with black, toxic smoke billowing into the air and into the terminal building. The building went into immediate lockdown and everyone was quarantined in sectioned areas, away from the fire. What an absolute mess, I thought.

This could have been easily avoided and I was kicking myself that I hadn't intervened in some way. More and more people were arriving at the airport and everything and everyone was getting buffered up. Flights were coming in and none were allowed to take-off so chaos was quickly forming. I contacted the others to let them know what was going on and some could see the smoke from miles away as they were driving towards the airport. Ben and I were getting shuffled around a circuit of the terminal building with everyone else and the place was jam-packed, such that you could hardly move. Now this wasn't at all safe!

We felt vulnerable and cut-off from the others. It was like a disaster movie. The airport was not handling this at all well and it was as if they had never encountered such a scenario! Surely, they do fire drills! I was shocked at their appalling communication and lack of coordination with each other. We did many laps of this circuit as they tried to integrate more and more people into the building.

About a couple of hours later, we finally saw Katy, Emma and her parents. We got our skis, boards and luggage checked in so we didn't have to carry them—at least they allowed us to do this! Others of the group were finally making it into the building and we tried to find small pockets of space where we could huddle together and work out what we do from here. Clearly, flights would be delayed now, but for how long? The airport was not communicating anything at all and then they made the announcement. The airport is closing so please make your way back to your cars and go home! What? We had just checked our bags in and what about our holiday! Everyone around us just looked totally stunned.

Emma spent the next hour trying to get our flights rescheduled or refunded, but they refused to cooperate and offered nothing! This was unbelievable! We were all totally devastated and couldn't work out how we could actually make this holiday work now! The airline refused to let us have our baggage back and said they will send it to our home address! We weren't intending to be at home and I had my medication in my bag so I needed it!

Now that they knew I was a cancer patient, they agreed to return our bags, but felt for those who were not able to negotiate in this way! We all decided to spend a night in a local hotel and see what transpired the next day. Any available flights were getting snapped up quickly and going for stupid prices, and there was no guarantee that they would be able to fly anyway.

During dinner, we all looked at all sorts of ways to get to Austria, and to cut a long story short, some were now driving and others trying to fly. We spent the rest of the day and night trying to find alternatives to get to our holiday destination. I didn't fancy driving that distance, but there were no flights going in or out of Stansted. We managed to eventually find a flight out of Gatwick two days after our original flight time, which we felt was better than nothing. We had to pay a fortune for them though, being short notice and not many seats left!

We left our cars in the carpark and headed down to Gatwick the following morning in a minibus, since we kept our return flights. We needed another night stopover in Gatwick before catching our new outbound flight the next morning. We were relieved to have found a flight. The others had begun driving already and we used an app to track each other and the entire journey became a race to get to the chalets first! This made it a bit more fun and it was like planes, trains and automobiles! Our flight left without any problems and we were soon in a transfer vehicle heading to our chalets. One of the groups had got there already, so we weren't going to win the race but we didn't care about that now.

We arrived second, for those wondering, and we all got settled whilst the final group arrived, blaming their adherence to safe driving speeds to their lateness! From this point on, we enjoyed a lovely sunny break in the Austrian mountains and the chalets were fantastic and had plenty of space for us all. No dramas on the way home, but the next battle was in getting our money back for the various outlays we all had to make in alternatives—that took over a year and needed solicitor involvement, which shocked me!

No sooner had we gotten back from our ski trip, the same family group were meeting in Paris for a family christening. I had managed to squeeze one of my Herceptin treatments in after our ski trip and had no problems getting this done before our next trip. We were hoping that we weren't going to face further travel issues and none of us did, thankfully! We were all staying in the same area, but not hotel. Emma and I had decided to stay on for a few days afterwards to make a bit of break for us both. We felt we needed some time out on our own, away from the more familiar environments.

Katy travelled back with Emma's parents and we had some space to gather our thoughts and explore some of Paris again. We had been to Paris quite some time ago and liked the feel of the city. We walked our legs off, but really enjoyed our precious time together. I had an opportunity to take some photos too, which I was really grateful for. It's nice to see new sights and iconic buildings when you are a photographer! I was in my element!

Unfortunately, they had shut the Eiffel Tower as they were refurbishing the area around the base of the tower. It was still great to be up close and we had some great evening walks in the dark, looking at the beautiful illuminations of these iconic buildings. We pondered about what might be in store for us in our future. Our lives had been seriously disrupted and we knew it would never be the same again. What will it be like though, we deliberated?

We wanted only to think of positive outcomes, so without discussion, we found ourselves focused upon that. We began thinking what we want from our lives, what is important in our lives and things like this. Once you strip it all back, you don't want or need much in your life we found and your appreciation from the smallest things are easily achieved. I had lost my ego and need for materialism. I still liked and appreciated nice things in life, yet my approach was now one of liking to experience new things or things I had always wanted to do. I never made a bucket list and never felt the need to write a list down. I always considered a bucket list was too cliché and I was not intending any of this to be final, so avoided that approach. My needs were quite simple really.

I was happy being in new amazing landscapes around the world with my lovely wife, Emma. I wasn't too bothered with things like bungee jumps or swimming with sharks. However, I do love flying and seeing the natural beauty in this world. The problem at the moment was that I cannot fly long distances, so we stuck to Europe and our own back yard to see what we could explore. We had trips still planned for Scotland, Portugal, Spain and Cornwall. Bring it on! I was enjoying 2018 so far—we both were and we didn't want our 'high' to end!

We arrived home from Paris and felt a little exhausted from the two recent, successive trips. It had been a good month of trips and we were making new memories. Our next trip was Scotland and neither of us had spent much time there to explore it a little more. My drone was definitely coming with us on this trip. We were flying into Edinburgh and had a small rental car to use as our 'explore' transport. We intended to drive through the Cairngorms and make a big loop around down the west side and back to Edinburgh—all the hotels were booked and it was something I was really looking forward to.

My love for dramatic landscapes was certainly 'ticked' and I was super-curious to see it for ourselves over the five days we had organised. I was not disappointed and was absolutely in awe of some the sights we took in as we drove through deep valleys, past vast lakes and over hilltops. I felt that there was so much more to explore in the wonderful arena and definitely recommend it to anyone! Sorry, this year is sounding a bit like a holiday diary here, but it was a year for trips—that is what we envisioned and how we wanted to spend this year. We both had felt really motivated to plan all these trips and we just went with that instinct. We were letting our instinct lead us for a change and we have experienced some years where we wanted to do all sorts of things, but never seem to have the impetus to book anything and it is usually for a good reason.

The year I was diagnosed, we had been planning to go to Australia, but we never seemed to be motivated enough to book anything in advance which is not like us at all—that's instinct speaking! I noticed that we had actually planned ahead, booking a whole year's worth of trips. Now that must mean we have more confidence in our future! We still were enjoying each day as they came and went, but the planned trips gave us something to look forward to and it motivated us, keeping our spirits high and our heads up.

I was again back to routines of appointments and treatments now. I had got quite a good programme with everything and felt that I was in control. I was not worrying about my tumour size or activity and just focused on moving forward with positivity and discipline. I was able to balance work well at this time and they were still being pretty flexible and understanding with my treatment schedules. I had to pivot everything around them to remain disciplined and consistent.

If this cancer was being relentless, then so would I and give it some of its own medicine! I was super-determined that it was not going to affect me physically or mentally. I was in a flow with it all and my life seemed somewhat effortless, despite the obvious disruption. I was not going to be phased with any of it and, in fact, it had made me so much stronger. I began to feel more and more fearless and invincible as each day passed.

People were beginning to wonder whether I was actually ill—I wasn't looking or feeling too ill and I had to question it to myself sometimes. I almost felt guilty that I wasn't looking or feeling at all bad, even though I had a serious, incurable disease. I hoped that I had come through the worst and now that I wasn't doing that horrid chemotherapy, I was seeing fragments of my life re-emerge and I had begun to piece them together in my mind. My life had been turned upside and smashed into little pieces—a little like the nursery rhyme 'Humpty Dumpty'. It would never be the same again and I didn't feel the same. I had now a great opportunity to reconstruct myself with these 'new' pieces and choose which to include and which to leave on the floor.

I was mentally recreating myself in a way that felt right and from my new learnings. I felt stronger, more loving, more courageous, impeccably strong in my mind and was getting more in touch with my spiritual side—remember, this isn't about religion, it's about believing there is more to us than just our physical beings and that we have the ability to use our consciousness to create our dreams and desires, as well as heal ourselves. This whole spiritual subject had intrigued me a great deal and I was determined to learn more about it, since I had directly experienced it and knew it was real. Those things we call miracles and coincidences are not truly the case, they are meant to be and you most likely attracted them through your thoughts, emotions and actions without even realising it.

The first part of becoming spiritual is to become aware. Aware of yourself, aware of what's happening around you and aware of your sub-conscious. We are generally programmed throughout our life and what we see, hear and read is often so controlled and mediated that it's hard to decipher the truth amongst it all. The world has evolved with so many controls, rules, guidelines and restrictions. Obviously, many of these are necessary, but I believe that we have been too conformed and channelled, upon reflection, and as such we end up not really living, but operate a relentless life of eat, sleep, work, repeat... We don't tend to question this and having stripped everything back in my own life, you can begin to see how we have evolved into these work horses. It is a situation that is not sustainable and someday it will all come tumbling down!

Now, it is interesting that as I write this section of the book, there is this emergence of a global Coronavirus pandemic and this is exactly what would have happened at some point, if this virus had not caused the world to stop in almost every way! Once you get off the conveyor belt of life and everything around you stops, it is a great time to reflect upon yourself and to observe where the ways of life are just not working, if we are to 'live' our lives. I will come back to the spiritual piece later in this book.

Our trip to Scotland was underway and I was excited to see it for myself. We were lucky with the weather and it was forecast to be around 28 degree °C most of the week—this is Scotland in May and it's certainly not a normal temperature for a) Scotland or b) May! I hadn't envisaged needing sun screen for Scotland, but I sure wasn't complaining—Emma and I loved the warmer temperatures so that box got a big tick in it! It also meant we will get some good views of the mountains from the mountains, which can be unpredictable in this region of the UK because of the unpredictable weather.

We arrived into Edinburgh just before lunchtime and got our rental car picked up. It was definitely small and I began to wonder whether it was going to be ok for us to drive around Scotland in. There was only two of us, so we decided to give it a try. The sun was already out and the clear skies were nice to see. It felt warm and I was down to a t-shirt already by now. Our first stop was not too far away and it was a spa hotel so was looking forward to starting with some relaxation.

The hotel looked pretty grand and it sat perched on this hillside with great views across a valley. Apparently, it was the area where the tennis player Andy Murray was from, to put it on that map. We ended up sunbathing in the outdoor loungers at the spa and were quickly looking a bit 'lobstery' because I don't think our bodies were used to seeing the sun! We weren't complaining though and nor were the other guests, equally amazed by the weather. We checked our route plan out that evening ready for kick-off in the morning.

We had planned a hot air balloon ride first whilst in Scotland and were really pleased that the weather was looking good for it! However, they finally said it was a wee bit windy, so they couldn't fly! OMG really! This weather hadn't been this good for years—how good does the weather have to be? It was a bit disheartening because the landscape from a balloon would have looked incredible! Anyway, we would have to rebook and find another location that was weather dependent!

Our first stop was in Aviemore and we drove up the 'Old Military Road' through the Cairngorms on the way there. Wow…Wow…Wow! I was blown away with the scenery and the road just wound through the mountains and the views were simply breath-taking. I was getting a bit of a pain in the arse though, because I was wanting to stop the car at every bend to take another photograph. I was truly in awe of the landscape and it was a photographer's paradise!

Eventually, we got to our hotel after some stop-starting. We both felt a little tired already, but we were chilled out and both enjoyed the drive at our own pace, well my pace! I did get the drone out on one of the valley sections and flew it almost out of sight above us so we could see the winding river below. There was so much space to fly in and I was absolutely loving it. I think Emma knew I was loving it and she was happy that I was happy!

We got a bit of an early night and woke the next morning to bright sunshine through the window. We felt so lucky to have this weather and could imagine how disappointing it would be to have a holiday planned here and it be raining and overcast the whole time! We had a lazy breakfast and got back in our super car for our next driving stint. We were heading to Fort William via Inverness and driving down through the lochs. It was a different type of landscape and it was great seeing the vast expanses of water amongst the steep hillsides and narrow roads surrounding the lochs.

I was wishing the car drove itself so I could look at the views some more. We got caught up in traffic on the way to the hotel and the cars were backed up for miles it seemed and we weren't moving at all. It must have been a serious accident and could imagine anything happening on such narrow roads with steep drop-offs. The trouble with the roads in Scotland is that there aren't many and any detour would consist of at least a two-hour drive on top of the rest of the journey!

In short, we decided to try a detour because the traffic hadn't moved for over an hour and it was at least another three-hour drive beyond that to our destination! The sun was beginning to set as we got to our hotel and we decided to chill out with a swim and jacuzzi before we ate. We had chosen some nice hotels and we were appreciating them after our day's driving. We had a one-night stopover and our next stop was a great hotel overlooking Loch Lomond, but before that, we wanted to take a look at Ben Nevis, the highest mountain in Great Britain.

We had an early breakfast and headed to the base of the mountain around mid-morning. It was already feeling warm and there were a few walkers out making their ascents, but also some already coming back from their ascents! We went to the information desk and got a route map and our bottle of water and got started. We weren't really that prepared in hindsight—a small bottle of water, not much food and not much stamina! We decided to go for it and see how far we get. The climb was relentless and there were many sections which were rocky steps that had formed into the exposed rock and you had to take big steps on many of them.

There weren't many shaded sections on the way either and if there was, it was packed with families trying to catch their breath and cool down a little. It was scorching hot today and we just kept marching at a constant pace. Just when you think you're at the top, you turn a corner and you have another steep incline to navigate. We didn't know how far it was and it was difficult for us to pace ourselves. We finally got to a small lake just below the peak of the mountain.

Actually, I should call it a tarn, not a lake! It was a welcome sight after such a long, hot climb and I was eager to dip my feet into it as we sat on its banks. We ate our lunch we had packed and I took a few photos of course. There were no clouds in the sky and probably only three small areas of shade on the way up. The rescue helicopter was flying about, above us and below us—I wonder who needed attention because I could imagine some folks would have heat exhaustion! I wasn't sure how long we had walked, but our thighs knew we had done it!

We rested for about half an hour and contemplated climbing the last section, but thought we need to drive to Loch Lomond yet so we headed back down. We thought it would be quite quick and easy going down, but it wasn't! You could not go quickly because of the terrain and your other muscles in your legs were getting a hammering now. We finally reached the bottom and we couldn't believe we both just did that after not being that fit for a while. We were pleased with our achievement and enjoyed our car journey down to Loch Lomond hotel.

Loch Lomond is quite long and narrow and we seemed to be driving down its coastline for quite some time. We were travelling from the north side and our hotel was nearer the south. We saw a sign at last for our hotel and turned left into the car park. We could immediately see the great view the hotel had of the loch and we felt instantly satisfied with our choice. The hotel room was awesome and it was almost in the loch itself.

The uninterrupted view was straight across the loch and we felt very lucky to have our final night here. We sat on the bed and just gazed out of our window. I think I almost dozed off! Even though we had driven every day, we felt chilled and we had managed to relax. The change of scenery had been both needed and rewarding. I was keen to catch a sunrise over Loch Lomond in the morning and set my alarm for 4 am! I know it's a bit keen, but some sacrifices are worth it, believe me!

The sunrises start early at this time of year and I didn't want to miss it. We had a nice meal in the loch view restaurant and reflected on our short, but sweet trip. We were impressed with Scotland and I was keen to explore more and some of the islands on the west coast another time. We both were tired and we couldn't have stayed up late if we tried. The next thing I heard was the beeping of my alarm. I silenced it quickly and couldn't believe it was 4 am already. It still looked a little dark out there! I drew the curtain back slightly so I could sit and watch the sky from my bed.

The sky had begun to become purple, and then more pink and the anticipation of the sunrise grew inside of me. I was imagining what it would be like. The sky was becoming lighter and lighter, pushing the darkness further away. I began snapping away because I wasn't going to miss any of this. The colours of the sky were looking fantastic as the sun rose higher and higher behind the mountain. The sun finally broke on the horizon and cast its rays across the very still loch and into our room. It felt warm and the sky continued to change colour as the night transitioned to day. There is something really magical about sunrises and sunsets and I am totally addicted to them both—they seem to recharge me!

I felt very satisfied with my captures and pulled the curtains back together and got back into bed for another couple of hours! We had a bit more time this morning so we didn't need to rush too much and enjoyed the rest of our time at this hotel. It was quite remote and it was peaceful and quiet in its surroundings. We have a few of these Scotland photographs on our walls in our house now and it is a lovely reminder of a great holiday together and some great memories. It felt like we were teenagers again, pleasing ourselves and exploring the world together without a care in the world.

We had only been away just under a week and Katy had been left to look after the house and our dog. She had done well and everything was still intact. Maybe the dishwasher could have been used a little more, but couldn't complain. Our dog was pleased to see us both—I wonder where she thought we had gone! It was soon back to business as usual and back to work and appointments and treatments! Oh yes, I remember that life now!

It was the way of life these days and it had become pretty normal to me by now. I slotted back into it and picked up where I had left off. It was tricky to remain strict with my regimen whilst away from home and eating in restaurants, so you always have to make compromises. I was glad to back to my regimen and have all the things I need at my fingertips. I had stumbled across the benefits of infrared saunas during my daily perusal of research. I was impressed with what I read and hadn't realised the broad benefits. I liked saunas and used to use one at my previous gym after a workout. I read that the 'infrared' saunas have the following benefits:

- Detoxification
- Stress and fatigue reduction
- Muscle and joint aches
- Weight loss and increased metabolism
- Immune system support
- Skin conditioning
- Heart health
- Diabetes

I had no idea that these saunas provided these benefits and I was particularly drawn towards detoxification, stress reduction and immune system support. Nothing like this is mentioned or discussed by the medical profession and it just fuelled my frustration towards their narrow-minded and one-dimensional thinking. These benefits were very relevant to my mission and I was keen to get started. I made a local search for infrared saunas and found a local swimming pool that had one, so I enrolled with them so I could use the pool and sauna any time. This was another therapy to incorporate into my regimen, but was pleased to include it since it serves multiple benefitting purposes. I was aiming for minimum of three times a week and included a short swim each time to keep my body moving.

See Learning Focus in Appendix: 1.5 Nutrition and Supplements

When we got back from Scotland, we rebooked our hot air balloon ride and chose a location that was only about 10 minutes away from us. We couldn't face another disappointing cancellation after travelling miles for the experience! We were lucky we had somewhere just north from us and we may see some sights that are familiar to us, but from a different vantage point in the air. It was June by now and the weather was still being really warm and dry.

I had another scan this month to look forward to and we were off to Portugal soon after with two of our close friends—this was our first really socialising we had since my diagnosis and we wanted to give it a go and see how we get on. Our friends are really easy-going so we knew nothing would be a problem for them. It was a nice sunny and warm evening as we headed to the balloon take-off site. There were a few clouds around which made the sky more interesting and would give us a sense of perspective when we were up there. We arrived to find the rest of the group looking at the pancake of a balloon lying on the ground.

There were about twelve of us—I had no idea there would be this many on the flight. The basket was huge and it was compartmented into small standing sections which we were all allocated into. We had to all help pull guy ropes as the pilot inflated the balloon. It was a huge balloon and it towered into the sky as we all hung onto the guys ropes to stop it blowing away!

The roar from the burners was really loud and the heat was much more than I had expected. We all climbed awkwardly into our allocated spots and up we went. Once the heat had gotten into the balloon, it was an eerie silence and I couldn't believe how much lift it had as we soared up, leaving the ground below at quite a rapid rate. It felt unnerving to think about the physics of it all and that fact that we were all in this woven basket, suspended underneath a material balloon—so I didn't think about it!

As we reached about 5,000 feet, we drifted wherever the wind took us! Apparently, there are different wind directions at different altitudes, so you can move around much more than I thought we could have. The burner was giving a loud roar when the pilot needed more altitude and it was burning my head, since I was closest to it and taller than the others—I wished I had brought a cap like the pilot! When the burners were silenced, there was an immense feeling of tranquillity and we just gazed at the small stationary and moving objects far below us.

We eventually got our bearings and could work out where we were and where we were heading. We had some friends in a village that we were passing close to and we contacted them to see if they could see us. They could indeed and we could just about see them waving to us from their garden, knowing that they couldn't see us at that range, all huddled in a basket. We continued to drift over other villages and fields and it felt like we were at the same level as the flat-bottomed clouds that had formed. I was snapping away and enjoying the new, amazing vantage points.

Eventually, we had to land and I hadn't realised that you can land in almost anyone's field, as long as you do your best to minimise any damage. Our pilot had spotted a field that had some sort of grass runway on it! We tried to land in the previous field, but we were travelling too fast and the animals in the field were running scared as we pretty much skimmed their backs! The owner of the new landing field was mowing the grassy sections as we descended. He looked at us all with a surprised face, suddenly hearing the roar of the burners as our pilot tried to scrub speed. I felt that we were being a little intruding, but we had to land somewhere!

We were still travelling at some pace and the pilot was pulling various ropes to try to stall us a little. The closer we got the ground, the faster our speed looked. We were running out of landing opportunity, so the pilot just ditched us down with a bump and we tipped over and skidded to a halt after several yards. Well, I have had worse landings, I thought. We were all still in our respective sections in the basket, only now sideways! We took it in turns to escape from the basket and get our feet on the ground again.

By the time we had all got out, the owner of the field had caught up with us on his mower. He was really pleasant and found out that he did in fact have a runway which was for his Cessna he had in his garage—different life, I thought! He was ok with us being in his field and just asked us to leave everything in good order and left us to it. I think we spent longer getting the balloon back into a bag than we did flying, but it was a great experience and would recommend it to anyone, making sure the balloon company is a reputable one!

It was yet another scan result day—I guess these are becoming familiar to you as the reader now and can appreciate the anxiety that always goes with these days! I grew particularly anxious about this scan because the last scans were showing an increasing activity from the tumour. I hadn't let Emma see my anxiousness, but she was most likely feeling the same. It's strange that we never talked about scan results prior to getting them—it was like a forbidden, hidden rule that we both seemed to be conscious of. We were now sitting in the familiar waiting room with the other unfortunate souls!

I sat wondering how everyone else is coping and how many are having the courage to supplement their treatment with their own methods... I reckoned less than 1%. I based this on discussions I had had with other patients and indeed the nursing staff. Many of them had thought I was crazy, but I stuck to my guns and my self-made treatment regimen. Whilst I was deep in thought, I was distracted by my name being called. The voice of my oncologist had become very familiar to me and we again followed him to his room.

As we entered the room, I glanced at Emma as if to reassure her. We were both going through the same emotional trauma of this disease and I hated that about this damn cancer. I hoped my oncologist was better prepared this time and indeed he was—he probably recalled our last appointment and got himself sorted. He didn't delay in conveying the results to us, since he could sense our curiosity about them. Like before, there was no real change in the tumour size which was the first relief point. At least this thing wasn't growing, I thought to myself.

Unfortunately, he continued, there seems to be another increase in activity. We both sighed in disbelief. We were so hopeful that we could slow this activity down with everything we were doing. This damn tumour was certainly stubborn! My brain was trying to process what else we could possibly do to restrict this tumour's activity and it motivated us to try even harder, although we weren't quite sure how we could achieve that yet! The activity rating had moved from 8.7 to 12.6!

I wasn't liking this increase of another 40%, but still didn't really know how impactful this was to me—I was feeling good at the moment and nothing seemed to correlate with this. I had to do something to buck this trend of tumour activity increases. I wondered at what point would this activity would start becoming a real problem for me and one which was probably irreversible. I didn't like thinking about things in a defeatist manner, but I had to be realistic at the same time as remaining optimistic. I didn't dwell on that thought for long and began to think beyond this issue and what could be done to address it.

By now, I had been trying to avoid dairy, preservatives, gluten, sugars and was consuming a plant-based, alkaline diet. I had been reading about people who cured themselves from cancer by doing only singular things like juicing or eating a particular natural food, but I wasn't personally convinced by this, because cancer fighting needs multi-pronged approaches in my experience. The armoury I was developing was certainly multi-pronged and it consisted of a disciplined diet, no sugar or alcohol fluid intake, exercise, saunas and an emphasis on power of my mind. I was being as consistent as I possibly could, whilst still living, rather than just surviving.

I was curious to learn what else I could do and I kept this challenge within my mind for now. We had another trip coming up, so focused upon that and told myself to enjoy the trip, recharge and get back to the driving seat afterwards. This trip was to the south coast of Portugal and a new location for the four of us travelling—Emma and our two good friends. I mentioned before that this was our first trip with anyone since my diagnosis and Emma and I weren't sure how it would all work out—it was just new territory. We didn't drink alcohol anymore and we thought that our company wouldn't be the greatest. Maybe I could allow myself a cider—I am sure one would not hurt me!

Half of me was desperate to be normal again, but the other half was fighting a difficult battle. Thinking about this some more, I wasn't even sure what normal was anymore. My normal had changed and I felt that I needed to re-calibrate myself. I felt like my mind and body was in some state of flux and until I stabilise, I won't know what 'normal' is—for now, I had to persevere and simply be patient.

Before we knew it, we were on a beach in the Algarve. The weather was just a perfect temperature and we were staying in a small hotel just on the edge of the old town. We could walk to the beach and walk to the restaurants, so we were happy with the location. You are never quite sure what everything will be like until you get there do you! The hotel had a small pool, but it looked pretty cramped so we preferred a sunbed on the beach. My mate had managed to book a round of golf in whilst we were there which I was both apprehensive and excited about. My stamina was still fluctuating and I was sure it was that damn chemotherapy that had destroyed it.

As I said before, our friends were easy-going and we were all happy to lay on our sunbeds and chill out, finally finding that book to read that had been sitting on the shelf for too long. Nothing felt awkward and I was happy with that. I didn't want to be a pain and restrict the rest of them from doing what they wanted to, but they weren't at all bothered and were happy doing nothing. I was lucky to have such understanding friends. I wanted to check out the sea and thought it might have been warmer than it was—it was freezing!

Not to be deterred or seen as a wimp, I continued to swim in the sea and after a while, I felt much warmer—or my body had become numb! It was so contrasting to the warm air temperature outside. I hadn't inspired the others to get into the sea after that exhibition, but could see the curiosity on their faces. We stayed on the beach most of the day, enjoying the sunshine until it began to cool. I was already seeing some great photo opportunities with the water, surrounding landscape and some of the historic architecture.

I was feeling happy with our trip so far, despite that crappy scan result we received just before we left. It wasn't going to ruin this trip and I didn't think about it anymore whilst we were away. By the evening, I was feeling quite lethargic and decided I would stay in the hotel room and rest whilst the others went out to eat. I was trying to listen to my body, instead of me usually over-riding it with my head! It wanted to rest, so I let it. I was disappointed in not joining the others, but thought if I rest now, I will have more for later.

I had to accept I was still ill with this disease, so couldn't expect to do everything as I normally would have done. The rest of them went out just to a local restaurant bar whilst I put my headphones on and rested my mind and body. I had rested for about an hour and began to feel more energised. I caught sight of an amazing sun glare shining through the window. The sun was beginning to set and was casting some beautiful colours across the sky. I was strangely, suddenly motivated and found I had a burst of energy.

I was curious about how the sun looked from the beach, since the sun may be reflecting on the stillness of the evening water. My curiosity got the better of me and I grabbed my camera and pushed my feet into my flip flops. I headed back down to the beach and took the quickest route I could, weaving through some of the many narrow streets. I could see the sun shining on the taller buildings and knew it would be setting very soon. Sunsets are my favourite time of day and anyone who knows me is that I will chase anything to see them! I was on the beach in under ten minutes and was greeted with a lovely orange sunset. The sun was reflecting on the tranquil sea as it ebbed and flowed lazily along the beach. I found a great position on the shoreline.

I was surprised that nobody else was here witnessing this sight. I was almost alone on the beach and it made me feel privileged to have this spectacle to myself! I snapped away until the sun had disappeared out of sight. The sky was changing its colour palette from orange, to pink and to purple as the sun sank over the horizon. I felt satisfied with what I had captured and couldn't wait to review the photographs and find that 'one'! I made my way back to the hotel and checked in with the others—they were still eating, but doing fine.

I was still processing my photographs when they returned and I said a brief hello to our friends before they turned in for the night. Beach days were pretty much the format for much of our short trip and the weather allowed us to do this most days. It was time for golf and my mate had arranged for us to be picked up and driven to the golf course. The courses are pretty good in Portugal and this one was no exception. It was lush green and immaculate. It was a very warm day with little wind, so I had no excuses for poor play.

We hired a buggy and loaded a few refreshments onboard. I wasn't sure how well my golf would be, having not played for a while. Not that I was any good anyhow ha-ha... Anyway, we got teed off and I was surprised how straight my first shot went after a reasonable connection with the ball. That was a good start, I thought, and I actually didn't play too bad at all considering. My mate won of course, but he's pretty good, although he always complains if he is only 'feet' off target. I am happy to hit the ball in most cases! He must hate playing with me!

We spent a good 4-5 hours on the course and caught a bit of sun on our faces. There was a nice cool breeze to take the edge of the heat—it was really nice to do something like this again and one of those things I could label as 'normal'! The rest of the trip went quickly and it was probably because we just didn't do much—it is what we all wanted from the trip though and we all had a lovely break. Our friends were grateful to spend time with us again and we were pleased that we had successfully achieved to get away like this under the circumstances.

We hadn't any trips planned for July, but we both had birthdays at the end of this month. We thought that the weather might be ok in UK and we could just do some local trips on our days off this month. Going from trip to trip can be quite tiring, but I certainly wasn't complaining—I was really enjoying the variety of trips we had this year. Now that we were back into our usual reality at home, I began to think again about what else I could do to hammer this tumour and restrict its activity.

I felt that I had exhausted most things, but then out of the blue, Emma gets a message from a friend we hadn't seen for years. She was now living about forty minutes away and she asked if she could meet us for lunch somewhere local. We both thought this was randomly unexpected, but then remembered that everything happens for a reason, so let's meet up and catch up!

Exploring New Places

Coconut on the Beach

Appreciating Time Together

Exploring Cornwall with Phoebe

Meeting Robert Swan, Explorer

Adventure with these Two

Balloon Ride Views

Precious Times

Austria Ski Trip

We chose a pub-restaurant nearby and we met in the carpark. It was good to see her again, but I couldn't help question why this was happening now. We have known her for many years and her parents are friends of Emma's mum and dad, so it goes way back. As we got chatting about my cancer and how everything was going, she mentioned that she knows someone fighting the cancer battle too and she told us about this great book they had discovered.

She began to explain some of the content and genre of the book and it sounded just what I needed! It was written by this couple who had beaten cancer through non-medical treatments and it was titled something like, "What we did to beat cancer". This was right up my alley and it suddenly dawned upon me why we had this seemingly random meeting like this—it was for us to be shown another way by the sharing of this book we had not yet discovered.

I was really grateful for her reaching out to us and I think we both felt uncertain why we were surprisingly just drawn together like this! That is what is known as a 'synchronicity' and it was something that happened for a reason. This had reinforced my belief in these synchronistic occurrences and made me pay even more attention to them, because they often come at the right time if you are awake enough to notice them.

As soon as we got home, we ordered the book online and waited impatiently for it to arrive. I was super curious about their methodologies and what I had missed out on up till now. Since my tumour was becoming more and more active, I was obviously keen to stop it in its tracks. The book finally arrived and Emma and I went through it meticulously, as if it were some kind of crime scene! We began making a list of all the things that they had done and did some sort of gap analysis against my own treatment regimen.

Two areas stood out for us relatively quickly and these were three detoxes and hyperbaric oxygen therapy (HBOT). It was reassuring to learn that we had been doing much of what was outlined in the book and this gave us confidence in our path we had self-developed. In my opinion, I was doing more than the book suggested since I had integrated meditation and other supplements that I had learnt from my own research.

I was feeling that we had developed quite a holistic package for myself with all of the self-learnt and self-taught aspects. Imagine if what I am doing actually works, I used to tell myself. My motivation was boosted by my new additions and Emma and I were now on the hunt for the ingredients for some of these detoxes:

- Colon cleanse
- Liver cleanse
- Parasitic cleanse

I was going to need some unfamiliar ingredients and wasn't sure how to obtain or make them to be honest. There were things like black walnuts, wormwood and special cloves amongst other items. I decided I needed to find an herbalist to help mix these potions up for me. Emma did some searching and found only a few that were in the area. She spoke to some and chose one, reaching out for some guidance. She was really helpful and arranged to meet me in a church hall in a village about 30 min drive from home.

It was a bit of a random location, I thought, but went with it. Ben was with me and I was grateful to spend some time with him as he was back from college now having finished with his course. We were a little early, so we had a walk around the church yard and looked at the views across the fields from the hillside. Ben was pleased that I was taking these natural approaches to fighting the cancer and he was an avid supporter of anything non-medical! I shared his view and we had developed a good bond over this and I think that helped him mentally handle the ongoing uncertainties about my health. We went into the adjoining church hall and it appeared empty. We wondered if we had the right place and time and as I was about to call the herbalist, she appeared from I don't know where! She greeted us and we all sat at a lone desk in the corner of the large, empty room.

I told her about the current journey and what treatments I was already doing. She was inspired and that gave me a bit more hope that I had a good approach to this cancer. She commented how well I looked and was wondering if I was in fact the Pete Adams she had arranged to meet, because of my wellness! I was glad I was not looking too bad—the last thing I wanted was to look ill and people sympathising with me.

Once I had rattled off all the details of my approach and the ups and downs I had faced so far, she got into the detox discussion. I had some specific cleanse solutions which I needed, as described in the recent book I had been reading. She was pretty familiar with much of them and it made it an easy conversation. However, she wasn't familiar of the context in which she was providing these. She hadn't met someone with a serious cancer disease requesting such detoxes. I don't follow the sheep and carve my own paths, I thought silently to myself.

"There is a first time for everything!" I commented and I saw that she was enthusiastic to help, given this scenario.

She agreed to make up the solutions and deliver them to my house in a couple of weeks. I was extremely grateful and she told me to keep her informed on my progress, because she could use me as a case study! I did feel like I was my own case study and I often felt like I was trying to blindly navigate a mine field without knowing where the best exit was! You can think of many analogies associated with how this whole situation felt. These were tangible ways in which to describe this experience to others who wouldn't know what this cancer journey is like. We said bye to the herbalist and headed home.

Ben was curious to see how these concoctions would affect me in a positive way. I was keen to get started and it felt like a long wait until we received them. At last, they arrived on our doorstep and we quickly began to get started with them. Emma was going to do them with me too for her own benefit and to support me which was appreciated. Some of these detoxes were horrendously tasting and to the point where Emma could not continue because she was vomiting as a result! I had more to gain from these, so I continued through the course until completion. Glad that was over! It was hard to judge how effective they were, but they must have done something to expel the toxins from your body.

During August, we had a couple more trips planned which were back-to-back! Our first was to an area of Spain neither of us had visited before in the north section of the Mediterranean coast, right next to the French border. We often holidayed in the south of France in a place called Narbonne when the kids were younger. We all loved the area and the close proximity to the Pyrenees. We had created some lovely memories here and we were curious about the Spanish side of this area. We arrived at the local airport and picked up our hire car. Since it was just the two of us, we opted for a small car and it was definitely small! We filled the boot with our small rucksacks and began our route to the hotel.

We were staying in an apartment that overlooked the sea in the Bay of Roses. We had no idea what it was going to be like and was part of our new adventurous approach. We arrived to a busy area and a funny one-way system which made it difficult to find the hotel. I decided to dump the car and find the hotel on foot and ask them where we can park. I found the hotel and was pleased to know they were expecting us. They informed me that they had a carpark, but it was down a couple of streets away and we needed a key to the padlocked gate. Sounded ok, so I paid a deposit for the key and off we went. When we got to the carpark, we found that someone had snapped the key off in the padlock and we couldn't get in, so we had to traipse back to the hotel and let them know so they could get it sorted.

Not the best start, but we waited patiently whilst their maintenance guy fitted a new padlock. The area was just a spare bit of land with gravel on it, surrounded by a high wire fence. At least we had somewhere to park, because there wasn't really anywhere else to park! Our room was nice and it had a balcony which overlooked the bay. It was nice to explore a new area and we were both excited to see what we could find. Below our balcony, was the promenade and it was busy with people and local sellers and the promenade seemed to go for miles around the bay. We dumped our things and went to check out our new local area.

It was mid-afternoon and it was nice and warm. We both loved the sunshine and we were grateful that the weather was looking good for the few days we had here. We grabbed a couple of ice-creams from a little stall we found and began a lazy walk up the promenade. We were enjoying our time together away from our reality which we left at home. We were really distracting ourselves this year with these trips and they were working for us. We didn't know what our future holds, but were enjoying the time we have now and living in the 'now'. The sun was getting low as we returned to our hotel and we had spotted a couple of places we could eat at on our way back. We decided to head out early evening, so we weren't late to bed and we could have a decent start tomorrow. We hadn't planned anything, so we thought we would just see how we both feel on the day.

It was a warm evening and was ok just wearing shorts and t-shirt. We enjoyed a nice meal, although they struggled with the vegan thing, but managed to find plenty of vegetarian options. We found that there were not many English speakers in this area and it was more of a Spanish tourist area. We kind of liked that, yet we felt like the obvious foreigners! We got back to our room and chilled for a bit on the balcony until heading to bed. It was nice to just sit and watch the world go by below us. As soon as we turned in for bed, we began hearing loud piano music and someone singing. Our windows were closed and it was still loud! Oh no, that's typical, we said to each other.

We opened the balcony doors and the sound was really quite intense, taking us aback. We looked below and saw that it was our hotel that had started some sort of show. It was about 11 pm and they are just starting this now! It was poor singing too, which made it tough to listen to. Emma had some earplugs and I had my headphones, so we decided that could be a solution to some alternative peace and quiet. The music droned on in the background until early hours and we both dropped off at some point.

We awoke to another sunny day and it was motivating for us. We were dreading what show might be on in the hotel tonight and braced ourselves for it. We had a big breakfast and grabbed our things and headed for the car. We had decided to drive up the coast and see what is in that direction today, taking our swim stuff and beach gear. The area was quite desolate and there were some small, hidden bays dotted around the coastline. After passing several, we opted to stay at one of them.

There were not many on the little beach section and there were a few nice sailing boats anchored offshore in the bay which made it look like a film set. I fancied a dip in the sea, but it was absolutely freezing! I hadn't expected the water to be so cold. I've got to get in though, so I continued to submerge myself, patiently waiting for my body temperature to quickly adjust! It wasn't motivating Emma to get in, so I had a quick paddle and got back to the warmer beach. There was a man selling fresh coconuts on the beach and as he passed, we bought a couple. He hacked the tops off them and gave us each a straw.

The coconut milk was refreshingly cold and the coconut was really tasty. We hadn't brought much with us to eat because we thought we might get something at one of the beaches. However, these secluded bays had no shops or any facilities, so we decided to drive further to find some food. We were surprised how barren everywhere was beyond the area we were staying in. We headed into a town and found a supermarket type shop and stocked up on a few things. We felt better now we had some 'backup' food and some tasty snacks for our evening in our hotel room later.

We expected another loud music evening, but it wasn't happening tonight. That was a nice surprise, so we ate early again then got back to chill in our room with our snacks and drinks. We were not ones for going 'out-out' really and enjoyed our time in the comfort of our own room! I had taken some photographs throughout the day, so I was flicking through these whilst Emma chilled on the bed playing Candy Crush or something similar.

We had a couple more days exploring the coastline and on our last day, took our hire car for a bit more of a rough track route. We found some routes that traverse the more hilly regions of the area and I was keen to see what views we could find on these. Unfortunately, the roads were more like gravel tracks and quite steep and narrow in places. Our poor hire car was getting a right hammering, but that's what they are for isn't it! Our instincts were right, we found some great views across valleys and bays that most tourists wouldn't find. That was satisfying enough for me and I snapped some good photographs along these routes. Emma had become very patient with my stop-starting in the car to get the next view photographed. I'm not sure if I would be so understanding!

No sooner had we gotten home from Spain, we quickly exchanged our bags and began our long drive to Cornwall. We were taking our dog on this little trip and she was really not sure what was happening or where she was going! We made a couple of stops on the way and by the time we arrived in Cornwall, it was already very dark. We had trouble finding our accommodation with the rubbish instructions we were given. There was no mobile signal which didn't help, but we eventually found it hidden along a dark track.

I didn't like the fact that our kids could not contact us if they needed to with no signal. The accommodation said it had Wi-Fi, but it was like on an intermittent drip! We were staying in what was called a chalet, but it felt more like a mobile home. It had a nice position though and we could walk about a mile to the beach. The weather was up to its usual tricks in the UK. We are in the middle of August and it was forecasting rain and the temperatures had noticeably dropped. WTF! We had packed all sorts of clothes because you just don't know what you'll need. We went to bed feeling quite tired from the travelling back from Spain and then the long drive to Cornwall.

We awoke to sunshine streaming through a small opening in the curtains. That's always a welcoming sight in the morning! I tried to check the weather forecast on my phone, but it was on the intermittent part of the wi-fi drip feed! Stupid wi-fi! You can't advertise this accommodation with wi-fi if it is like this, I thought angrily to myself. Anyway, I stopped trying and got up to make green tea. Yes, I was still enjoying my green tea in the mornings.

Emma was still asleep, so I managed to do things quietly and slip back under the covers to drink my tea. Our dog was feeling a little left out, so I lifted her onto the bed and she snuggled down against my legs. We didn't have any expectations from Cornwall and simply wanted a short break in somewhere we hadn't been before where we can take the dog. I had found some maps that had been left in the chalet and I was looking at what was around us and where we could explore. There appeared to be a lot of coastal paths and I liked the sound of that if the weather was going to be kind to us.

I remember the forecast showing the weather becoming wet as the week went on, so if we can do as much outside stuff as we can sooner, then at least we will have managed to see things. I was keen to check out the beach and see what our route was like to get to it. Once Emma was up, we had some breakfast with some food we had brought with us and headed along the footpaths to the beach. It felt quite a way, but it was a nice walk through trees and small valleys.

As we neared the beach, we could see quite a large bay forming with steep hills either side of it, making it look dramatic. Part of the beach merged into a series a large rock shelves that formed a huge staircase up one side of the beach. There were surfers in the water and nice steady waves rolling in. We were happy with what we found and there was a little shop, cafe and a pub just off the beach. We treated ourselves to a Cornish ice-cream each and sat on a bench which overlooked the whole bay area. The sun was shining and it was casting a welcoming, warm heat upon us. We felt energised, so decided to walk along the coastline path that ran southwards from the beach. It meandered up and down and around the coastline, providing some lovely views of little hidden bays.

The water was clear and aqua in colour, looking almost tropical, but it was deceptively cold. I was glad I had brought my camera with me and was happily finding new views to capture. I just loved taking photographs of landscapes and found it satisfying seeing these new compositions which I hadn't experienced before. Even our dog had got used to me stopping and taking photographs and often posed in them too! We looped our walk back so that we ended up back at our chalet for some lunch. We were pleased we had got out and we were getting our bearings now. Our dog was looking quite exhausted. She was getting old now and hadn't as much stamina as she used to have. I think the same applied to me!

We chilled around our chalet area for the afternoon and I decided to give my drone a quick fly from our adjacent field. I was curious to see what everything looked like from above. It was soon high in the sky and almost out of sight. The sky was clear and I could see the sea and the bay we had started our walk from. The whole area around us and towards the coast is covered with trees. I aimed the camera directly downwards and the trees surrounding the field I was in looked like broccoli all bunched together. I took a few photographs of the views and brought the drone back to me. It was great to see things from any altitude and any angle from the sky.

We spent the next few days exploring different areas around us, trying different coastal paths and hill sides. We had begun to have our breakfasts at the local beach café because they served fresh cooked food and catered for my diet too! Well, we did until it became colder and more drizzly. We found that there wasn't much to do as the predicted rain set in. There were times when it was just a torrent of rain and there was no point in even trying to go out in it. I was grateful our instincts had caused us to make the effort earlier in the week to explore!

Over the last couple of days, we found ourselves stuck in a chalet with no mobile and no wi-fi connection, but it gave us time to chat, read and play games instead. The rain hadn't stopped and we were ready to get home and get ourselves straight for the coming week of 'back to normal'. I hated to wish our time away, but we hadn't been home properly for a bit and sitting in a cold chalet in the rain isn't much fun to be honest! We packed up our car in the pouring rain and began our drive home. We had had a nice chill time in Cornwall and we felt ready to get back to the challenges of normal life!

When we got home, I began looking for oxygen therapy centres. It seemed quite specialised and was concerned that there wouldn't be anywhere local and it could cost a small fortune for the treatment. Eventually, I stumbled across a multiple sclerosis (MS) centre that had an oxygen chamber. I was pleased to have found somewhere pretty local, but I didn't have MS so believed I wasn't eligible. I contacted them anyway via email and they do support cancer patients so I would be welcome to use the facilities. It was a charity-funded facility, so this made me even keener to support them.

I needed only to pay a small joining fee and then it worked out only £10 per session. I decided to go for 2-3 sessions per week and they each lasted an hour. I discovered that you have to initially saturate yourself with oxygen, which means having twenty sessions in close succession before moving to the less frequent format. I arrived for my first session, not sure what to expect. The MS centre was a small unit on an industrial estate and there was the oxygen chamber, which looked like some old-fashioned deep-sea dive pod—it was about 10 feet in diameter and almost spherical. It had small portholes around the perimeter and a huge submarine style door.

I felt a little apprehensive thinking I was going to be locked in there for an hour, so I had taken a book and other things to keep me occupied. You are not allowed any electronics in the chamber because of the pure oxygen that is administered. There were other therapy rooms where they did massage, reiki and other helpful, physical treatments for MS patients. There was quite a mix of individuals in the centre—all ages and different levels of frailty.

I felt a little bit fraudulent because I looked and was quite able in comparison to many of the others. I got chatting to everyone and we got to know one another. I had already made out the characters of the individuals—the cheeky ones, the miserable ones, the quiet ones and the loud ones. Once you suss all that out, you know who you are dealing with and how to engage with them at an individual level. They showed me the ropes and grabbed my oxygen mask from the rack. You have to wear the mask for the entire hour and it fits over your nose and mouth so that you receive the pure 100% oxygen.

We got sat inside the chamber, where about 6-7 seats all faced each other. You connected your mask to the oxygen supply and then felt like a fighter pilot about to take off for service. When everyone is connected, they shut the thick steel door and then pressurise the chamber to the equivalent of 32 feet under water. This makes your ears really hurt initially, but you gradually get used to it. The pressurisation is important, since you absorb more of the pure oxygen at higher pressures. I was fascinated by the science and was really pleased to have found this centre where I can add more to my treatment regimen.

I found out that a lot of professional sports people use the chamber too to aid and accelerate healing of pretty much anything from torn ligaments to broken bones. I met many professional footballers and even racing motorcyclists! I had many cancer related books to read and soon got stuck into my reading. The hour passed quickly and we were soon ascending from our depths of 32 feet. Your ears popped and felt as if they were unblocking as you rose, similarly to when you descend in an aircraft. I felt good after the session and this became another regular activity for me from now on.

My treatment agenda was getting quite busy and it was like a full-time job to remain consistent and disciplined. I had made my own timetable so I could see everything on one page. You can see why many people don't venture out on their own paths, because it takes a lot of effort and courage. Many just want to be told what to do and will only consider 100% medical treatments. I felt sorry for these people because their own limitations will likely be the death of them!

More reading of the new book revealed that bitter apricot kernels help the cancer fight too. There is mixed literature about these kernels, some saying that they will poison you and not help with cancer whereas others rave about them and how they kill cancer. You see a lot of polarity in most cancer-related content and you have to cross-reference a lot of things to come up with your own judgements. I believed that much of the negativity towards unconventional approaches are fuelled by the pharmaceutical corporations, since they don't want us to stop taking their synthetic drugs which they make a fortune from!

There are certain chemicals found within apricot kernels which are said to kill cancer cells through what is known as 'apopotize' where the cancerous cells self-destruct. The kernel's chemicals will only target cancerous cells, not like chemotherapy which targets every cell! I ordered some of these kernels online and intended to take 3-4 per day as another supplement.

I was meditating one morning and I felt such energy surges from where I placed my hands on my body. It felt good and it was as if the energy was doing something to my body, stimulating it in some way but wasn't sure exactly what or why. I began to research this some more after my meditation session and 'reiki' was cropping up a lot, so decided to look into reiki a little more. I wonder if reiki could help stimulate some sort of healing of this cancer, I thought.

Reiki is a form of energy healing and much of what I was reading resonated with my own experiences through meditation and from my spiritual awakening and new awareness. I began searching for a local reiki healer so I could try this out and discuss this some more, first hand. We are so lucky to have the internet at times like this—it would have taken years to build up the knowledge I have gained in a matter of months from various content. I found a reiki healer who was only 5 minutes away—would you believe it. I contacted her and arranged a session for general healing. It would give me an opportunity to talk to her about this further and I could then judge its relevance to my situation.

I arrived at the reiki healer's house and she had a room dedicated to healing with a couch you could lay upon. There were crystals, stones and candles dotted around, and an herbal aroma filled the room. It felt very calm and I climbed onto the couch and lay on my back. I had no idea what to expect, so just kept an open mind. She spoke to me about the treatment and I was having a general energy clearing session.

Apparently, there are seven major energy centres within your body called 'chakras' and they provide different functions to support your wellbeing. I was already fascinated and curious to learn and experience more of this. The energy used in the healing practise is all around us and reiki channels this energy to perform various functions. I had had acupuncture some years ago for really bad hay fever. I used to really suffer from it and had tried everything medicinal to no avail. I had a few acupuncture sessions and have not suffered from hay fever since! I was, therefore, positively aware of these alternative treatments which considered the energy flows and meridian lines within your body.

The session was going to take about 45 mins and she was going to be stimulating my chakra energy centres and then go from there. Sounds easy enough for me! She explained how reiki works by channelling a 'force' or 'energy' through her hands to my body in order to stimulate my Chakras. As I lay on the couch, the healer told me to close my eyes and relax. She began clearing the negative energy within the room with burnt sage and waving a smouldering wood around myself and each corner of the room. She began at my head and worked from one area of my body to the next.

She placed her hands in close proximity to my body and I could feel a tingly heat as she did that. Some areas felt more vibrational than others and I learned that this means that more work is required in those areas. I think I fell asleep in the last part of the session and felt totally relaxed. She woke me from my slumber and asked me how I was feeling. I almost forgot where I was, I was that zoned out! I felt energised, yet so calm—it is hard to describe the feeling exactly. I really liked how I was feeling and she was telling me more about the energy centres and how the energy healing can unblock things within you. She explained what she had discovered from my own Chakras that there was some blockage in my throat and solar plexus areas.

I wasn't sure why I had this blockage within my throat area, since this relates to communication problems, but maybe I am frustrated with my current situation! My solar plexus blockages were likely to be attributable to my frustration too and this correlates with my throat Chakra. It was good to know my other areas were functioning well despite my traumas! I was fascinated by this whole subject and the fact that these Chakras can actually become blocked.

For example, you store any pent-up emotions in your lower abdomen and these can build and build over time as each emotion is not properly dealt with. At a certain point, these stored up, un-processed emotions can begin to block the flow of energy through this part of your body and you will begin to notice physical manifestations such as poor digestion, organ problems and weight issues amongst other things. Each chakra serves a different purpose and each one can become blocked for different reasons. I was thinking what role this could play in my own healing. In that moment, I decided that I would like to learn how to do reiki on myself and maybe also help others at the same time.

By chance, my new reiki healer was just beginning to teach reiki and I enrolled for my first-level reiki training! I couldn't wait to learn more about this healing art. I was wondering if people would think I was going crazy turning to all these new findings of spirituality and reiki, but I did not care anymore what people think. I was carving a new path for myself and was enjoying the new learning I was collating. In a strange way, I was becoming increasingly grateful for getting this cancer because it was forcing a whole new outlook upon myself and discovering about how life and energy really works within ourselves and our world.

This was 'real' science that is still being discovered and proven—this was a clear fascination for my mind and was inspired by new quantum physics findings that are now starting to validate some of these energy and reality theories. Let's get back to chakras once more, because there is a bit more to learn here!

Please learn about Chakras in the 'Spiritual Enlightenment' learning section in Appendix.

Emma was doing her usual evening research and found an NHS hospital in London that catered for more of the homeopathic medicines. We couldn't believe that this existed and nobody had told us about it, or even knew about its existence. It was called 'Royal London Hospital for Integrated Medicine' and was almost attached to Great Ormond Street hospital. They provided alternative medicine as well as other services such as the following, which stood out for me because of their relevance:

- Integrated cancer care service
- Hypnosis
- Integrated Medicine
- Mindfulness

We contacted them via email to see what they could offer to myself at this time and we waited for a reply. It seemed so odd that this was an NHS facility that complimented the approach I was developing myself and the fact that we hadn't found it until now surprised us. I couldn't wait to pass this one by my oncologist at our next meeting. He is going to get tired of my 'alternative path' nonsense I am sure, but I was intent on pursuing every avenue to beat this thing! It wasn't long until we received a reply from the London hospital and they said you just need a referral from your GP.

My GP had been great so far and I made an immediate appointment to get this moving. She presented no pushback on my request and produced a referral for me there and then! I was impressed and very grateful for her diligence. I duly sent this referral off and soon received an appointment for next month, just after my next oncologist meeting.

We both travelled into London for the appointment and we found the reception on one of the many floors. We checked in and waited. We were looking at the others in the waiting area and there seemed to be a whole mix of people and it was quite busy. A lady soon appeared and called my name. She looked friendly and she showed us to her room. She wanted to know the full background and journey so far, which I hadn't prepared for, but I talked her through everything. I could see the amazement on her face about all of the aspects to our self-developed treatment regimen and she was impressed by it all and what I had learnt. She was learning from me too, which made me feel good about what I was doing.

Eventually, we got to the interesting bit about what she could recommend. Since I was doing most of her offerings, she suggested mistletoe drops and two other remedies that help with healing within my oesophagus. I had heard about mistletoe and only thought it was available by injection, so was keen to learn more about the oral drops. Mistletoe is shown to stimulate the immune system, thus helping fight cancer cell and reduce tumour size. Mistletoe was also reportedly good for reducing inflammation and to ease digestive and gastric conditions. Ok, I am sold!

We were prescribed six months' worth and I only had to take the drops morning and evening on my tongue. Another one for my list! We arranged another appointment for six months and we went to their pharmacy to collect our new herbal medicines. We both felt this had been worthwhile and it re-assured us to know we are doing as much as we possibly could to fight this cancerous disease—we were hitting it from all angles from diet to mindfulness, from therapies to self-healing.

Katy hadn't liked using the word cancer when she talked about my illness, so she had begun calling it 'Clive' and she wanted Clive out of here as soon as possible! He was an unwanted guest as far we she was concerned! That helped her deal with this and I was happy she had found a way to refer to it! Bye Clive…you do need to check-out now and leave!

Emma and I were becoming anxious once again—you know what time is looming again. These scan result times seem to come quickly and this one was no exception. We had seen successive increases in tumour activity from the last two scans and we were needing to see a level of control or stabilisation with it. We couldn't possibly, or practically, fit anymore into my regime. I was still trying to work amongst all of this and still enjoyed the sense of 'normality' which this provided. I was thankful that my employer was still patient with me and allowed me to be flexible in my work because of my appointment and therapy schedules.

I kept meaning to put everything into a timetable, but I resisted since I didn't want to focus too much of my energy on the scheduling, but more on the activities themselves. I felt like I was in this weird place right now where I felt ok, I looked ok-'ish', I was consistent as I could be with my regimen, but this cancer was still festering away at me without me really physically feeling it. I continued to push these thoughts away and focus on the forwards and believing that this cancer will soon be gone somehow and I had to continue to have faith in my journey and trust that it will lead me to this outcome.

This is the part where spirituality comes in and your need trust your intuitions, instincts and guidance that can appear in many forms. I was strangely feeling guided and protected and it was re-assuring to me, like someone's got my back and can look out for me!

It's already scan results day! Mixed emotions again—excited about the prospect of better results, yet obviously apprehensive at the same time! It was a familiar feeling for both of us and nothing can eradicate this feeling, despite how confident you are. This waiting area was becoming a second home to me because I was spending much of my time here with various meetings and appointments. I still wasn't liking the atmosphere and it was feeling more like an old people's home.

I felt totally out of place and too young to be submerged in this environment. I could see from the faces of many of the patients, that they were putting all their faith in the doctors' decisions and I could hear snippets of conversations that confirmed this. I felt sorry for them in that they didn't know any other path and probably wouldn't ever have the courage to try another way! How could this change for them, I always thought. My thoughts were soon interrupted by my oncologist calling my name.

Off we followed him to his room. He knew we were anxious and could probably see that from our faces, since we couldn't really hide this emotion. He appeared up-beat today, which was unusual for him. He was almost smiling and it was refreshing to see him like this because it was easing my anxious thoughts. After about 5 minutes of faffing around to get his computer to work, he found my scan results. I don't think he had looked at them yet so we all found ourselves scanning the report information, looking for clues!

He found the ratings area and proceeded to read the results verbatim. "Your tumour size is 3.3cm—that's hardly changed for about a year so was really happy to see no real growth, since this is an aggressive cancer! Your activity," he continued, "is 11…11.3."

I repeated this back to him to ensure I heard him correctly. "11.3 activity rating?" I asked.

"Yes, that's right!" he replied. Wow, what a relief! We had stopped this cancer in its tracks! The last rating was 12.6 only four months ago so we are winning this battle! That is about a 10% reduction—not massive, but a turning point! Emma and I hugged awkwardly in front of the oncologist and he was pleased for us. He knew that he wasn't really contributing much towards these results, but he was happy nonetheless! He didn't really believe how the hell we were achieving this and I could see this in his facial expressions.

The problem I have now is to fathom out which part of my treatment regimen is truly fighting this cancer off! I will never actually know that, but it was a frequent thought which entered my mind. It was really the whole combination of things which was restricting many avenues that the cancer needed to grow and survive. I proceeded to tell my oncologist about my visit to the 'Royal London Hospital for Integrated Medicine' and what I had been administered following my consultation. He looked a bit put out, but I pointed out that it was an NHS facility and it provided 'integrated' medicine, which implies complimentary! He would be formally informed about the details of the consultation, as will my GP, so I was being transparent about things.

My oncologist should know me well enough by now that I will pursue every valid avenue and he knew I was probably the most determined patient he had had to manage! I curiously asked how his other patients are getting on who have a similar diagnosis to myself because I was keen to gauge how I was doing against them—not as a competition, but as a way in which to validate my approach really. He turned to me with his head tilted forwards so his eyes peered at me above his glasses and simply said, "You are running a totally different race to the others!" He sat back in his chair as he said this and smiled. That was not the detail I was expecting, but felt reassured by what he said and how he said it!

He was right, I was running a different race so it would be hard to compare me with others who are on the single-track path. In comparison, I felt like I was on the highway and was able to change lanes and avoid obstacles. I had options and was driving a juggernaut that wouldn't stop for anything if it got in its way. This was a good day and I again felt in control of this cancer.

It was October now and Christmas will be here soon enough. This was a Christmas I wasn't sure I would see at the time of my diagnosis. I was pleased with my progress, but the constant nagging reminders of cancer never leave you. I kept myself busy with working from home and my other full-time job called 'my treatment regimen'! It really was a full-time job to keep consistent with everything to ensure I didn't drop the ball at any time. I felt like I was winning a little after my last scan result and this renewed my focus and motivation to maintain what I was doing.

By now, many friends and family members had become used to me having cancer, so were wanting to resume normal life with us. We just couldn't resume just yet—we were at a critical point in our journey and one mistake could ruin the entire process. It was hard for people to understand this and it was especially hard for Emma, who was the communication channel to the outside world. She was having to keep everyone at bay to give me the space I needed and I felt sorry that she had to cope with this on top of everything else. If people see you looking ok, they assume you're better and it was difficult for them to properly understand what we were actually going through.

Christmas holidays soon arrived and we were spending it at home this year. Emma's parents were coming over to stay for a couple of nights and this made a change to our normal routine of staying with them. Ben was also home for a few days, so was nice to catch up with him. He had now moved from Guildford and was now living in Brighton, setting up his videography business there. We all were feeling exhausted from this year and I was appreciating our more relaxed approach to the festivities. Ben and I were the only vegans, so we had the alternative to the traditional turkey. It was good to have some vegan alliance with Ben at home!

We spent New Year with Emma's side of the family as we normally do. This time, the destination was….Cornwall. Cornwall! We felt like we had only just got back from there! We were strangely staying less than a mile from where we had stayed in the summer. Emma and I remembered how damp and cold it got there in the summer, let alone winter! We headed down with the dog. Ben and Katy weren't joining us this time. They were getting independent now and had wanted to spend a New Year with their friends for a change.

We had reasonable weather for winter time and got some nice walks in along some coastline we hadn't been to on our last visit. The dogs were loving the beach and going into the sea—must have been freezing! Emma's brother usually goes for Christmas swim in the sea—it's a tradition in some places around the UK. Before you knew it, he was in the sea in his swim shorts…Crazy!

Once we got back home, Emma and I pondered about what sort of year we would have in 2019 and we couldn't really see anything much different to 2018. We were both re-assured that we were seeing some control of this cancer, but that's as far as we could see. I couldn't imagine not having it now and we had gotten so used to living with it. I always remember the oncologist saying at the time of diagnosis, "We can try to control it, but won't be able to cure it!"

That meant that I was on a palliative care regime and this was a one-way ticket to nowhere. Just when I was getting my head around my next move and building up a mental focus for the next six months or so, my dad told me he had been diagnosed with cancer! I could not believe it! My dad was one of the healthiest people I know and his was as strong as an ox. He was 75, but as fit and more active than most 30 year olds. How can this be? Could I not get myself sorted before my dad has to start dealing with this as well? More "Tell me whys"!

My dad lived on his own and didn't have the support that Emma had provided me, enabling me to do so much of what I am managing to do now. He lives two hours away so I couldn't just pop in! I began sharing some of my knowledge with my dad, but had to be careful of information overload. He was a man who always did what the doctor asked, so knew it was going to be a challenge for me to convey my non-medical learnings to him. He had been diagnosed with primary bladder cancer and secondary lung cancer. He had never smoked!

I began to wonder why either of us had gotten this horrid disease and nothing made sense. I always tell myself that everything happens for a reason, but I could not fathom this one out at all. My getting this cancer was a wake-up call to change my stressful lifestyle I am sure, but my Dad? I gave Dad one of my books to read and regularly travelled to take him to his appointments and be there for him in the early stages of consultation. My brother and his family live about 5 minutes from Dad, but he was often busy with his work and everything else to help in work hours.

There were many consultations and I quickly noticed that his hospital was not managing this as well as mine. They frequently messed up appointments, his oncologist meetings were often substituted by a nurse and it just appeared that there was poor communication between everyone involved. This obviously angered my Dad, since his appointments were usually a 30-minute drive from his home and resulted in wasted trips. Not good at all when he was going through all of this! It took them almost six months from initial diagnosis to him starting immunotherapy treatment. He had found out that one of the pipes from kidney to bladder was blocked, so they fitted a bag to catch urine from this side whilst they figured out the next move.

So, now he had a bag he had to empty and the connection of this to his body was frequently becoming infected, resulting in the need for antibiotics! It was a mess! It distracted me for the first part of the year though and I was glad I was able to spend time with him and help him out. I was still trying to work myself, but this was becoming more and more fragmented. I was feeling like the entire world I knew was slipping away and I could not imagine what was going to replace it.

I felt that there was a definite change coming—it was a gut instinct without any detail for now. My intuition levels were primed and I kept feeling that how we are currently living is going to reach a point of permanent change—not just for us, but for everyone! I just didn't know how, but definitely believed it was for the better.

Emma and I had made a spontaneous decision to go skiing, just the two of us. We love to ski, but it had taken a bit of a backseat whilst all this was going on and we certainly didn't want the stress of the last ski trip! We were curious about Bulgaria, since we had never ventured to this region before. As soon as we arrived, we noticed that it wasn't as well kept as the Alps and it felt like we had gone back to the 1980s in many respects! We hadn't bothered taking our own skis this time because they were cheaper to hire than it was to bring them with us as sports luggage!

We had a two-hour commute from the airport to our hotel. It seemed a long, bumpy ride and the driver couldn't find the hotel initially, so ended up driving around somewhat aimlessly. We noticed a lot of partially build hotels and it felt like there were abandoned building sites in many places. This didn't fill us with confidence, but as we finally arrived at our hotel, it looked finished and in good order. The staff were friendly and we were happy with the facilities.

Our room overlooked the mountains and we chilled for the rest of the afternoon, just exploring the vicinity of our hotel. There was nothing around us— just partially built buildings and no shops. Hmmm… this isn't what we are used to, we thought. There was a free shuttle bus to the ski lifts and main resort, so we decided to keep an open mind and go with it.

We had a relatively early breakfast and found that our hotel had a ski hire shop, so we conveniently got our skis and boots fitted here. Now kitted up, we headed for our shuttle bus. It was a minivan and there were many others from the hotel queuing for it too. We didn't make the first run, but soon got our seats the second time around. As we arrived at the main resort, we found the lift pass office and got this sorted. The lift passes are about a third of the cost of the French Alps! As we looked at the ski run map, we noticed that there was only one lift up to the main section of the mountains. It was right in front of us and it had the longest queue I had ever seen! What the hell, I thought!

We didn't delay in joining the back of it and found it was moving very slowly. This wasn't something we were used to and hardly had to queue for more than a few minutes, if that, usually. It took us over 45 minutes to reach the gondola lift! We squeezed in and began our trip upwards. As we rose higher, we could see the layout of the resort and how it was the only civilisation you could see for miles. The runs were shorter and fewer than the Alps and I told myself that I must stop comparing it to the Alps!

We soon found our favourite runs, but since there were only a few different runs, most of the lifts were busy as a result! Nevertheless, we enjoyed our first day skiing and it was simple, knowing we only had ourselves to think about. We had a nice lunch in a mountain restaurant and I managed to take a few landscape photographs with my phone, which I was pleased about. I even sneaked some of Emma skiing, which she loves me taking…not! We spent much of this short ski break doing the same each day, but finding new run routes.

We found that we just couldn't avoid the massive queue at the start of the day, which disappointed us somewhat. We had never experienced anything quite like it and didn't fancy coming back to the resort because of this—it didn't have the same atmosphere as the other resorts we had been to. However, we managed to relax and got some skiing in, so we ticked the boxes we needed to and it was all part of the experience!

I was finding work difficult to manage by now and my mind was struggling to tune into it. It seemed so trivial compared to what was going on in my personal life. It was an increasingly mental challenge. I didn't know what my future holds, or indeed my Dad's now. So many unknowns and uncertainties were surrounding me, surrounding us! I just didn't know what I could commit to with my work and I was fast becoming an unreliable entity in my opinion. I just couldn't change the situation, which frustrated me a lot. By this time, I had a new manager.

My previous manager had been moved to another project and I was really worried that I would not get someone who understands what I am going through. I recalled a previous manager I had in an earlier role and he used to bully me and be extremely awkward and inflexible. He made me want to leave my employer and I would have done, had I not gotten my new role I was in now.

We soon heard on the grape vine that we had a new manager. The whole team were curious about who it was and what they were like. It was an external hire, since they wanted some fresh views within the organisation. Finally, we received the announcement. We had a new lady who had joined us from O2's head office. Ok, sounds promising, I thought.

She soon arrived on the scene and got to know us all individually at first. I took a trip to our London office to meet up with her and to inform her of my challenging situation, that she too had to become involved with—I felt sorry for her already! As soon as we met, we seemed to be on the same page with everything and quickly formed a bond that gave me the reassurance that she would support me through this. I was totally relieved that she had been chosen to manage us. It was a blessing for me.

I felt as if she had come out of nowhere and has all the attributes and intent to support me fully with whatever direction I need to take with my situation. I felt sure that this was one of those synchronicity times, when the person you need suddenly appears in the right place, at the right time! The timing could not have been better because I wasn't sure if my previous manager knew how to deal with this situation—that did make two of us though! I didn't know if I was coming or going half the time, so I already knew I was going to be challenging to deal with!

Despite this, I was finding new ways in which to contribute to the business and support others with knowledge and guidance. I hated to think that I was not valuable to the company, so this was motivating me to find innovative ways to add value that was mutually beneficial. I had loved my work and the people I work with. The last thing I wanted to do was disappoint and let them down—

that is definitely not my style! By now, I was having more frequent engagement with our company doctor who spent a few days week in our health centre at the head office. I had kept him informed throughout my journey and neither of us knew what outcome to expect or to plan for, so we just played it by ear in a way.

My new manager was being extremely supportive, as was her leadership team. I was certainly blessed to have this kind of support, because many other organisations would not have been so understanding in my experience. I could never fault their tolerance and allowing me to take the lead on my work pattern— thinking back now, I am so very grateful to all of them.

Emma and I were really breaking up the year as we did last year, with many short trips to new places we hadn't been to before. We were now off to Verona for a few nights with a couple of old friends. The weather was looking good and I was looking forward to this trip, since there was a lot to see and a lot of history in Verona with the likes of Romeo and Juliet, for one! I liked Italy and it had some beautiful landscapes which I had seen from other photographers on my photography forums.

Our hotel was walking distance from the relatively quiet airport and was situated in a little village type location. Well, I say walking distance but I was quite a walk away in the end! It was a spa hotel and that is what attracted us to it. Upon checking in, the receptionist was querying our reservation, since we should not have gotten it as cheap as we did! I began to think that they wouldn't allow us to check in, but after a quick discussion with the manager, they accepted the circumstance.

I wasn't complaining and it turned out the agency who we booked it through should not have sold it at the price we paid—we had gotten about 50% off! We had hired a small car, since we wanted flexibility to get about easily and to see the sights. The hotel didn't have much around it, so we were glad we had it. The next morning, we headed into Verona city. The sun was shining and it was t-shirt weather. Since this was our first visit, we dived into Verona centre and acclimatised a little first.

I was struck with the grandeur of some of the buildings and the architecture itself. There was a colosseum, similar to the one in Rome. We were keen to take a look inside! Emma and I never went into the one in Rome whilst we were there some years ago. We continued to wander the streets on foot and were grateful for the shady narrow streets as the sun was getting hotter and hotter as the afternoon continued. After we had worked out where the main city sights were, we sat and had a drink in the plaza area and decided what we wanted to see or not see.

I was keen to walk up the hill that overlooked the city and watch a sunset, but that's a pretty normal request for me! I loved watching sunrises and sunsets, as if they are some type of sacred event for me! We found a route and agreed to do that on the next day. For now, we can check out the Romeo and Juliet balcony and the colosseum. There wasn't much of a queue for the colosseum, not like the one we had seen in Rome. This one was oval in shape and very intact, considering it was built in 30 AD! They still host concerts inside it, which would have been fantastic to experience had we come later in the year.

It was still an impressive structure and I enjoyed being able to access pretty much all of it. I may have taken a few photographs too! It was cloudless today and the sky looked very blue against the architecture. The heat was tiring us, so we decided to find an ice-cream shop to cool down. You don't have to look far for one of these in Italy! We continued to have a lazy wander around the streets for the rest of the afternoon and then headed back to our hotel to check the spa facilities out. This trip was quite chilled and none of us had any real expectations, so were happy to take things as we wanted to.

The spa met our needs and was a refreshing end to our first day of exploring. We were all feeling tired—we had an early flight this morning and none of us were any good at staying up late any longer. We all turned in for the night to give ourselves a good start for tomorrow—after all, we had a hill to climb! We had unoccupied room separating our rooms which were the only three rooms on this level, so it felt like we had this section of the hotel to ourselves.

Well, the quiet night we thought we would have didn't actually happen. The empty room became occupied by around midnight and needless to say there was quite some activity until around 4 am! Emma had to call reception to ask them to be quiet, but that only worked for a little while! We met our friends outside their room in the morning before we headed to breakfast. I could see by the looks on their faces that they had had the same experiences as us during the night! We had all felt like we had been part of the action and it angered us a little that the hotel didn't seem at all bothered by it.

I saw that there was a 'Do Not Disturb' sign on the door, so I thought I would repay the occupants by removing it for them! We spoke to the receptionist at the desk about our experience as we went to breakfast, but he just smirked. I think he knew what goes on and he could only shrug his shoulders saying, "Continental!"

Oh, so they expect this behaviour because they are continental! After returning to our rooms after breakfast, there was a guy outside 'the room' talking angrily to the cleaner. My removal of the sign on the door must have done the trick, so I was quietly happy about that. We found out later that this guy had the cheek to ask to move rooms! Whatever…continental!

The next day we had a chilled morning and then headed back into Verona late afternoon. We walked along the meandering river before proceeding up the hillside to catch the sunset. We didn't quite realise how high up we were by the time we finally arrived at the top. There was some sort of church at the top, but nothing was open. We were out of season so it seems, because there was also a nice restaurant behind which was also not open! We could have done with a nice drink by the time we had gotten this far.

Having said that, the views were amazing. We could see the entire city and winding river below us. The sun was setting already and casting reflections upon the river. The rest sat and chatted as I was here, there and everywhere with my camera. It's interesting how many photographs you can take and then choose only one as that 'one'! I often think I have got 'the one' until I see the next opportunity. In fact, the front page of this book was taken from this location!

Whilst we watched the sun set, we discussed where we could go whilst we are in the location of Italy. We all agreed that Lake Garda would be worth seeing and it wasn't a difficult decision for us all to make. We had a car, so we may as well use it! We had a much quieter night in our hotel and woke feeling much more refreshed. After a quick breakfast, we worked out our route to the lake. It was about an hour's drive and we found ourselves in quite a touristy area at the south of the lake. We could hardly find a parking space, so god knows what it's like in peak season!

We parked up and began walking along the lake shoreline. It was a fairly big lake and the waters were very still and calm. We found a busy little village area with bars, restaurants and boats. We saw that the boat rides were available, so we jumped into one and it took us around the peninsula of the lake. The driver of the boat spoke good English and he told us all about the thermal activity under the lake and I could see that he enjoyed his job—it wasn't very stressful! Once we docked, we were getting hungry and thought we could get back in the car to head up the shoreline a little further to find somewhere to eat and chill until the evening.

We found a secluded place by chance and it had a long promenade with bars and restaurants all the way along it. They were all facing west, so we could watch the sun set here too whilst we ate and chatted. This was heaven for me and I couldn't wait to see what the sunset over Lake Garda looked like! Well, I wasn't disappointed—the sky remained clear and the sun got larger and lower as it disappeared over the horizon of the lake. The glow of the sky and reflection upon the lake was out of this world and the still, calm waters promoted a nice atmosphere. Once I was done, we began our drive home. I was enjoying out little trip to Verona and was inspired to do more exploring in this region another time. But for now though, it was back home and back to work!

Realize deeply that the present moment is all you have. Make the 'Now' the primary focus of your life

You must be the change you wish to see in the world

We do not learn from experience, we learn from reflecting on the experience

Every mountain top is within reach if you just keep climbing

It got to the point where I was really struggling to focus upon work, with myself battling mental and physical aspects of cancer and now my dad too. I was trying to keep occupied with a variety of distractions. However, my mind was becoming over-occupied with everything and I believed I needed to focus on getting well, or at least give myself the best chance. If I become stressed again, this is going to further impact my already weak immune system and the disease will infiltrate more and more. I could not risk it! My manager agreed and I was permitted to hand over my work to my colleagues and put primary focus upon me!

This was now a period where I was needing to use some of my permitted 'sick' leave and try my best to achieve a positive outcome with this disease. I had no idea how, but I was determined to give it all I had! Whilst all this was going on, I decided to explore Reiki some more and contacted my Reiki healer for advice. She had started doing teaching courses now and so I enrolled on the first one I could. I believed that I could really use this to provide another angle of healing for myself.

The whole subject of Reiki still captivated me and I was super keen to explore what I could achieve. There were about six of us enrolled for the Reiki training session. It was refreshingly casual and we all sat in a circle in a room in an old church building. It was definitely an old building, and apparently haunted! I had to duck for every doorway because they must have been a lot shorter people back in the day.

The room felt calm and peaceful, there was some relaxing music playing and crystals strategically positioned around the room. I had no idea what to expect, but entered into this with an open mind. We were all at the same level and each of us had different motives for wanting to do the training. It was interesting to hear other people's journeys and it provided a purpose for us all. We were taught about the background of Reiki and its origins. There are theoretical and practical techniques to learn and there are three levels initially—Level 1 and 2 and then Master.

I was only planning on doing Level 1 so I could begin using the techniques to heal myself. By the afternoon, we were practising the techniques on each other and providing feedback from both a 'healer' and 'being healed' perspective. I was amazed by the sensations you could gain through your hands and it was like another language to learn! I was really pleased to have completed this first level training and it had definitely left me wanting to learn more. I went on to complete the Level 2 as soon as I was able and this built on the previous learnings, being able now to treat others, even if they weren't physically there! This was called distance healing.

I was practising Reiki on myself most days by now and added it to my busy treatment regimen! It was so hard to know what was going on inside my body. You put all these inputs in and don't get any feedback, other than the occasional scan or twinge. I felt that it was such a blind way of managing the disease and increasing the frequency of feedback would make it a lot easier to manage and know what is helping what!

I reflected upon my treatment regimen and, my god, it was becoming a full schedule. I was happy that I had packed as much as I physically could into it. I was disciplined, consistent and hopeful in my mental approach and this gave me the strength and courage to continue moving forwards. I was not letting anything discourage or distract me from my path and I continued to learn about cancer and how to deal with it.

I thrive on learning, so I was actually enjoying this process from that respect. I used to think that if I come out of this alive, I want to be a much better person from what I have learned along the way. I had read so much related material that my learnings had now covered everything from psychology to science and from the physical to the nonphysical. I had become a holistic learner! I had become grateful for my learnings and I was longing to continue to live so that I could apply the learnings and share them with others somehow. Maybe this book is the way I was meant to share this knowledge with you, who knows?

One thing that I have taken from this is to appreciate every day, be grateful for the small things and don't be egotistic, materialistic or selfish. If every day you can learn something, be kind to someone, inspire someone, create something and love someone, then you will grow as a person and feel fulfilled with your life.

I was really loving my photography, but still hadn't got to grips with shooting in manual mode! I was more into compositions and no matter how much I wanted to learn more about the manual settings on my camera, something was not motivating me to spend time on this. I was listening to these instincts fully by now and I can only assume it is for a reason. If I want to do something and everything is aligned, then there is such a flow of energy, inspiration and effort that completes the task easily and quickly.

I had become familiar with this approach now and when something is hard to focus on, for example, just don't! Move on to something else, because maybe the timing isn't right or the direction isn't right. I began to use the analogy of pushing 'shit' uphill, because this is what life will do—it will make things twice as hard if you're pushing a direction that is not right for you at the time. I made this mistake earlier in my life, trying to make a quick fortune—if it isn't right for you, then everything will go against you to deter you or to force you to learn something!

With my photography, I was simply enjoying finding new perspectives on everyday things and capturing some of the natural beauty in this world, or even on your own doorstep! I was finding that it helped people see things they hadn't really noticed before and, for me, it was creating a memory of what I had seen and where I had been. Memories were really important to me at this time and I felt that you can never take material things with you when you die, but you will always have your memories, because they reach your soul! That was deep, wasn't it? Deep, but true!

We had another break to our routine. This time we were off to the Peak District for a long weekend. Emma's parents had bought us a helicopter ride and we thought this could be a good location to experience this. Neither of us had ever flown in a helicopter, so we were both apprehensive and excited at the same time. We had a nice hotel booked just a few hours' drive north from our home. I had always wanted to explore a bit of the Peak District, but Emma didn't share my enthusiasm.

We weren't staying long in this area, so we couldn't be too elaborate with our schedule. Our hotel was pleasant and the weather was looking good for the few days we were here. We managed to get some short walks in and see some of the more immediate views available within the area we were staying. I didn't have the energy to get up to watch a sunrise or anything similar, so we took our time and paced ourselves to suit our mood. I didn't think we would do as much as we did the last year, but we have been able to pack these trips in and I haven't even told you about our short break in Spain after our ski trip!

It was the day for our helicopter ride. We headed to our take-off location on top of one of the many hills in the Peak District. We checked in and found that I wasn't even on the flight list! Oh no, that's just typical, I thought. Maybe that is for a reason? We found out that Emma had checked herself in twice, so luckily they were able to fit me in on the flight. Phew! We had a pretty basic safety briefing and awaited our turn. They had one helicopter that seemed to be piloted by a 12-year-old boy! Why do people look so young as you get older! It was now our turn!

We boarded the aircraft as instructed and buckled ourselves in. There were about 5 of us on this flight and the flight time was about 15 minutes around the local areas. Emma and I were sitting opposite each other and I was feeling the same as her. I knew how she was feeling by her body language and I squeezed her hand briefly before take-off. The engine was started and the blades began slowly spinning. They soon became a blur and before I had realised, we had already lifted off the ground. It was effortless!

The pilot pointed the helicopter between a gap in the trees down the far end of the field and suddenly propelled us forward at about a 40 degree angle with the tail high in the air. I felt like I was on a marines mission! He then lifted us high into the air and banked sharply right so we were now looking almost vertically down when peering out of the side window! I was in awe of the manoeuvrability of this thing. I absolutely love flying and would like to pilot an aircraft myself at some point! We flew over the hills, valleys and quarries in a long, wide loop.

The time passed so quickly and before we knew it, we were landing back in the field which we had left only 15 minutes earlier. I really liked our hot air balloon ride, but this was the next level! I was pretty apprehensive of helicopters, and still am to be honest, but the buzz you get when flying in them is something else! I felt like I was in my drone. I think I might have to book a flying lesson soon!

As we drove back home, we were both feeling grateful for the time we have been spending together recently and appreciating each other's company. Neither of us could predict our future, so we continued to focus on the shorter term aspects of our lives.

Breaking Free

Whilst life continued in our 'new normal' fashion, we had had a couple more oncologist meetings, but I was finding these less and less useful as they had become secondary to my own 'primary' plan! They were not benefitting me and my regimen was so unconventional for my oncologist, that he must have been wondering himself where he can add value! I remember him saying in the last meeting, "You have been on my books for a long time!"

I kind of liked this remark, since it was an interpretation of my survival so far! He was now bringing surgery up into our conversation again. I believed that I was not able to ever have surgery and I didn't want it anyway. It seemed far too invasive and life-changing for my liking! The only benefit of going down the surgery discussion route, is to get another PET scan. He asked to keep an open mind at this stage and just have another scan to see how things were looking.

I agreed with this and it was scheduled for June and that would have been eight months since my last scan. Whilst I had accepted the scan, the usual anxiety began with that. What if it has spread? What if it has got bigger?—the familiar negative thoughts! As soon as you have scans or scan results looming, you will associate every twinge and every change with a cancer onslaught! You cannot stop your mind doing this, but you can stop how you react to your mind doing this, so I just let those thoughts just pass by! Even you, as a reader, will be familiar with my scan anxiety, so I will spare you the details.

After the scan, we were heading to Portugal again with the two friends we went there with last year. This was another welcome distraction whilst I await scan results and these trips began to feel almost strategic in their timing! Upon our return, it was soon time for results day. These results were feeling quite decisive and I could sense that they would determine a path at a crossroads I was fast approaching.

We arrived at the hospital for the meeting and I could feel my palms had become sweaty. I was trying so hard not to think about negative outcomes, but my mind was tormenting me. I wanted to remain strong and focused so that I could make the right decisions. We soon found ourselves sitting in our familiar seats in the oncologist's familiar room waiting for the familiar IT issues to be resolved until we could talk. He hadn't even looked at the bloody results yet! He apologised yet again, but felt pretty awful that he hadn't prepared himself for our meeting. We waited patiently and I tried not to react to this situation, remaining calm and collected as he accessed my notes.

I allowed him time to read my results notes, watching his facial expressions to try and determine what the results are saying. He finally began to read some of the notes out loud. I only wanted to really hear about the activity. I believed that the tumour was not significantly growing enough to worry about at this stage. "Ah, here it is," he soon remarked. I assumed he was talking about the nugget of information that he knew I wanted to know about! I was right. "Ok..." he continued. "The activity rating is measuring 18.0," he finally stated.

What! That is the activity rating I started with! The tumour is much smaller, but I wasn't liking this activity rating. I am still at a loss why I cannot sense any difference in my body whether it is at 5 or 18! I felt pretty downtrodden at this point. I think my tumour had found another way to fuel itself, but how and where! Before I got too concerned about this new situation, my oncologist suggested that I have a chat with the surgeon and just see what he thinks about all of this. He was telling me to keep an open mind again.

He knows I don't want surgery and have heard about many cases where the cancer has gone rife as soon as it is operated upon! However, we didn't have anything to lose and maybe he could at least stick a small camera through a keyhole to see what it really going on in there that would help me make some future decisions. We left the meeting accepting a chat with the surgeon based in Oxford. He had a good reputation apparently, so it wouldn't hurt to see what he thought.

We soon met with the surgeon in Oxford at the same hospital where I have my PET scans. He was the loveliest chap you could meet and was really empathic and just put you at ease. He said, "Why don't we take a look inside and see how the tumour is formed and what it is attached to?" I didn't like operations, but this was a small keyhole which shouldn't be too much of a problem. I was soon in the day surgery ward having this quick exploratory operation. It didn't take more than an hour and was able to go home the same day.

I was doing this using my private medical insurance to expedite things. I have never used it before, so found it quite fulfilling to claim back for what I have been paying in for years! About a week later, we met with the surgeon to find out what he discovered. This was another highly anxious time because nobody had looked at this thing since my initial endoscopy at time of diagnosis and certainly not to see it from outside my oesophagus.

We sat and waited for him to call us in. He had already seen us and waved as he passed by. It was nice to be recognised, since he has only met us once. It was our turn next and in we went. I couldn't read his face so wasn't sure what he was going to say about his findings. "Well…" he said. He came straight out with it, because he could see the anguish on both of our faces. "The tumour looks clean, contained and not attached to anything else!" he explained with an excitement in his voice.

This sounded good, right? I trusted his judgement about this and it was good to hear. I felt that it gave us more options than if the tumour was wrapped around a main artery, for example. He went on to tell us that he could fairly easily remove it and you would technically be cancer free! Emma and I looked at each other in total bewilderment and Emma quickly burst into tears. The mere thought of ever being cancer free had been far from our thoughts since I was diagnosed! We had to ask him to clarify this so we had properly understood what we had just heard! I hugged Emma tightly and tried to control my own emotions as we digested what we had just been told.

At the beginning of this journey, we learned that I would never be cured and it could never be operated on. What a change of events we were now witnessing. The surgeon has weekly meetings with my oncologist and was well aware of the progress I had been making and self-management path that I had formulated. He already kind of knew me and was impressed with how far we had come, so this was so re-assuring to hear. We left this meeting feeling like we were on a whole new level now. This was like a game with many levels and we felt like we had created options for ourselves once again. Creating options relieves the feeling of being trapped in a corner and allows your mind to relax, knowing that there is more than one escape route. Today was a good day!

From this point, Emma and I kept replaying the remark from the surgeon in our minds. Cancer free! We were struggling to adjust to this potential reality because our mental preparation was for the complete opposite in a worst-case scenario! I was still extremely apprehensive about the surgery due to its life changing and major intervention nature. It was a serious operation and one which you do not take lightly. I did not want to make the wrong decision that I am unable to retract from.

The surgeon briefly explained the procedure to us so we could get our heads around it all. He would basically remove about a third of my oesophagus and the top section of my stomach and join it all together. Getting into this area was the challenge and they would have to almost cut me in half to get access! After the operation, you would be expected to spend a few days in intensive care and then move to a gastric ward for a further seven days or so. It was down to the individual in how quickly you recover.

You then have to learn to eat again with certain pureed food and frequent, small quantities. I was constantly trying to compare the outcomes of this surgery with the continued uncertainty that exists with the tumour and its activity inside of me! It was a damage limitation decision rather than a choice of the most favoured. Emma and I talked and talked about this constantly. The more we talked, the more we became excited about the prospect of being cancer free and you begin to realise that you are willing to trade a lot to remove an unpredictable and active tumour from your everyday life.

I wasn't naïve enough to acknowledge that the surgery may go wrong or that the cancer may return at some point, but the 'damage limitation' lens which I was now applying to this pretty much made the decision for us. The prospect of being free from cancer was a tempting ticket to now be holding! We had found a new hope for our future and while the journey to this new cancer free life was going to be tough and would need us to remain patient, it provided renewed energy and our determination should pull us through it.

We decided to go for the surgery and doing it privately meant it could happen quickly. I updated my employer on these outcomes and decisions, agreeing to continue using my 'sick' leave for my recovery. I still could not thank them enough for their continued empathy and tolerance as I navigated this horrid experience.

We contacted the surgeon and my oncologist and informed them of our decision to proceed with the operation and to get things booked in. I had to have a fitness test before surgery which was a mandatory requirement. This was in Oxford with one of the anaesthetist team. There were various checks that formed the basis of this evaluation and it was to ensure that my body would tolerate this major surgery. I didn't like to think about this much and focused more on proving my fitness! It was time for the bike! They wired me up and put a breathing mask over my nose and mouth. I then had to maintain a constant speed whilst the load was increased, simulating a steepening hill.

I was definitely wanting to prove my fitness at this point and maintained and maintained my speed as the load was continually increased. I could see the anaesthetist looking bewildered that there was no evidence of any slowing as yet! That motivated me to push harder and he continued to wind up the load! Eventually, he said, "I think we could be here all day with you!" He said he has never found anyone who has gone that far with that much load before! Yes! I shouted to myself quietly. He confirmed that there was nothing wrong with my fitness and I ticked all the boxes for surgery.

There wasn't much time to wait until surgery day. I had been dreading this day, but knew it was a necessary evil that would hopefully allow me to be cancer free at some point! This was a point of no return, which made this decision very impactful. We checked into Oxford hospital and Emma was being my usual rock! I could see she was worried about this surgery, as indeed I was, but I tried to remain brave to reassure her as best I could. She stayed with me until I had to go to the operating theatre. We said our goodbyes and briefly hugged.

I was doing so much wishing that this would all work out for us. We had been through a lot of mental trauma and we needed a positive break point. We had given absolutely everything in our fight and this felt like the last battle! I entered the theatre prep room and they inserted an epidural into my back. I was then laid on my side in this foam mould which was supporting my body in a certain position. I was feeling pretty nervous about this. It felt like I was being prepped for an execution! The team was great though and doing their best to put my mind at rest.

I don't remember much after that and found myself waking in a room somewhere. I opened my eyes slowly, gradually remembering what I was here for. I could not move much and had wires and tubes all over my body, connected to various machines. It felt very sore despite the quantity of pain relief I had been administered. I began to recollect the procedure I had just undertaken over the last 7-8 hours.

I was glad to be awake and know that I survived the operation! I couldn't wait to see Emma again and let her know I am ok. I was wondering whether the operation had been successful and I would not know that until the surgeon came to see me at some point. A nurse checked a few things over and I was then transferred to the intensive care ward. They had to keep a close eye on me and there would be hourly checks day and night! I tried not to move, but could not get comfortable. I actually couldn't move my body without it hurting like hell! I was on my back and that's where I stayed.

Soon enough, Emma and Katy came to see me in intensive care. I was so pleased to see them, but I couldn't hug them like I wanted to. Emma's face looked relieved to see me—I was relieved to see me again too! We felt like we had conquered the first stage of a battle to a better life, although it was certainly not feeling that way right now! Emma and Katy stayed with me, but I felt exhausted and was drifting in and out of sleep. I was so loaded with pain relief that it was sending me to sleep. I was already dreading what the pain would be like without pain relief. I had a button that I could press throughout the day and night and it would inject morphine directly into my spine—I certainly needed it! The surgeon called by to see us and check how I was feeling. I put my brave face on again!

He explained a little about the operation and he deemed it very successful and he had managed to remove the entire tumour. However, he continued, I did need to remove your entire stomach and use some of your bowel to join things together! Oh my god, I thought. I have no stomach? How will all this now function? I didn't even know you can live without a stomach! He said that the tumour had penetrated too much into my stomach, so to be sure he got everything, he opted to remove the whole stomach. I valued and trusted his decision, but was still confused how my body will now function!

Emma was staying at her cousin's house in Oxford during this time so she didn't have the one-hour commute from our home each day. I was pleased of this arrangement because it made things much easier for her. My first night in intensive care was tough as I didn't know what to expect. The pain relief was not enough, but I couldn't have anymore and was feeling myself shuddering trying to cope with the intensity of the pain. I had got some relief from the remnants of the anaesthetic, but this was now gone.

The pain was inside and outside yet difficult to describe in words. I was on my back and not able to move, not appreciating how uncomfortable lying in one position can be even after a short time. I couldn't move because of the attachments in and out of me and because I had an incision from the middle of my back to the middle of my front, at a diagonal angle. I had a chest drain into the side of my back which was digging in as I lay on the bed. I had never been so compromised in my life and felt totally dependent upon everyone for anything. I accepted that this won't change until I become more able and mobile, but could not even think that far ahead.

During the night, I was on hourly observations which included temperature and blood pressure checks. There was no way you could sleep properly with the pain and disruption. If it wasn't you the nurses were attending, it was to someone else, so there was constant noise, movement and lights on and off. I am a light sleeper anyway, so told myself that I would simply have to endure this until I can hopefully move to the ward. The morning took a long time to arrive and I was finding my focus was on pain relief, going from one pain control to the next, within the allowable intervals.

I was grateful for my epidural, so I could boost things occasionally, but was finding that this was not quite targeting all the areas of pain. I always felt that I had a high pain threshold, but this was next level! I couldn't imagine being without pain right now—it became a seemingly endless cycle. I was allowed to drink some water now and was worried how it would feel with my new internal plumbing, consisting of just a straight through pipe! I was still struggling to understand how my body can now function properly without my stomach and without the sequence of organs that assist digestion and control blood sugar levels.

This was something to discuss further with the surgeon at an appropriate time, but my questions I needed to ask were stacking up. I am an engineer and a logical thinker, so was trying to solve this problem in my mind, but I was missing vital information about what's actually left of my digestive system. I couldn't help think that whilst I had physical parts now missing from my body, how does my brain and nervous system learn that these are not there anymore and adapt accordingly—that's the bit I was struggling to understand because in any other system, this would result in total chaos! Emma had messaged me to see how I was and what was the best time for her to see me. I was desperate to see her, but I didn't feel much company! I was still quite drowsy from the medication and needed frequent naps. She was fine with that and would be quite happy to just be with me.

She was soon by my side and I was really pleased to see her again. Emma had really supported me throughout this journey and she could not have done anymore for me! I was eternally grateful and I hoped she knew this. We began thinking about how I could be cancer free now and this helped me focus forwards, beyond this intensive care unit. It made me determined to get mobile again as quickly as I could so we could get some normality back to our life. We had forgotten what normal was and we didn't want to totally revert back to the normal we used to know because we had learned about a better normal where stress is reduced, nutrition is improved and outlook on life is enhanced. I was excited about our 'new' normal that we could achieve and begin living!

Time passed more quickly when Emma was by my side and by the afternoon, we were visited by the surgeon and his team once more. We were able to talk in more detail about the operation and about how my body will now function. He re-assured me when he told us that he had done over a thousand of these operations and his anaesthetist team could not believe how stable my body had remained whilst this major surgery was going on inside of me. They said it just looked as if nothing was happening to you and they had never seen that before!

This gave me some strength in knowing my body is pretty resilient and will hopefully bounce back from this! We learned that my body should gradually adapt itself to the new configuration, but could take up to two years. That seemed a long time, but small price to pay to be cancer free and leading a relatively normal life, I thought. For now, I was taking each day as it came and not setting any expectations just yet.

The surgeon was extremely pleased with how my operation went and he was hopeful for a good recovery from it. He was very happy with my recovery already and instructed the nursing team to move me out of intensive care and onto the gastric ward. Wow, that was quick! I was still all tubed and wired up, but he believed that I was making quick progress and didn't now need the intensive care. I was happy with that, since that means less disruption at night hopefully! However, I wasn't moved until the next day, so had to endure another night as before. The morning eventually arrived and I was happy that I now had my headphones to distract me and to silence much of the noise around me.

I was excited about the prospect of moving to the ward now because that was signalling progress. I messaged Emma and told her I was moving and I would let her know when and where I was later that morning. The porters arrived quicker than I expected and I was off, being wheeled along corridors and in the elevators. We arrived at the ward and I was expecting to have a private room, but there wasn't one available at that time. They put me onto a ward with three other older men. To be honest, everyone was generally older than me and it made me ask myself 'why me' again!

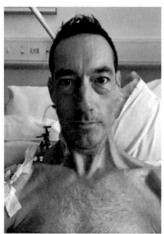

Recovering from Surgery

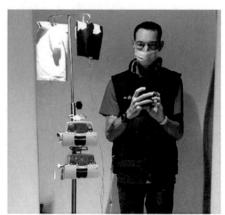

More Chemotherapy

Blue Lagoon in Iceland

Me and My Electric Bike

Waiting for the Sunset

Hair Gone!

Catching Up with Dad

Our Two Little Doggo's

Finding this Heart on the Coastline

Always Something to Capture

Lockdown Walks

The others had had similar surgery, yet slightly different variants and all had different outcomes. I was expecting to have a feeding tube in my nose, but didn't have one. Some of the others did and they were all at different stages than me in terms of their recovery. I had had the most recent surgery and these chaps became a useful benchmark for my own recovery. They were all still struggling with different things, such as infections or insufficient nutrition.

I was worried about what complications I may face as I tried to make progress. Emma soon found me and saw that I had settled well into the new ward. I had inclined my bed a little now so could see forwards instead of upwards. I still couldn't move much and daren't move, if I was honest. I was now able to try and eat very small portions of certain pureed foods. I initially found this daunting, not knowing what response to expect from my body. I think it was pureed carrot to start with. I tried a little and didn't really notice anything different, so tried some more and it was feeling pretty good. I was trying to imagine where the food was going and wondering how I am getting the nutrition from the food now!

Now that I am on this ward, the team try to get you as mobile as quickly as possible. Before I knew it, they had me sitting up on my bed and standing. I was still attached to a lot of equipment, but had managed to get rid of the heart monitors that were fitted in intensive care. They encouraged you to take a few steps and build on this each day. I felt very wobbly, but had my drip stand that I could use as my walking aid.

A nurse was able to hold my other arm as we began walking, further and further. I found I could only do this soon after my pain medication, because the movement was still quite painful. Every twist, bend and reach felt like I was ripping my incision open. I began to understand what milestones to expect towards recovery and ensured I demonstrated my mobility at least once per day, walking further than the last time on each occasion. It was time for my epidural to be removed and I started to wonder what my pain control would be like after this. It came out easily enough and I made sure I had one last dose before it was removed.

I now had to revert to oral pain relief and this transition was an extremely painful one. I found that the medication that they were giving me instead just wasn't touching the pain and I felt so sore all over. The pain would not leave me despite the cocktail of medication I was being provided with. I was almost in agony and once they have given you a set of medication, they cannot give you anything more or try anything different for several hours. This was now a trial and error exercise to find a new combination of pain relief that worked for me.

I wasn't enjoying this period and it lasted a couple of days until things restabilised. It really felt like I had gone backwards with everything during this time and the pain was exhausting me. It was time to check how my scar was healing. It had been taped up, so hadn't seen the extent of the external damage as yet! Many areas of the incision were still numb thank goodness, but the mere removal of very sticky tape was making me cringe as it tugged at the incision.

Wow, that's a big cut, I thought to myself as the incision was becoming more and more revealed. There was staple after staple, holding the skin together—a total of sixty staples in fact! This was going to be one hell of a scar, since it traversed half the circumference of my torso and it looked like a shark bite, so that was how it was going to referred to from now on! I was quietly proud of it actually—it was like a memorial for the start of my new 'cancer free' life! I have passed the stage of worrying what I look like, to be honest.

When you are literally fighting for your life, you are only wanting your life. This is your primary intention and you are not worrying so much about your appearance, as long as you could still function and had my senses and had my limbs. There are people who are far worse off than me, so I wasn't ever in a position to complain. You take what you have and be grateful for it, simple as that! As every day passed following this operation, I had felt that more and more of the shackles which had held me down were being released, allowing me to re-emerge into the world as this new, wiser person.

I eventually got to my own room with a lovely view over the adjacent fields. It was summer time, so I was appreciating this view and being able to open the window. I felt like I was abandoning the others from the previous bed on the ward, but they were fine about it and insisted I would keep calling by! They were now on my walking route and we would be comparing notes each day! I was recovering well and the doctors and nurses were pleased with my progress. They said I was sailing through it. It didn't feel quite like that, but I guess in contrast to other patients they had seen, I was doing pretty well!

I found that I was able to eat more and more each day and was testing different foods to see how I would respond. This was very early days, but I was gaining confidence that I would recover from this operation relatively quickly and that motivated my determination. Looking back, the whole hospital experience is a bit of a blur since you are quite focused on small things and dealing with pain and little steps in progress.

By day 3 after the operation, they had got us doing gym exercises in their rehabilitation facility. I say 'us', but it was just me and the three chaps from my previous ward. We were instructed to rotate between step-ups, push-ups, cycling, weights and things like this. We were assessed in how many reps we could do in a set amount of time, being encouraged to push ourselves as much as we were able. Some of the lifting and pushing exercises were highlighting the pain from my surgery and had to back off my enthusiasm for these!

I was still only a few days from this major surgery and had never envisaged doing this just yet! They gave us an exercise band to continue to use on various muscles. I managed to snap mine after first use, so got the next one up instead. Emma was still seeing me every day and I enjoyed her company. It was nicer that I had my own room and we could chill out a little more and even watch a movie. I was still getting tired easily and needed a nap in the afternoons. This didn't bother Emma though and she stayed by my side as much as she could— she is a real soulmate!

We began to feel that we were winning this battle and this may be the final battle for our freedom and opportunity of a new life. The stressors were still with us, but there was a new hope, a different hope and one we felt was in our grasp. My surgeon called in to see us and check on things. He always seemed to have a happy and positive demeaner about him, which I appreciated. He explained more about the surgery experience and the ins and outs of it all. I could see from his expressions that he was really satisfied with the procedure and he couldn't believe how well I was doing and looking. They were doing a biopsy on my tumour to check its composition as part of their routine evaluation.

The surgeon was confident he had removed the tumour, but you never know what's still lurking within your body and it takes time and subsequent scans to confirm this status. I had had the consultant in doing his round that morning with his entourage of junior doctors. They were all fascinated by my story and the particular procedure that I had just undergone. Two of the junior doctors called in afterwards to see if they could ask more about it and we had a good chat about my events leading up to the surgery and we discussed their aspirations for their future careers too. I felt like a case study or mentor!

By day 4, I was to have my chest drain and catheter removed. I was looking forward to both these being taken out because they were a pain and restricted my movement in and out of bed. I wasn't looking forward to either procedure though, but remained focused upon the outcome. I now had a new nurse from America and she had different standards and ways of doing things—she loved to keep telling me this! This irritated the other staff, as well as myself, and there was always tension when another nurse was with her in my room. They were literally arguing about the dressing to apply to my chest drain after its removal and this American lady was insistent, and somewhat bullying, in her defiance in any other approach.

Anyway, to cut a long story short, she was wrong and the nurse sister was not happy about it. She was now going to be disciplined which made me smile— that's karma for you! The other nurses used to roll their eyes at me when the American nurse was preaching about one thing or another—it was nice to see a bit of humour amongst a tense situation. The chest drain removal wasn't a nice feeling because it felt like pulling out a huge, fat worm from inside your body and it sounded just like that too, if you can imagine that! I was so glad that was out!

Catheter was out too now and I began to feel my freedom emerging as the shackles which were holding me down were slowly being released! I no longer needed to walk with a drip stand and was whizzing about the corridors, looking for longer and longer routes. It reached day 5 and was allowed to be discharged. Wow, I had mentally thought I would be in for 10 days, so this was nice to hear!

I had made such good progress in my recovery that there was no apparent need to stay in hospital. I felt a little nervous and still quite vulnerable, but certainly wasn't going to waiver the opportunity to go home! I felt that familiar feeling of apprehension in leaving the hospital. I liken it to when you are going home after the birth of your first child and the worry about going it alone from that point forward! I was so glad I had Emma and she was determined to support my recovery at home. She seemed to have endless energy at the moment and I was very grateful for her diligence with my new eating schedule whilst my body acclimatised to its new surroundings.

I had to eat a limited range of pureed food and gradually ramp up, broadening what I could eat and eventually becoming less pureed! I felt like I was eating baby food half the time, but learned to remain patient until my body was able to cope. I was still amazed how my food was being digested and processed without my stomach in the loop. I had been reading all these symptoms and side-effects to be aware of after this operation.

It wasn't the lightest of reading and there were many things that can go wrong after this operation, but I focused on positive outcomes and channelled my energy here. By the second day at home, my chest drain was leaking quite profusely. The fluid had penetrated my dressing and was all over the bedsheets. Here we go, I thought. I did not want to end up in hospital again after having done so well, so far. Emma contacted one of the nurses from my hospital ward and got some advice. I was lucky that Emma is a nurse, so she had some dressings and knows what she's doing!

She was told to remove the dressing and drain the fluid, redress the wound and monitor for more leaks and my temperature, in case infection had resulted. When she removed the dressing, fluid was pouring out of the incision. It worried us both, but it had to come out! She applied a new dressing and it felt a lot more comfortable. I thought back to the argument when I was in hospital, between the nurses on the correct choice of dressing for this wound, so I wasn't surprised it had become an issue already! Luckily, the leaking fluid became less evident after a couple more days, so no trips back to the hospital required!

For the first couple of weeks, Emma was making some pureed versions of what they were eating where possible. So, it could be things like pureed Bolognese with pureed mash potato with cheese mixed into it. I had to eat little and often which felt like I was constantly eating and you are told to eat even if you are not hungry. I was beginning to wonder what I had signed up for, because it felt like my whole eating experience had become a constrained schedule of baby food, whether I was hungry or not! Could I no longer enjoy my food, I often thought.

I kept trying to supress these feelings, but they continued to haunt me. I loved food and I was determined to get myself back to as near normal as possible, focusing upon the vision I had for myself coming out of all of this. I believed that my body will adapt to how I wanted to live, rather than my body dictating how I should live. I now had to have vitamin B12 injections, since I did not have a stomach anymore and I could not absorb this vitamin from my food or supplements.

A vitamin B12 deficiency could leave you anaemic and if untreated, it may lead to heart palpitations, digestion problems, nerve issues and vision loss. I would need injections to be administered every three months and would need them for rest of my life.

Following this surgery, I had to almost flip my previous, disciplined regimen on its head. I was now having to consume high calorie, high protein foods, which included sugar and dairy products! It has been a while since I had consumed these and felt I was cheating myself and going against my principles in doing so. However, at this time, I needed to put on and maintain my weight. You are extremely susceptible to weight loss after this surgery and I was already under weight.

I found some high protein snack bars and yoghurts, which I didn't have any problem eating. I was constantly eating something and felt that my life was now revolving around an eating schedule! There have been so many phases to this journey up till now and you find yourself having to continually adapt to new learnings, new treatments, new regimes and new fears, whilst maintaining a sound and focused mind. Talk about multi-tasking!

The scar from my surgery was healing well and hadn't needed to be covered for a several days now. We counted sixty staples in total and they all needed to come out at some point! I certainly wasn't looking forward to that. When we left hospital, Emma was given a staple remover since she was going to be removing them at home. She actually loves doing things like that—must be a nurse thing! The staple removal day had arrived. I was looking forward to their removal, but not the process of removal! I just didn't know what to expect, but they need to come out at some point.

I delayed the removal for a couple of days, but then it was indeed time! Emma was itching to take them out and already had the tool in her hand. She made a start on the first one and it came out really easily, to my surprise. They weren't all like this though, many had become rather stuck and needed quite a tug to remove them. I was trying to count down as she was removing them so I knew when I was approaching the staple removing finish line!

I lost count, but it was over quicker than I had anticipated—not that I knew what to anticipate really! Phew, one less problem now. All of these things were a kind of release from the last phase of my journey and I was emerging with a different, or modified, body, a fresh outlook, a strong will and a wise mind. I often reflected upon the journey I had taken from initial diagnosis and it was a winding one. I felt like I was a new person in so many ways and the combinations of learnings and experiences across nutrition and lifestyle, mindfulness and meditation, non-medical treatments and regimen, spirituality and energy healing had indeed reshaped who I was now becoming.

It has transformed me into a person who is appreciative of life and living, more understanding of others and self, more trusting of intuition, less egotistic and materialistic, seeks to inspire others and of course, more healthy and content with a high vibration level. This vibration level is an important concept which I would encourage you to grasp and I refer to it more in the 'Spiritual section' in this book.

Well, as if we hadn't had enough trips, we had a sneaky one planned to Spain just seven weeks after my operation. Probably a bit soon, but should be doable if I am careful with eating and physical stuff. Some good friends of ours had let us borrow their house for a week near Murcia on the coast. It helped me focus on being well and able that was for sure and we headed over for a bit of sun, relaxation and change of scenery. We hadn't planned to do much whilst we were there, so that helped with expectation setting! We arrived ok and picked up the car and headed to the house. The weather was great and we quickly unpacked and sat on the balcony to take in the view of the sea and to take stock of where we were on our journey back to normality?

However, neither of us knew what normal was anymore and figured we would have to redefine it for ourselves. The next day we set off to a beach in the car which was a little way up the coastline. We hadn't ventured this direction before and were curious about it. As we entered the first town, we noticed that there was so much mud and sludge everywhere. It was very deep and all over the roads, the pavements, the cars and the buildings! What had happened! People were walking around in shorts and welly boots! We later found out that there was a storm last week and the sea had flooded entire villages and towns along the coastline with powerful rivers of sludge!

Wow…I was glad that was last week and not this week! We continued our drive in a strange awe. It was like we were driving through devastation and felt a little awkward being there. We eventually reached our beach, but found we couldn't drive the usual route because entire roads had become washed away in the storm. This must have been quite a frightening time for the locals! We found people having to climb over huge boulders, massive holes and missing chunks of roads and pavements to access the areas around the beach and bars.

We got settled on the beach eventually and had prepared some pasta beforehand for lunch, so could stay put for a bit. The sea was pretty cold this time of year, but I went in anyway—even if to just prove to myself I can! It's a man thing! I was still getting used to what I could eat, how often I need to eat, etc. Not something I had to ever consider and felt a bit of a chore now, losing much of the enjoyment about eating. I was still struggling with eating too large a portion and not chewing enough. This was still being recalibrated between mind and body! We decided it was lunch time and we got stuck into our pasta we had prepared. I was finding myself really struggling to eat it and it was not going down at all well! It was extremely painful and it seemed to just lodge itself somewhere and radiate the most awful pain across my chest.

It was making me salivate copiously and was getting a constant urge to regurgitate. I have experienced this before many times, but this seemed much more severe. It usually passes after 10-20 mins and I can usually continue. This time it did not stop and showed no signs of lessening. We hadn't anticipated this at all and was very self-conscious of how I must have looked to others on the beach not knowing what I am going through. This is why I cannot really eat in restaurants—it can be so unpredictable! We decided to pack up and head back to the house. I was still salivating like crazy and had to use a carrier bag to expel it all. I was not really in the right frame of mind to drive, but I persevered by continuing to use the carrier bag on my lap all the way home.

The pain was not subsiding much and I was trying not to worry myself, or Emma, about it! We finally arrived back to the house and I just went to lay on the bed and took some codeine to try and numb the pain that it was creating. After several hours, I began to feel better but the experience had really shaken Emma. She felt that I was not ready to do things like going to the beach and she suggested we just chill at the house around the pool and keep local for the rest of the week. I was happy with that.

It is nice to be able to retreat easily when you need to and certainly creates less anxiety as a result. We continued the rest of the week by the pool, taking walks and biking up and down the coastline on our doorstep. We were simply enjoying each other's company away from the all of the usual day to day events at home. I managed to get out with my camera too, finding some gorgeous sunrises and sunsets. We felt like we had had a break by the time we got home, so it was definitely a worthwhile trip.

We hadn't planned to do much for the next few months and I continued with my recovery from surgery step by step. I felt I was quickly gaining strength and learning how my new body was now functioning. I still found it hard to believe that my cancer had been removed from my body and I had a chance now!

However, I did not become complacent about this and continued my focus on healing—both physically and mentally, which are equally important.

Ben decided he was going to move out of Brighton now and head to more of a village location about 30 mins north of Brighton. He was still working part-time in Brighton so couldn't venture too far away. We found him a newly refurbished apartment above a refurbished old pub in a village. He seemed to like it, so we got organising the move for him! I managed to get down to see him on the train each month which I enjoyed. He wasn't managing to get home as often as he'd like, so he appreciated my visits. We would walk, eat, explore and talk about our futures. We were on the same wavelength in many ways and it was good for both us to connect like this. Ben was continuing to produce promotion videos and work part-time in the community centre in Brighton. He liked the vibe of the place, which was in a large converted church where different businesses had occupied different office spaces creating within the huge ceiling vaults.

Katy had finished her fashion marketing diploma and was in the process of setting up a part-time business on the side to do eyebrows and eyelashes for clients. We converted the study into a clean and contemporary salon and she began marketing her services after several training courses in London. This was a good distraction for Katy and it allowed her to focus on something positive and rewarding.

For me, I had made a massive decision to retire from the work I love! It had been a very difficult decision to make, since you feel like you are losing your purpose and contribution in life when you retire and I was only 47 years old! I felt like I was deserting my colleagues and all those great relationships I had built-up over many years. I will certainly miss all of it and will cherish my time with a great company.

We could manage financially, which is one of the important consideration factors, but it was my health and recovery chance in life that was outweighing much of the decision process. I was still not out of the woods, so to speak, and I felt that I had to take this unexpected path into a new chapter in my life. I handed over all of my equipment, ID badge and my work. It was a sad time in many respects and a seemingly permanent end to my career and how people knew me in the professional world.

It wasn't long before the distraction of Christmas arrived—they seem to come around quicker and quicker, don't they? We were spending it in our home town of Stroud where most of our family resides. Katy was still working at Michael Kors and so she had to drive back home on Christmas Day evening for her Boxing Day sales shift! We had a fairly chilled Christmas and it was nice to relax with the family and catch up with each other. By the time we arrived home, we seemed to be then packing for our usual New Year away. This year we're off to the Dorset coast. We are staying in a farmhouse we have been to before, so we knew our whereabouts and were familiar with the property. It was in a lovely area and a proper place to chill out and reset yourself.

We finally entered into a new decade of 2020 and I was filled with fresh hope having recently retired. I began to mentally plan my year out and how I going to occupy it. I was not intending to sit around, but my stamina and concentration was still impaired so I could choose when I needed to rest. It was a strange feeling being retired because you are not timetabled in anyway and you can dictate your schedule. I could imagine that you could become quite lazy if you lacked motivation. I was still finding it hard to believe that my cancer had been removed and I was technically cancer free! It was my intention to build back my stamina now and begin to define my 'new' life with my 'new' body. This was a project in itself and I was keen to put time into it for obvious reasons.

Katy was keen to get her business off the ground and now needed a treatment room in the house! We decided that she could use the downstairs study, since I was not using as much as I did when I was working. In fact, I found that I could almost cut and paste all of the fitted desk units into the room above the study, so moved the entirety of it upstairs. This created an empty room which we could configure to suit her requirements. It was adjacent to the front door too, so clients would not be wandering around the house! I got to work now that I had the time and we created a clinical looking room that was modern and professional looking. She was soon up and running and began to create a good income for herself. She had just left her job with Michael Kors and had learnt enough to know that retail was not for her!

I was still having oxygen therapy to assist in my healing, although I was not sure how much this was helping me. Again, you can never determine the individual effectiveness of any treatment or nutrition because you just don't have the feedback on the contribution of each of them. As I was driving up to the therapy centre, my mind was mulling this over and I was undecided in whether to continue this treatment.

I approached the last turn before reaching the centre and noticed that an articulated truck had parked opposite the entire junction, making it awkward to pass and turn. A bus was approaching in the other direction at quite a pace and I slowed until a gap appeared between the truck and the bus for me to pass. As the bus began to pass, I turned to go around the truck and the bus seemed to suddenly stop leaving very little gap for me between the truck trailer and the rear of the bus. I was already still moving slowly and was committed to the manoeuvre so did my best to squeeze through the narrow gap.

Alas, it was probably one inch too narrow and my front left wing of the car caught on a bar sticking out from the truck trailer, opening it up like a can opener! I was gutted and the sound it made was gut wrenching! I didn't want to get out of the car to assess the damage! I was driving my pride and joy, Jaguar F-Type, and could not believe what just happened! The bus was totally oblivious to the issue that had been created by how it was being driven and was well down the road by now. I pulled over to the side of the road and reluctantly got out of the car to see what it looked like. Half of the wing was just pulled open and was sticking out precariously. The bodywork is made of aluminium, so it doesn't take much to damage this relatively soft metal. I pushed bits back as best I could and picked up bits off the road.

Everyone passing was looking at my car and I felt embarrassed about the whole situation. I kept thinking 'what if' in my mind, but that's normal in these predicaments! The truck driver wasn't bothered too much, since there was certainly no damage to his steel trailer bar. Great, now I have an insurance job on my hands! Great start to the year! Luckily, I could still drive the car and my insurance company dealt with the claim really well. Needless to say, I did not attend my oxygen therapy session and ceased attending any of them in the future! That must have been a sign for me to tell me that I don't need these anymore. I just wish the sign had been a little more subtle!

Now that I had more time, I was intending to see Ben a little more and was soon on a train down to see him. The train was a much easier way to get down to Brighton than driving roads which often get so congested—it can easily take three hours and we had experienced this enough to avoid it. Ben was still working in the community church and producing independent promotion videos at the same time. Although he liked the village where he was living, there was not much going on and he was feeling a little isolated. This gave me more impetus to see him more often and he was happy about that.

We enjoyed each other's company and had a chance to catch-up on some really deep subjects that interest us both, where many others would not have a clue what we are talking about! Ben picked me up from the train station and we grabbed some food on the way back to his flat. He was keen to cook me up something for tea and he really seemed to like cooking, which surprised me. We managed to get a nice walk in and take some photos of course. We're both into our cameras and related equipment so this was another common interest point we had.

It was quickly time for me to head back home and Ben dropped me at the station again. I could sense that he was not feeling settled where he was living and felt that another change was on the horizon at some point. We said our goodbyes and told him I would be back soon for another catch up. I wished I could get to see him more often…

I was again due another CT scan to just check-in on my body to see if all was ok after the surgery. I was pleased to have this because it was the first check since my surgery last August, but wasn't pleased that it was just a CT scan. I was assured that they had new scanners now, so this gave me more hope in their ability to detect anything festering which was unwanted! The track record of the previous CT scanners had not filled me with confidence. Not long after the scan, we found ourselves in the oncologist's office reviewing the results. It was a short meeting, since there was nothing untoward detected and this reinforced my hope for the future—'our' hope for the future.

I felt a little closer to freedom at that point and Emma was equally comforted by this news. We set another scan date for mid-year so the monitoring could continue as I ween off the need for treatment and interventions. I was still having to go into hospital every three weeks for my Herceptin treatment, but this had become part of normal life for me now.

Anyone living in 2020 knows what happened next! The COVID virus struck and it seemed to swamp the nation and the entire world rather rapidly. It was a little news item one minute and then we found ourselves in total lockdown the next! What just happened to the world? I will spare the details, since nobody has been unaffected by any of this, but I did feel that my initial enthusiastic start to the new decade was being quickly eroded. Lockdown meant we were all isolated as households and sudden restrictions upon our lives were unimaginable.

No sooner had Katy started her business, she had to stop and Ben was also now restricted in operating his business. Emma was as busy as ever being a nurse and her surgery had to adapt quickly to ensure that their patient care continued. One respite from this lockdown was that the weather was excellent and I walked my socks off every day, making this part of my stamina rehabilitation routine.

Ben had some friends staying with him in his flat when lockdown was announced and they stayed with him for the first three or so weeks. After that, it became a bit too much as Ben had little space for himself. The novelty can soon wear off after a short while and the restrictions and confinement can become quite a mental battle.

Katy found that she had time to think about her future during this lockdown and she became interested in the medical world. To cut a long story short, she ended up deciding to do a nursing degree and soon found herself enrolled to start in the next study year. Wow! Emma and I could not believe the apparent U-turn she had now made in her career. Well, it was more of a total directional change rather than a U-turn, but it did make us laugh because we had ridiculed her for wanting to be a midwife at some point in the not-too-distant past!

I was already feeling that a lot had happened this year despite our restrictions to our movements. I am sure that many of you faced holiday and flight cancellations and then joined the millions trying to get refunds and re-schedules! What a total mess. You cannot actual plan anything right now because you do not know when these restrictions will be lifted and each country has its own controls in play. We only had flights booked to South of France, but it was still a pain in the arse trying to get refunds.

I was finding that I was able to get down to an allotment that we have and this was a welcome distraction from lockdown. I was growing a mixture of fruit and vegetables and experimenting with what grows best—with least effort! I was a novice at this and some of the older folks had their allotments looking like a garden show. They spend a lot of time down here though, so it's a case of prioritising your time. That was my reasoning anyway. It was unusually hot for March time and the allotment needed a lot of watering.

This was all good exercise for me though as I wanted to get my strength back, so win-win! I actually enjoy growing organic food and it is strangely rewarding when you eat the food you have grown. I always like the saying, "Reap what you sow!" It can apply to many things in life and it formed a connection for me between watching my crops grow from seed and investing time in myself to be a better person.

In spite of developing quite a routine myself during lockdown, I was finding that the weeks were flying by. Many people were not really knowing which day of the week it was anymore because every day was very similar to the last. It was such a weird time and nobody had experienced anything quite like it. I was seeing people on my walks that I had never ever seen before and, ironically, there were so many people out walking and exercising than times when they weren't in a restricted lockdown. I saw this as a positive and the lockdown was really helping people appreciate the outside!

However, I was very aware that many people were doing their best to avoid any form of contact or near contact, even up to the point of not even acknowledging you or saying, "Hello!" This made me quite angry because this lockdown was creating a division in the community and the general courtesy of people was being lost. Emma and I used to play a game on our walks—when people were walking towards us, we would guess whether they were going to say, "Hello!" or just ignore us. I would say about fifty percent totally ignored us, as if we didn't exist!

Katy was having too much time to think and her latest brilliant idea was to get a puppy for herself! Emma and I didn't want another dog and we were looking forward a little more freedom in the near future. Anyway, our advice counted for nothing and we soon found we had a little Pomeranian puppy in the house—well, it was just a little ball of fluff really! I already knew who would be looking after this puppy once the novelty had worn off and it wasn't long before the walking and feeding of it was integrated into my day.

He was very cute though and he does actually smile, attracting a lot of attention when we are out with him. Pomeranians are pretty yappy dogs though, which I didn't sign up for! This challenge is still being worked on and we are often having to apologise for his 'yappiness' to passers-by! The Pom was keeping us busy in our continued lockdown as he was growing and being toilet trained. It wasn't long until Ben was going to be back home for his birthday. We hadn't seen him for so long, so this was a special family time. He arrived with a fully loaded car so we knew he was planning to stay a while.

He was getting a little lonely down in his flat on his own and it made sense for him to be back home until work picked up again and lockdown restrictions eased. In the meantime, he had managed to get some local work with his friend's mum's glazing business, which we thought was proactive of him. He was up and out early for his first shift and had enjoyed doing something different for a change. We were glad he was occupied and earning a bit of money too, which is always a bonus. Anyway, to cut a long story short, Ben was soon not liking this work as he ended up deployed in the spray booth and the fumes were affecting his breathing and skin. It wasn't long until he decided to leave and he was then back to square one. However, he was enjoying being at home, at least for now, so we were a family again for a while.

The lockdown was gradually easing and we were able to move around a bit more freely. I took this opportunity to drive over to see my Dad because I hadn't seen him for some time and he lives on his own, which makes lockdowns all the much harder. He was pleased to see me and we got out into the local docklands for a coffee and catch-up. Dad lives a simple life and doesn't expect anything from anybody. He had made some good progress during the lockdown in clearing out things he didn't need in the house, which also helped declutter his mind.

Our day together went by so quickly and I was soon having to say goodbye and head home. Dad was still having cancer treatment every two weeks and a good friend of his was helping to get him back home afterwards. I wasn't sure when I was going to see Dad again if further lockdowns ensued, but we keep daily contact on WhatsApp so know what each other are doing and, more importantly, I can check on how Dad is feeling and keep him in a positive mindset.

The time had come for my PET scan. All of those familiar anxious feelings quickly returned and I headed over to Oxford and went through all the usual processes of measurement. I had not given any of this much thought since my scan back in Feb, so began to wonder if I had become too complacent, too early. I was feeling really good and had been building my stamina progressively and had gained a little more weight too. It was only a couple of weeks wait until the scan results which wasn't long in the scheme of things.

I hadn't met with my oncologist for some time and was not missing these meetings, if I'm honest. Emma and I were soon sitting back in front of him, watching him trying to gain access to his computer once again. At least this time, he was expecting us and appeared to have already looked at my results. Don't keep us in suspense, I was thinking to myself. I could not read his face as he turned to talk to us both. I was hoping to hear good news, but as soon as he began talking, I knew something had been found. My heart sank! Here was me thinking I was cancer-free and now this! Why had the CT scan not seen something back in Feb?

The oncologist went onto explain that a lymph node behind where my stomach used to be had become cancerous and was showing up as quite active on the scan. I began to question why this wasn't removed during my surgery and wondered if it was just attributable to the pre-surgery cancerous mass which was festering inside of me last year. There was no point in dwelling on the past now though because I now had another cancer issue that needed attention. I wondered what they may suggest in dealing with it and they were adamant in removing it surgically. Oh great, another body intervention!

I was getting sick of this journey and the hidden obstacles which trip you up as you try your hardest to make progress. A date was duly set for surgery and it was the day after my birthday! However, this meant I would be in hospital for Emma's birthday which is three days after mine. I was gutted and felt hopeless in the current situation. Emma did her best to be positive and was more interested in getting rid of this cancer.

Earlier in the year, I had booked a photography course in Wiltshire, which was a gift from my employer upon leaving. They knew how much I was into photography and I was keen to learn more about the camera settings and what to use for which purpose. I often shoot in 'Auto' for those camera geeks and focus more on the composition.

However, this doesn't always work and especially when doing astrophotography or wildlife. I wasn't sure if the course was going to go ahead, but it ended up being in a period of little restriction so I could proceed as planned. The course was in a village not far from Emma's Auntie's home, so she planned to drop me at the course and then spend the day with her Aunty and Uncle. That worked out really well and I was able to complete my one-to-one course successfully, learning how to set my camera up better so just need practice now.

During the afternoon, we walked around the village to take photographs of various aspects. The weather was scorching and it was like I was in another world for a while. The village was used to film some of the Harry Potter movies, so it attracts many tourists from around the world. Once I was all finished, Emma picked me up and we drove back to her Auntie's house so we could all have a catch-up over a cuppa! Much of the family were also over, so it turned out to be a nice family reunion in the end.

My birthday was fast approaching and that only meant one thing to me—surgery the next day! I was not at all looking forward to more aggravation within my body after I had been trying so hard to heal everything. All this hard work would all be undone and it had left me feeling quite frustrated and disheartened. I had thought the operation would be fairly quick and easy, but I soon found out that it would not. The lymph node was right at the back of my abdomen, near my spine. This meant that they would need to carefully unpack a lot of my insides in order to gain access.

My surgery day was soon upon me and Emma dropped me off again as before. She didn't come in with me this time, since we knew what was what. I met with my surgeon once again and he was still cheery as I remembered him. He was keen to get this thing out as much as I was and felt I was in good hands. He assured me that he would contact Emma and update her post-surgery, so that was reassuring since I was likely going to be a little delirious afterwards.

Back I went into the familiar theatre environment and was soon receiving the anaesthetic. I had managed to jump the queue after the previous chap had a high temperature, so was told to go home! I did feel sorry for him though, knowing how you prepare mentally for such events. Before I knew it, I was out for the count. I came too in the recovery section and felt totally out of it. It felt like I still had a ton of anaesthetic in me and could hardly keep my eyes open and remain conscious. A nurse saw me stir and came over to check on me. I felt I was slurring my speech, but managed to assure her I was ok.

Well, at least I think I was ok—my body had not yet fully communicated with itself so was a bit of an assumption at this stage. However, I was once again intact and assumed that the surgery had gone as planned. I had no idea what time or day it was and kept frequently drifting into a slumber. I had not enough energy or consciousness to find my phone and let Emma know I am ok, but remembered the surgeon was going to do this so didn't continue to worry. I could not remember feeling so out of it after surgery last time, so I was wondering why I was feeling like this.

I don't know how long I was in this recovery section, but people were coming and going to see me and I could not recall any of it! I was later moved to a private room on a ward so I could continue to recover there. It was late afternoon by now and I began surgery in the morning. I had managed to be re-united with my personal belongings and searched for my phone so I could let Emma know how I am doing now. I looked at my phone and found many messages and missed calls from her. I wondered what an earth was the matter. I replied to one of her messages to re-establish communication and she replied instantly with messages of relief.

I found that she had been trying to contact everyone in the hospital for most of the afternoon to find out how I was doing. The surgeon had not contacted her as he agreed and this really upset me. Emma did not need this additional stress and she was worrying so much about me because she could not get any clear answers from anyone and was beginning to fear the worst. I really felt for her and was bewildered why my surgeon, who I considered extremely diligent and professional, had clean forgotten one of the most important tasks after surgery. Was there a problem with surgery and he was trying to avoid talking about it?

All sorts of thoughts were entering my mind as I began to convalesce in my room. Emma finally managed to console herself and was soon on her way to see me. She almost was on her way over anyhow because of the lack of communication she was facing. In the meantime, my surgeon popped in to see how I was. I told him I felt ok, considering the obvious intervention, but I did feel more bruised and battered than I had expected. He then explained that it was a more difficult task than he had expected and it took around six or seven hours in total. That may then explain why I was feeling more drowsy if they had given me another dose of anaesthetic, I don't know! I continued to ask why he had not contacted Emma and described her worry to him as a result. He was incredibly apologetic and believed his busy schedule for this. I can appreciate how busy he must be within this time of this virus, but I still believe that contacting next of kin after such events is of primary importance and someone should be monitoring the completion of this task. Emma soon arrived to see me and I could see she had tears in her eyes from the trauma she had been subjected to that day. I really felt for her and was still quite angry about an unnecessary situation that is already traumatic in itself! We hugged as much as my body would tolerate and enjoyed each other's company until visiting time was over. She was much more upbeat now she had seen me for herself and we said our goodbyes until tomorrow. I was feeling noticeably crampy in my tummy and was trying to imagine the trauma my organs had been under today. I hope my insides have been put back together correctly. What if there was a kink or twist in something I began thinking because I was feeling a moderate level of cramping pain. Off your mind goes in any of these situations and you cannot seem to stop it doing that! I did recall some discomfort for a few days after my last surgery until your body begins to function normally again. My surgeon was noticeably not so diligent this time around and he wasn't as attentive as he usually is. I had explained my cramps to him and he did not seem too concerned and thought it may be due to inflammation caused by the surgery. I kept this in mind for now and continued to see how I felt going forwards. I was needing regular pain relief for this by now and could not work out what was going on inside of me. Google was indicating all sorts of things, so I put all that to one side for now. This cramping pain was exhausting me and could not seem to relieve it in any way. Maybe I was super constipated, but it didn't appear to be that either. Despite my discomfort, I was discharged a few days later and Emma and I were now tasked with another recovery and recuperation phase once more. I was finding that I needed a hot water bottle on my tummy to help relieve some of the cramping feelings and continued with regular pain relief. I did not feel well and this did not feel right. I contacted the surgeon again through his secretary. Not finding any response, I again contacted several times. I felt a noticeable absence of support and consideration here.

Several weeks later, I eventually get a call from the surgeon. He could not work out why I was feeling like this and referred to the possible inflammation cause again. I was not convinced and pushed for a scan just to rule things out. Forward winding from here, I did not get that scan until October, which was three months after surgery! I assumed the delays were again virus related, but who knows! The scan came and went and found nothing conclusive. Great! I was still feeling bad and I am not seeming to move this forward at all. The cramps had become less severe, but they still flared up frequently on a daily basis. I felt like I just couldn't progress my recovery.

My oncologist called me for a scheduled telephone consultation and he asked the usual questions about my well-being. I explained again my situation and the discomfort I was still feeling, but I got a distinct impression that he was not overly concerned, which implied I should just give it time and shut up. How much time though, I thought to myself! When is this going to be taken seriously? Anyway, he moved on to the subject of his call and proceeded to tell me that they want me to have chemotherapy again. The medical team believed that it would 'mop up' any remaining cancerous cells that may be lingering within me.

Whilst I could see their point, I was really not expecting this and saw another set-back for my recovery on the horizon! Whatever next! Chemotherapy! That almost killed twice me last time. My oncologist knew of my justified reservations for such treatment, but indicated that it would be beneficial to me longer term. My heart sank once again. This journey is so relentless and every time you seem to stand up on your feet again, you are knocked right back down with something else! I was becoming exhausted and was still trying to recover from the surgery.

After much thought and discussion, I agreed to proceed with the chemotherapy treatment. I was between a rock and a hard place with this. I didn't want the treatment, yet didn't want the cancer to return either! I was already approaching a four-year interval with this fight and didn't want to fall at the final hurdle. What have I just agreed to? I was not looking forward to this whatsoever and worried about the side-effects, both during and after treatment. I was being given a treatment known as FLOT, making an acronym of the horrid chemical names of the drugs within it! I read of many of the familiar side effects, which conjured vivid and traumatic memories for me. It's a lottery to see which side-effects get you, so it becomes difficult to prepare yourself.

I stopped reading about the treatment because it wasn't making me feel any better. I just accepted that the period of eight weeks of treatment was going to have to be 'head down' and focus on the finish line. The difference with this time when compared to my previous treatment is that I needed to have one of the drugs over a 24 hour period and it consisted of a pressurised bottle which I had to carry around with me and sleep with! I would need a permanent intravenous line put into my arm for it and this was another procedure that required a thin tube to be pushed through your veins from your arm up to an area above the heart. I hate things like this and wasn't looking forward to it!

Whilst all this was going on, Emma's parents had randomly purchased a motor home. They were super-excited about it and thought they could explore more of the UK, considering ongoing restrictions to international travel. They were also keen for us to use it, which was very kind of them. It was a big wagon and sleeps seven. We hadn't been on any holidays this year, so made a quick decision to go to the Gower in South Wales for a few nights in September. We could squeeze this trip in before I start my chemotherapy, so seemed like a great opportunity. The weather was looking good for the days we had planned, which reinforced the need for a bit of therapy and change of scenery.

We picked up the motor home from Emma's parent's house and began our three hour drive to the Gower. This was a big motor home and had to quickly get used to driving it and working out where the edges were! It was fun though and most oncoming traffic got out of your way. As we drove, Emma and I were recalling the last times we had been to the Gower.

It was over thirty years ago, which surprised me. It was a lovely area, especially if the sun is shining! We arrived at the site and it was refreshingly quite empty. We parked up and got settled in. We were a stone's throw from the beach and the sun was shining. We were happy so far and it was so nice to be able to spend some time away together at last. We didn't plan to do anything too strenuous for the few days we were there and had some fantastic short walks, which often ended at the ice-cream shop each time! The coastline is incredibly pretty around this area and we watched a sunset from the hillside overlooking the sea on our last evening. It seemed to give us hope and energy to tackle the next coming weeks.

Before we knew it, we were back home and I was being prepared for my treatment. Because of this damn virus, Emma would have to work from home during my entire treatment, since she could not risk me picking up anything nasty whilst my immune system is compromised. I felt sorry for her as I was once again disrupting her with this again—an already frustrating time, complicated by the virus! I was hearing of some hospitals cancelling or postponing cancer treatments because of the virus, so was at least fortunate to not experience this at my hospital. It was all very much business as usual in the hospital, apart from the obvious precautions that had been put in place. I headed in for my first treatment. Emma dropped me off and got back home to work.

Nobody was allowed any accompanying visitors during treatment now and I really felt for the elderly and frail patients who could have done with some company and support! I got seated in the new cancer centre that had been built recently. I had experienced three different treatment centres in this hospital whilst being on this journey and appeared to have evolved with them! Many of the nurses had moved on over the years, but there was still a core of regulars that knew me quite well by now. Some of them still mock my veganism, but they only did in jest. I was in for a full day of treatment, so came prepared with the technology and the food snacks. I was still getting these cramps and was still needing pain relief.

I just could not seem to find a position that I could sit or lie where the pain would be relieved. The nurses plugged me in with my first treatment and I got stuck into a book I was reading. I found that I was reading a lot of factual books during this time on subjects that related to the power of your mind and subconscious. I was still fascinated by this new world I was discovering which often sits under the banner of spirituality.

I continued to receive the successive drug treatments throughout the day. I was already feeling tingly in my fingers, face and tongue from the treatment. Some really strange sensations. I remained optimistic and hopeful that I would not suffer any extreme side-effects as my treatment day ended. I am on the treatment journey now, so no turning back.

Love asks me no questions and gives me endless support

The state of your life is nothing more than a reflection of your state of mind

Sometimes a ray of hope is all the sunshine you need

A new day is dawning, giving you another chance to make a difference in the world

I was feeling tired once I got home and sat in one of our reclining chairs to take stock of my body's response to treatment. I was feeling a bit nauseous and had feared that this would escalate like I had experienced before. I was ok so far and just felt a bit bluh! You know what I mean? I had my drug bottle with me and had to get dressed and undressed with it, which took a bit of getting used to. I would often forget it was attached until something tugged me back—it felt like I was in shackles.

I took my medication and anti-sickness drugs to help combat the nausea—nah, didn't work and never worked to be honest. I was going to just have to endure these feelings and get on with it the best I could. My treatments were going to be every two weeks, so was looking forward to the side-effects subsiding as time went on. I slept ok considering I had this bottle still attached to me. I had not been physically sick and was tolerating things ok so far. Although I wasn't feeling at all great and lacked energy, I was coping. This comforted me strangely, because part of me was expecting much worse!

In the middle of all this, Ben had decided to move back to Guildford because the dynamics in and around Brighton had changed for him and there weren't many opportunities here that interested him. He was still at home and his flat remained vacant near Brighton. I tried to get an early exit from his tenancy agreement, but they were having none of it, even with all the virus impacts that were disrupting everyone. They did manage to let it one month early, so at least that was some reprieve.

Emma and I went down to help pack up and put the flat back to a respectable order so that he, or should I say we, could get the deposit back. Wow, Ben had a lot of stuff! We had arranged for a man with a van to come around midday so all the stuff he wanted to keep with him could go directly to Guildford. Whilst we were packing, I decided to check-in with the van man and he proceeded to tell me that he was double-booked and could not move us today after all. What! What is the matter with people!

I was fuming. I told him that he better sort something out in that case, because we had planned everything around this day. He soon called back and seemed to have gotten his dad doing the job with some random refrigerated van! He didn't speak much English either, so lots of gesturing required in our communication. With all of us moving boxes and furniture, the van was soon packed and Ben headed over to Guildford with the van and its man to unpack. We loaded the car up with all the stuff he didn't want and tidied the place up before we headed to

Guildford too. We wanted to see his new house that he was sharing with a friend and to help get him set up.

Ben appreciated that and we soon had him settled. He loved Guildford and felt much more at home there. He had developed a good network whilst he was there previously and could seem to pick it back up again now he had returned. He was keen to find some part-time work in the town to help pay the bills. Good to see him motivated as his videography business had taken a massive hit with the virus restrictions to businesses and the whole entertainment industry. Emma and I eventually headed home after a long day and treated ourselves to some chips to keep our hunger at bay.

I was finding that I was again in a treatment routine and when you are in these, it is hard to focus upon anything else. This is because you are often physically exhausted and, at the same time, your mind is fully occupied in focusing on winning whilst also coping with the trauma that the treatment inflicts. I hate these treatment cycles and longed for it to be week eight when I finish my last treatment. The side effects were unrelenting and I noticed that even walking in the cold air made my whole face feel like it was being pricked with a thousand needles all over it.

My tongue had become numb and I had lost all of my appetite. I just wasn't hungry because of the nausea. I was fast losing weight as I was getting daily diarrhoea on top of this, so wasn't properly getting the fluids and nutrition that I desperately needed. On top of all this, I still had these cramps to contend with which were still flaring up at least once a day. I felt an absolute wreck at this time and could not imagine being or feeling well ever again. The odds were stacking against me here and I needed to find some new hope to keep my focus positive.

My treatments seemed to be coming around quickly and I was soon on my second treatment cycle. I was familiar with the process now and knew what to expect. Emma was still working from home and insisted in taking me to my treatments. She was still adjusting to working from home and coping with all the distractions and interruptions that an occupied home presents. She usually works three long days a week, but she had to work five regular days for now. This was a shame, because it was always nice to catch up and do something together on her days off, even if it was a simple walk.

The progression of the treatment was also worsening some of the many side-effects that were expected to be experienced. I was noticing that some of the effects were intensifying as more of the drug effects were building inside of me. My fingers and thumbs have now become numb and weak. I often could not even pick up a pencil because of it. I did not like these impacts at all and was thinking whether these would have any long-lasting effects to me in the future. I was beginning to notice that my hair was starting to now shed too.

It began as noticeable hairs on my pillow to chunks falling out if I pulled any of the hairs only slightly. I was half hoping that I would manage to avoid this, but alas I did not. As if all of this isn't bad enough, losing your hair is a huge visual identity issue and I disliked the impact this was going to have on how others perceived me. I was fast losing my entire identity that I, and others, were familiar with in so many ways. I was finding it hard to remain motivated and positive when all I could see of my reflection in the mirror was a tired, frail, bald and weak man staring back at me!

I didn't recognise this person anymore and longed for our life to be normal again. How do I get back any sense of normality ever again? This thought pestered me a lot and could not see a clear way forward that would satisfy this desire. I talked about my hair loss with Emma and we decided to visit a local salon that specialised in hair treatment and wigs. I didn't know what I wanted to do at this stage and thought a wig maybe even more obvious than a bald head! We entered the salon and the staff were really welcoming and understanding of the situation.

We talked through various options and having seen their wig options, decided to go for something as close to my style and colour as possible. The wigs were all named and made of real hair—this particular style was called 'Mike'! Well, Mike, you better deliver on this one I thought. It took a few days to arrive into the salon and I made another trip to have it fitted. At this point, I had all my remaining hair shaved off to make a clean start. They put the wig on my head and I felt like a right pillock. The hair was much longer than my normal style and felt like some eighties throw back! They soon told me that it could be styled and cut, so this was reassuring to hear.

It is real hair, so why shouldn't it I guess. They began clipping and snipping. They were careful to take too much off because you cannot re-grow it and you could not get too short or the wig base becomes quite visible. When the trim was finished it did look a lot better, but it was still longer than I am used to and it looked like a needed a haircut. Many of you will now know the term, 'lockdown hair' whilst we were unable to get any haircuts during our lockdowns! This was me now!

I left the salon and headed back to my car. It felt like I had a hat on and I was looking diligently at everybody, trying to gauge whether they thought I had a wig on or not. I could not detect any suspicion from anyone as yet and began to become more confident in wearing my wig on a daily basis. I would sometimes tell people it is a wig and they were often shocked by this, since it looked so real. The wig was working for now, so this brought a bit of comfort to me.

I was wearing my wig on a daily basis now and was getting used to putting it on and caring for it. You have to wash it as you would normal hair, but not whilst it is on your head! I wore it to my third treatment session at the hospital. I wasn't getting any funny looks, but felt I had to confess that it was a wig. They were all amazed how real it looked and they just thought my hair had grown and just probably needed cutting. I was feeling more confident in wearing it and felt like I had disguised my bald head well which meant I was not attracting those unnecessary questions and sympathy from people.

My treatment regime was very familiar to me now and could pace myself throughout the sessions. I was getting used to the side-effects and it was a good job, because they weren't subsiding. I was not doing much during my chemotherapy period—I simply had no energy, motivation or enthusiasm. I was still focusing on the finish line, where I could be back in control and begin to re-build and reconstruct myself once again. I hope this is the last time I have to do this since my body needs to do a lot of recovering. My mind was feeling a mess and could not seem to concentrate on anything at all.

Emma was noticing that I wasn't as coherent as I normally am, which confirmed this. This year was turning out to be quite crap. The hope I had for this year had been extremely shadowed by the virus, the cancer and my general wellness. This huge contrast wasn't helping me remain positive and I was feeling somewhat trapped in this weird world that you would expect to be more of a bad dream.

We hadn't hardly seen any of our friends or family this year and it was starting to feel a bit unrelenting now. The government were switching the lockdowns on and off regionally now and we simply were not permitted to see anyone. Everyone was living in their own social media world, which they had to trade for the more traditional form of socialising together. I just found the social media world so fake and really it isn't me. I like to see and feel people in person—you cannot read people properly in a social media world and, for me, I feel like some of my senses have been taken away from me.

We were fast approaching the end of the year and could not foresee us exiting this lockdown world for some time yet. How any traditional business was surviving this year was beyond me. They had been dealt a really bad hand and most had zero income. Our world had quickly become virtual for almost everything now and I fear that this prolonged situation will be enough to permanently change people's behaviours, meaning that new norms will begin to emerge which probably aren't ideal for those still enjoying the physicality of the world!

The weather was not so nice now and only the more hardy ones were still getting out for their daily exercise. I wondered how unhealthy we may have become during the lockdowns—little exercise, lots of eating, drinking, take-away deliveries and lots of watching television. Actually, television had become really rubbish and they had a distinct lack of content. All the old repeats were coming out and we would often find little that was worth watching. What was this world becoming? It definitely felt like it was in a transitional state—a state of flux and chaos until a more stable world was established.

Let's see if my instincts are correct, because I cannot believe for one minute that we will ever return to the 'normal' that we are all familiar with. It looked like our Christmas was going to be at home with just the four of us after Boris Johnson was teasing us in relaxing the rules for Christmas! This will feel very strange, but I'm not sure that many people are feeling very festive. I think the boredom of lockdown was taking its toll as many households were putting up the Christmas decorations and lights early in November! Jeez, I was still having treatment and it was the last thing I could think about.

Katy was going to be twenty this year and her usual extravagant birthday celebrations could not work this time. Ben had managed to come home for few days and we did at least all go out to a restaurant for a meal on Katy's birthday. The staff even presented her with a cake and everyone sang happy birthday which she quietly loved really! It was so nice to go out and be 'normal' for a while and Katy enjoyed it.

At last, my final treatment day arrived. I will spare you the usual detail and all went to plan. It felt a little strange to think this maybe the last treatment I will ever need again and won't need to visit the hospital all of the time for tests and treatments. This had become my life for almost the last four years and it was another change, another chapter waiting to be achieved. I was still getting those cramps and they have continued since my surgery at the end of July.

Surely, things should have settled by now. It was still affecting me and my appetite. The cramps were often getting worse after I had eaten, which I couldn't help think that there was some sort of blockage! Christmas would be upon us soon and I did not want to be compromised during a special family time. Talking of Christmas, we had better start thinking about it and getting organised. The planning and ordering started and it began to feel a little more festive as we entered into the spirit of it.

Christmas day arrived and we were all together as a family. Ben and Katy liked being in their home for Christmas for a change, since we are often never here. They could please themselves and chill out. I think we all needed to chill out, especially Emma who had been working relentlessly for too long! We enjoyed our own company and watched a few of the classic movies. Emma had got the games out—she was quietly competitive and loves a good game. If it is one she is good at, then that will be played the most! It was nice to see Emma more relaxed and taking some much needed time out.

I was finding my cramps were returning with a bit more intensity—the Christmas food and drink may not have helped here, but it is Christmas! The hot water bottle was out again and I was having to lie down a fair bit to help relieve the discomfort. Once Christmas had passed, Emma was questioning whether my cramps were to do with 'what' I was eating. Maybe I had become intolerant to certain things or maybe certain things were aggravating an already inflamed insides.

She recalled her Mum had suffered with certain foods not that long ago and followed a diet which included foods on what is known as a FODMAP diet. FODMAPs are types of carbohydrates found in certain foods, including wheat and beans. Studies have shown strong links between FODMAPs and digestive symptoms like gas, bloating, stomach pain, diarrhoea and constipation. Low-FODMAP diets have shown incredible benefits for many people with common digestive disorders, which I could associate with some of my symptoms.

1.6 Nutrition Part 2 choosing the right foods

We began researching this further and also consulted the dietary advice post-surgery when I had my stomach removed. Emma thought if I started at the beginning again and stuck to only foods that were allowed on the FODMAP plan, then we could see if that makes any difference. I was willing to try anything and it made sense, thinking about it. We reviewed the food lists and went shopping to stock 'my' cupboard of only the foods which are low in FODMAPs. I also went Gluten Free where we could too so we could give the best starting chance for my body.

By day 3, I was feeling so much better and many of the familiar cramps had subsided. I had adjusted my portion sizes too, so I wasn't over-loading my insides too much. I was absolutely gobsmacked! How could this advice not have been given or considered by any of the medical and dietary teams? Another credibility knock for those folks I am afraid! Emma and I felt like we had solved a puzzle.

I continued eating low-FODMAP foods for a couple of weeks and later began to reintroduce other higher FODMAP foods to test my tolerance. I was improving and my tolerance to food had increased a 1000%! I have been so amazed in how quickly my cramping was resolved that prompted me to include a second part to my Nutrition learning section to outline FODMAP a little more for those of you who may be interested or have experienced something similar.

So, where does life go from here? I am technically cancer free. I am retired. I have no pain. My challenge now is to remain cancer free and to build up my stamina and weight again. I still have much of my life left, so hope I can seize opportunities as they arise. I still apply much of what I have learnt over the last four years and I hope that I have encapsulated my journey so far in this book effectively, so that you as the reader can appreciate the journey, the challenges and the learnings along the way.

Out of anything, I would encourage you to read the learning sections of this book. Your increased awareness of yourself will empower you to achieve more than you could have anticipated and it should also help you remain healthy and well during any challenging times. I hope I have inspired you to check-in with yourself and evaluate the type of life you are currently living. Make some time to do this because it is an investment in 'your' future, your life. Enjoy life in the 'now' moments and appreciate the world and people around you. Love your life…Never stop learning, never stop living, never stop looking for the signs and never stop believing in yourself!

Closing out on a positive note—I just had the results from my recent PET scan and it shows that I am still cancer free! This has significantly helped us to emotionally start to move forward in our lives and begin to remove the anchors and chains which have constrained us for so long. This is not over and nor is it an overnight transformation, yet one which slowly rebuilds as confidence increases as trust is progressively restored in yourself. The worry of cancer returning will always continue and you simply learn to live with this situation, but I have become a stronger person and have established a resilient faith in my ability to deal with future life challenges.

Go and live that life you have been given!
I will leave you with some final quotes that I find quite poignant from my journey:

The fullness of life is only accessible in the present moment.

-Eckhart Tolle

Learn from yesterday, live for today, hope for tomorrow. The important thing is not to stop questioning.

-Albert Einstein

No matter how many mistakes you make or how slow you progress, you are still way ahead of everyone who isn't trying.

-Tony Robbins

Everything you can imagine is real.

-Pablo Picasso

Look for the thing you notice, but no one else notices.

-Rick Rubin

All meaningful and lasting change starts first in your imagination and then works its way out. Imagination is more important than knowledge.

-Albert Einstein

Don't let the fear of losing be greater than the excitement of winning.

-Robert Kiyosaki

Rise above the storm, and you will find the sunshine.

-Mario Fernandez

A mind that is stretched by a new experience can never go back to its old dimensions.

-Oliver Wendell Holmes

This inspiring poem suddenly came to me as I walked through the woodland one day and I felt compelled to write it down, so here it is! The words seem to resonate with my gratitude and appreciation for my opportunity to continue living:

Thank you for the beauty
Which surrounds me everyday
Thank you for your guidance
That helps in every way
Thank you for the strength
You provide in such abundance
Thank you for the hope and light
Which keeps shining in the darkness
Thank you for this world
The one in which I live in
Thank you for this new life
This one I have just been given.

Appendix Summary

1. **Learning Focuses:**
    1.1 Impacts of Diagnosis—how does it affect you?
    1.2 Personality Analysis—how well do you know yourself?
    1.3 Stress Management—how to recognise and moderate?
    1.4 Spiritual Enlightenment—a new perspective on life and living
    1.5 Nutrition and Supplements—making changes to your diet
    1.6 Nutrition Part 2—choosing the right foods
2. **Levels of Consciousness**
3. **Your Vibration Signs Test**
4. **Recommended Reading**

1. Learning Focus:

1.1 Impacts of Diagnosis—how does it affect you?

When you are diagnosed with something serious and terminal in nature, you soon realise that everything which defines you is put on hold or ceases to prevail with an almost immediate effect. These 'things' that define you, and are you, are shown in Figure 1. You quickly realise that it doesn't matter how much money you have or what you own—it means absolutely nothing and you cannot buy your health, so if you have no health, you could have nothing.

The diagnosis impact not only affects you, but also your close friends and families. This can be burdening and supportive at the same time. However, not all friends and family will react in the same way. Some will step up and some will retreat. You can certainly see this landscape with renewed perspective and it was an interesting dynamic and one which can become permanent in many cases. I am not sure what drives this dynamic, but it I believe it relates to each individual's personality and coping mechanisms that come to the surface.

I found myself initially retreating from all engagements and wanting my own precious time with my own little family. I wanted to ensure we had stability here first and it became my instinctive focus. I was fortunate that my wife, Emma, was the communication channel to the outside world and this helped me shield myself and keep my mind concentrated on dealing with the cancer journey. At the time, I had not appreciated how burdening this was for Emma as she was also having to deal with her own emotions in this situation.

Figure 1—Diagnosis Impacts upon Your Life

You can probably relate to these areas of your life which you hold value against and ones which you may simply take for granted in everyday life. Some are life goals and you can literally spend your entire lifetime trying to achieve them and often forget to live in between! I was always one who pushed myself and constantly strived for the next and the next (i.e. the future) and was not taking enough time to appreciate the 'now'. Do you live for tomorrow or do you live for now? It is quite a profound question, but one which I found very insightful.

The only time that really exists is 'now', so the more we live in the past or in the future in our minds, we are missing all of the 'now' time and this is the time which is real and happening right under our noses. We are of course in the 'now' physically, but not always within our minds. If we are not aligned within ourselves, then we are surely not making the most of the 'now' and what 'now' is showing us. You could liken this to a radio which is tuned into to a particular station called 'today'.

However, the station only broadcasts tomorrow, so we will never get to hear the 'today' show today, because the 'today' show is always broadcasting tomorrow. We could only listen to the 'today' show as a recording and so any actions we could have taken at the time of the broadcast are not possible. The point here is that if 'we' are not tuned into ourselves and our lives at the time of happening, then we will miss things—we could miss signs and signals, interventions, opportunities, etc. We could only look at things retrospectively and we don't tend to allow time for this either.

The Figure 1 shows the few remaining aspects that now define you and your life after diagnosis, or any other life-changing event. They are not a great trade-in for who you were, yet you have to let go and become almost a nobody to focus on resolving the challenges you now face. However, these are only one aspect of what's left of you and there are other aspects that are physically and emotionally related and it is the power of your mind which now needs to step up and run the show! Your mind now has a pivotal role to play in fathoming out a survival package for you to execute and a buoyancy aid to keep you afloat during the 'storm'.

When you are considering 'who you were' and 'who you are' now, there is quite an interesting perspective to think about—who you are versus how you are perceived. What 'you' are is projected outwardly into the world and how you perceive 'yourself' is what is reflected internally within you. A little self-reflection is always beneficial and can help you identify any mis-alignments with the perception of yourself. It is also important to consider these against your personality characteristics, since you may not be doing or thinking in alignment to the character of who you are—this is discussed in the 'Personality Analysis' section, so take a look at this.

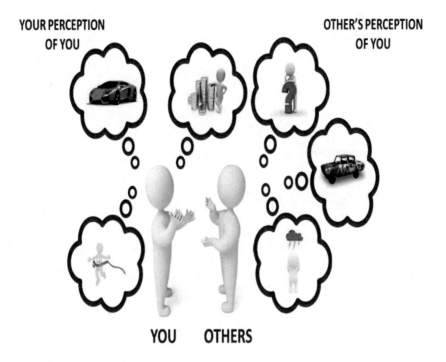

YOUR PERCEPTION OF YOU

OTHER'S PERCEPTION OF YOU

YOU   OTHERS

The table below in Figure 2 is what I noted when jotting some attributes down about myself—it will help you to see how I have applied it. You can always use others to help you define your outwardly projections, since they are the ones which will see this more than you! This has just been a mental model I have had in my mind and it's quite enlightening putting it onto paper.

I have used these simple questions, which should encompass most of the high-level aspects about you:

> **Who** → your key personality and characteristics which define you and people would remember you by
> **How** → your mental and emotional state
> **Why** → things that motivate you or you're passionate about
> **Where** → your progress and plan against your desires and ambitions
> **What** → what do you want to achieve in your life

Outwardly	Your projection to the world
Who you are	Kind, empathic, optimistic, determined, courageous, intellectual, inspiring
How you are	Strong willed, resilient, in the flow, positive mindset
Why you are	Innovation, nature, photography, helping others, being inspirational, bettering myself
Where you are	Striving to continuously improve upon myself and learn how to improve. My energy level is above average and live for the 'Whys', but also have begun to set new goals that are within < 5 year timescale - any longer just doesn't seem to resonate any longer
What you are	Happiness, health and family are primary, being able to photograph different places in the world, being able to inspire others to change for better, invent something that others will find useful

Inwardly	Self-reflect on your outward projections
Who are you?	I think that I am true to myself in who I am and I understand myself very well now
How are you?	I have always been strong minded, to my detriment sometimes if too inflexible. I find my resilience helps me bounce back quickly from any learnings and further reinforce and empower my mindset for the better
Why are you?	I am a creative person at the core, but also like complexity and analytical challenges. There are many facets to what motivates me as you can see and I love being active in all of them
Where are you?	Feel in a happy place and not much phases me now, allow life to flow more intuitively and continue to learn more about life and myself, live more for today and set shorter term goals - well, more of a vision board where it will happen when it's meant to happen
What are you?	Since my goals are more short-term, I am enjoying living for the moment more and taking in more of the 'now'. I have been lucky enough to retire at 47 and have a unique opportunity to rebrand myself and consider opportunities should they arise - I don't tend to chase these days and try to attract them to me

Figure 2—Get to Know Yourself

Whilst it may take time to develop this understanding of yourself, it should correlate with your personality and a true reflection ought to show alignment with these areas. The purpose of this exercise is to simply analyse yourself both externally and internally, taking the opportunity to learn more about yourself, what is important to you at your core and where there are any gaps.

I think I have lived my life this far being fairly true to myself, but this whole experience has taught me to get rid of the ego and just be yourself—don't worry about what others think, this is what often fuels your ego! Be yourself and be true to yourself and you will find a new fulfilment in your life that is more satisfying, more rewarding and less stressful.

Once you better understand yourself, then you will have a better opportunity to deal with a crisis situation, knowing your strengths and weaknesses. Remember 'like' attracts 'like', so if you find life is not meeting your expectations or you seem to get the same crap all of the time, you might be projecting an outward energy signal that is not quite what you think it is and you will, therefore, think, "Why did this just happen?" If the crap just keeps coming, try to analyse it and determine what might be the source of the recurring problem—there is usually a reason and a pattern to recurring themes.

1.2 Personality Analysis—how well do you know yourself?

I have always been fascinated by people's personality traits—it tells us a lot about ourselves and if we are more aware of ourselves, and others, it makes working and living together so much more harmonious.

There are many sources for determining your personality and I decided to use three independent sources and compare them to see if there were areas that resonated and if they did resonate, where are they resonating.

I believe that your star sign personality is often quite correct in my experience, so I included it here against my blood type and my character analysis produced using the Myers Briggs principles. These then provide three independent sources in which to begin analysing.

Leo Star Sign	O-Neg Blood Type (7% of the population)	INTJ – The Architect* (one of the rarest personality types)
Optimistic Caring and lives a good life Natural leader	Optimistic Loyal and reliable Leaders	 Leader
Kind and protective Intelligent Courageous	Generous and kind Above average IQ Daring Focus on big picture	Good listener Intellectual Curious and ambitious Focus on big picture
	Set high standards Calm and confident Adapt well to change Determined Outgoing	High expectations Confident and hard working Open-minded Determined Introvert—prefer to work alone Logical and objective Control and order
	Go-getters Flexible and resilient Warriors (accord to Japanese) Intuitive	Perfectionist Analytical and innovative Future thinking and possibilities Complex problem solvers Imaginative and strategic Dislike too much structure

*Myers Briggs classification

Wow, I was surprised by the amount of synergy between these independent traits and characteristics—I shaded those characteristics where there was this synergy. I believe pretty much all of them describe me fairly well and I have always stayed true to these throughout my life—even my first life (life before cancer)! I am sure for those that know me that there are a high proportion of these that resonate. I have always been an optimist and never given up on anything. I usually know what I want and develop strategies and solutions to achieve them. I like complex challenges and always think that there are solutions to almost everything.

Most of my working life has been aligned to many of these characteristics, so I have positioned myself in the right roles from that point of view. On reflection, I am proud of who I am. I don't want this to be taken as an arrogant viewpoint, but I simply like who I am and feel blessed by having these characteristics. I think that there are a lot of people in society who do not know who they are and if they do not know this, how can they possibly be in touch with their lives and be fulfilling themselves in the process of life!

I would encourage everyone to get to know yourself better and position yourself in this world. If you have a personal datum, you can track yourself better and determine how much progress you have made. Check-in with what you are doing with your life now and see if it aligns to your own traits and characteristics—if you don't know your traits, find a way of measuring them using on-line tools and do some research on yourself. If there is no alignment or misalignment, then ask yourself if you are satisfied and fulfilled doing what you are doing!

This is the first stage of change—recognising and believing that change is necessary. Be honest with yourself and maybe ask your peers and friends who they think you are—you cannot always see your own true-self. We so often wear a mask of who we think we are, hiding our true self. This might be to fit in with a certain crowd or to emulate someone who inspires you. The trouble in doing this is that we forget who we are at our core and your life is not being lived or fulfilled authentically.

Here is a quote about Myers Briggs INTJ personality characters and this one is me down to a tee: "Difficulties are highly stimulating to INTJs, who love responding to a problem that requires a creative solution."

Just for information, here are some famous INTJs—some of them I like, but not all: Dwight Eisenhower, Stephen Hawking, Mark Zuckerberg, Elon Musk, Arnold Schwarzenegger, Sir Isaac Newton, Nikola Tesla, Charles Darwin.

I think I was leveraging these characteristics in my fight against the cancer and solution finding was top of my agenda! This is important to recognise. Aristotle once said, "Knowing of yourself is the beginning of all wisdom." This is not a new concept, but one we tend to not acknowledge or act upon.

In addition to my interest in personalities, I have also been curious about astrology and tarot card reading, but never really believed that it worked in predicting your future. However, you search every corner of your existence at times of crisis and you find some weird kind of support and guidance from them.

Numerology was more tangible for me, because there was something more mystical about it and had an apparent structure that defined the relationship between astrology, numbers and letters. Sounds like an interesting concept that my curiosity could not let slip! This was another personality assessment as far as I could see and I decided to do a numerology assessment to discover more about myself from this perspective.

Let's see how accurate it was and what it's got to tell me—that's my analytical hat on now. I provided my full name, date of birth, place of birth, etc. and waited to see what this numerology report would tell me about myself. Wow, I was actually blown away with the accuracy of the analysis, not only in my personality and character, but in the life stages too! <u>Everything</u> correlated with my other personality assessments, but there were some other aspects of the report which I found inspiring and surprising how this report picked up on these—here a few that resonated with me:

- *Inner knowing and can predict things*—wish I had seen this disease coming, but maybe I was shown the signs and I just did not see them!
- *On a different mental playing field and far from a common person*—well that sums up how I thought of myself in my younger years and maybe that contributed to why I was bullied!
- *Incredible insights, ideas and perception*—this is how I have always been and ideas seem to overflow in my mind. I am only just now actually following through on an idea I had during my early stages of cancer because I thought, "You only live once!" and why not give it a try!
- *Inspire others, appreciate others and those needing support are drawn to you*—I never saw myself as an empathic person, but on reflecting back on my life I have found many examples where this holds true. I quite like the fact that others see me as someone who can listen to them and I find that I can often see that need in people too. I often find that people I have never met can comfortably share really deep situations about their lives with me.

One particular aspect of the report which I was really quite shocked about was the life stages. It mentioned the following:

Around your 44th birthday, there will be a big change in your life. Any health issues that you have late in life are likely to be due to your refusal to slow down; learning stress-management techniques, like meditation, are highly recommended.

Some coincidence that I was diagnosed with cancer when I was 44 years old and I have always considered stress was one of the primary reasons that I became ill—I never listened to my body and just kept ploughing on! This cancer was a definite sign to change my lifestyle and develop strategies to reduce stress. However, had I read this report ten years ago, I would have dismissed it and thought nothing of it. I didn't read the signs and I never thought I would have health issues at this age, but I didn't know what I didn't know!

The lesson here is to listen to your body, listen to your instinct and intuition more than you do now. Reflect upon both positive and negative things that have already happened in your life and try to determine why they occurred and whether there were any signs before they occurred—my bet is that the signs were there and you may not have noticed them or interpreted them incorrectly. Once you tune in to this and can see, feel and believe the signs, you will be better armed to handle situations or avoid them all together and your life will flow better!

In life these days, everything is so fast paced and we have become incredibly inpatient in everything we do. We get annoyed if we don't get a reply to a text message within 5 secs, upset if our food order hasn't arrived within 1 min of ordering it and frustrated when our video streaming is briefly interrupted by a poor network signal. What are we becoming? We are losing patience with life itself and not taking time to enjoy it! We are rushing it and wanting the next, then the next, then the next. The 'now' is not getting much look-in these days.

1.3 Learning Focus: Stress and Managing Stress

Occasional stress is normal for your body to handle and it will typically stimulate a chemical reaction within you to provide you with the ability to respond. The stress response should enable our focus on the immediate task or threat in hand to mitigate any risk to ourselves. Whilst this response is not usually related to a need to escape from a ferocious animal, for example, we find stress builds as a result of high workloads, un-paid bills and un-resolved tensions with others, to name just a few. These could be on-going threats in themselves and you may feel under constant attack and strain from them.

Once a stress response is triggered, a combination of nerve and hormonal signals stimulates your adrenal glands to release a rush of hormones, including adrenaline and cortisol. The adrenaline will increase your heart rate, raise your blood pressure and provide you with an energy boost. The cortisol element increases the glucose in your blood stream, heightens your brain's use of glucose and increases the availability of tissue repair substances. Cortisol is also responsible for effects to the immune system, suppression of the digestive system, reproductive and growth processes. Furthermore, it can affect your mood, motivation and fear.

Whilst these responses are necessary under certain circumstances, continual activation of this response can disrupt many of your body's processes and puts you at increased risk of many health problems, including:

- Depression and anxiety
- Pain of any kind
- Sleep problems
- Autoimmune diseases
- Digestive problems
- Skin conditions, such as eczema
- Heart disease
- Weight problems
- Reproductive issues
- Thinking and memory problem

That's why it's so important to learn healthy ways to cope with your life stressors, since the persistence of this can deplete your immune system making you vulnerable to diseases and illnesses. Some experts claim that stress is responsible for as much as 90% of all illnesses and diseases. It must also be stated that exposure to stress can cause the body to become more acidic, which creates its own set of problems as outlined in the 'Nutrition and Supplements' section of this book.

How do you know if you are stressed? Here are some of the signs—do you recognise any within yourself or others?

Cognitive symptoms:

Memory problems
Inability to concentrate
Poor judgment
Seeing only the negative
Anxious or racing thoughts
Constant worrying

Emotional symptoms:

Depression or general unhappiness
Anxiety and agitation
Moodiness, irritability, or anger
Feeling overwhelmed
Loneliness and isolation
Other mental or emotional health problems

Physical symptoms:

Aches and pains
Diarrhoea or constipation
Nausea, dizziness
Chest pain, rapid heart rate
Loss of sex drive
Frequent colds or flu

Behavioural symptoms:

Eating more or less
Sleeping too much or too little
Withdrawing from others
Procrastinating or neglecting responsibilities
Using alcohol, cigarettes, or drugs to relax
Nervous habits (e.g. nail biting, pacing)

(Ref: https://www.helpguide.org/articles/stress/stress-symptoms-signs-and-causes.htm)

Since there are so many factors that can induce stress, and I guess everyone has varying degrees of tolerance, it is important for you to be aware of these symptoms that become more than an occasional issue. For me, once I had started eating more of a plant-based diet, got rid of coffee caffeine and made meditation part of my daily regimen, I really noticed the difference in how I felt within myself, how I thought about things and how I responded to situations. Emma noticed these changes too, so I knew I was on a benefitting path of improvement and I was even more motivated to continue and try even harder. I was feeling like I was only just getting to know my 45 year-old self!

Sounds crazy, doesn't it, but that is the reality. I have always considered life as a bit of a conveyor belt—it is constantly moving in only one direction and if you fall off it, it is hard to get back on. You are soon left behind and few are there to pick you up and help you because they too don't want to be left behind...and so it goes on! Whilst you are on this conveyor belt, you don't get much chance to stop and reflect due to the simple pace of life which is why you could look in the mirror 40 odd years down the road and wonder who is looking back at you! Who are you? What are you trying to be? Have you achieved any of your goals yet? You're not aging well, are you!

I can imagine the conversation you could have with yourself here. Your subconscious thoughts are right to question and the more you listen to this, the more you will begin to observe yourself from new perspectives. We often only seem to see ourselves in one dimension, which means only a limited perspective! Once you shift your perspective, you will start to see the other dimensions of yourself. Whilst this is an analogy, it is valid in that there are aspects of yourself that you probably need to get to know better or have not yet seen or do not want to acknowledge?

Maybe the only dimension you do know about yourself is a façade which you have positioned to disguise something about you. Get to know who you are at your core and begin to integrate things into your life that slow the conveyor belt down and give you the time to get to know the real 'you' more and allow yourself to be the true 'you' more. I have found that through all of this journey so far, I have had to press all the reset buttons in my life, which has been necessary in many respects.

After resetting everything, you get the chance to reconstruct yourself and surroundings with the new knowledge you have gained and can adjust your lifestyle to better align to your passions and what your mind and body need to operate effectively and efficiently. I have digressed a little, but I thought that these points are important for us to consider as we live our busy lives.

Here are some typical stress management strategies to consider:

- Eating a healthy diet and getting regular exercise and plenty of sleep
- Practicing relaxation techniques such as trying yoga, practicing deep breathing, getting a massage or learning to meditate
- Taking time for hobbies, such as reading a book, walking or something creative
- Fostering healthy friendships—find friends with which you resonate with
- Having a sense of humour
- Volunteering in your community
- Seeking professional counselling when needed

First step is to recognise and acknowledge your stress levels and then try to work out where the stress is coming from. If the stress cannot easily be removed, then look more into how to develop coping mechanisms to reduce your stress response to them. You shouldn't have to go through this alone, so sharing your problems or stressful scenarios with those who you trust would be very helpful too! It is a self-learning game and there may be several causes of stress, so start with one at a time and work your own strategy to firstly recognise it, then respond to it and either temper any negative responses or remove it!

1.4 Spiritual Enlightenment—a new perspective on life and living

During my extensive research of every facet of everything in my cancer survival journey, I was fascinated by the science behind what is known as spirituality. I am not, nor have ever been, a religious person and believed that we are the only ones really responsible for our actions and what we achieve in life. Having experienced much of what I have read about from journals, anecdotal evidence and a breadth of scientific and spiritual research, my belief has now become increasingly more defined and the mystery of life and our purpose here is very intriguing and I am super-fascinated by it.

Finding information that resonated with my personal experiences and my analytical understanding have strengthened me from within beyond anything I thought I was capable of. I have never felt so whole and certain about myself, where I have learned about the power of life, self-healing, love for yourself and others and manifesting your true desires through your authentic intentions! Once you see the world from this perspective, it is a magnificent, mystical and wonderful place. One in which I appreciate much more and can fully immerse myself within now.

The definition is Spirituality is a difficult one to explain and can be quite a personal interpretation, yet I have found this description below:

(Ref:www.pocketmindfulness.com/definition-of-spirituality/)

Spirituality exists within a unique, unbreakable relationship between the heart and the mind. It is an internal harmony that allows one to endure the most harrowing of circumstances.

Even when lacking in material possessions and physical freedoms, this relationship endures and enables its host to continue to offer compassion to others.

Spirituality is an internal sanctuary, free of the rules and expectations of the physical world, it is a place where one can submit to one's mortality and rest properly, without worry, anxiety, desire and striving.

Spirituality offers liberation in the knowledge that as long as one has the freedom to think for oneself, one will always have the freedom to positively influence the lives of others through love and kindness.

Within this relationship, between heart and mind, there is a deep-rooted understanding that simplifies existence and removes the mental suffering surrounding the constant compulsion to grasp, acquire and succeed.

In the arms of spirituality, one is comforted by an understanding of the transient nature of life; that no matter who we are and where we come from, we are all part of the same interdependent, impermanent cycle of life.

So, what exactly did I learn to bring this much more positive outlook on life, I hear you ask! Firstly, being spiritual means that you are aware of your own existence down to a soul level and appreciate the connected life that surrounds you. You live less from the ego and more from the heart whilst being a positive influence upon others. You acknowledge the divine connection and trust your inner guidance, your intuition much more than ever before.

So, how are we connected?—let's start with energy and vibration. The term 'vibration' does not mean we visibly shake, but we do have a natural frequency about ourselves, which is termed 'vibration'. The Consciousness Scale in Figure 3 was developed by Dr Hawkins (ref)—not to be confused with Stephen Hawking though! Hawkins developed the scale through his work in kinesiology—the scientific study of human and nonhuman movement addressing physiological, biochemical and psychological dynamic principles of movement.

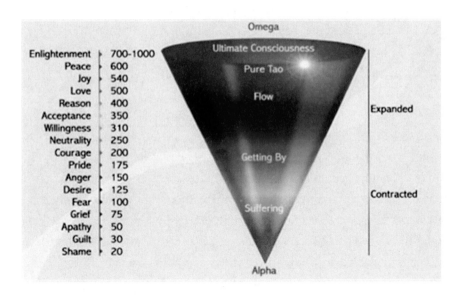

Enlightenment	700-1000	
Peace	600	
Joy	540	
Love	500	
Reason	400	
Acceptance	350	Expanded
Willingness	310	
Neutrality	250	
Courage	200	
Pride	175	
Anger	150	
Desire	125	Contracted
Fear	100	
Grief	75	
Apathy	50	
Guilt	30	
Shame	20	

Figure 3—Hawkins Consciousness Scale

Most of us have an average vibration level of around 250 on the Consciousness Scale, which is considered 'Neutral' as you can see in the diagram. We tend to remain at this vibrational level due to the negative emotions or conditioning and hidden energy blocks that we accumulate throughout our daily lives. Go and see the 'Chakra' pages within this section where it explains more about these blockages. Until we acknowledge and deal with these accumulations, we will not be able to reach higher vibrational states of being. However, we often don't know what we don't know, meaning that we may be totally unaware of our energy state or what we may have been doing to affect it!

For me personally, I believe I am now between 'Reason' and 'Love' on the scale from how I perceive myself at the time of writing this book. I have included the recognised descriptions that are associated with these states in the Appendix of this book, so have a look to see where you believe you are.

Everything within your everyday environment will affect your level of consciousness, your energy, your vibration—TV, movies, social media, websites, news, people, places, objects, food. You can consciously decide how much you allow or disallow these to affect or influence your state of being.

All matter is vibrational in nature and every one of us is vibrating at different frequencies. The higher our vibrational state, the more the positive circumstances we may attract and vice-versa. You behave similarly to how a magnet would in many respects and you can literally attract or repel circumstances or opportunities, for example, based upon your natural operating frequency which is driven by your thoughts, intentions and actions. I just wish I was taught this at a young age because this could really positively influence the way in which you live your life.

There is what is termed the 'unified field', which is all around each and every one of us and throughout the universe. It connects all things and it acts as an invisible information highway. There are other definitions of this 'field', which include 'life-force energy' and other cultures refer to it as 'Prana' or 'Chi' energy. You have probably experienced it without really realising—when you get that call from someone you were just thinking about or when you are thinking exactly the same thing as someone else at the exact same time. We transmit our awareness (consciousness) into this field as an electro-magnetic force or EMF!

The frequency contains information of your thoughts, intentions and emotions and you are literally broadcasting this into this field like a transmitter. It is much like a wi-fi network, but many different frequencies exist within it—some will resonate and some will not. Once you make your broadcasts, you will attract realities or circumstances to you that resonate with your broadcast. You are a transmitter and receiver without even knowing it, so be careful and conscious of what you think, how you feel and how you act!

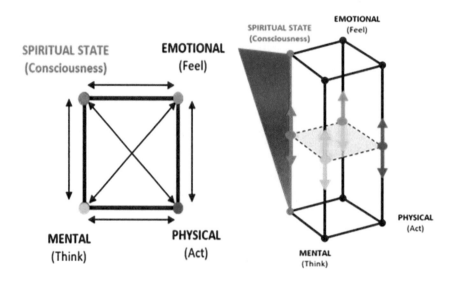

Figure 4—What Affects the Consciousness Scale?

You can see in the diagram above how your thoughts, emotions and actions are all related to your vibrational 'spiritual' state on the consciousness scale. You need all elements to raise together and you cannot just rely on positive thinking, for example, which this diagram demonstrates.

Once you tune in and are conscious of this energy and as your own vibration levels raise higher, you may begin to recognise what is known as 'synchronicities'. Synchronicity is a term originally devised by psychologist Carl Jung that refers to the meaningful (or even miraculous) coincidences that occur in your life. When you experience synchronicity, you'll have experiences that seem far too significant to be mere day-to-day serendipitous encounters or coincidences (Ref: https://lonerwolf.com/synchronicity/).

A growing number of people believe that synchronicity is like a powerful 'wink' from the Universe telling us that yes, we're on the right track. Synchronicity is also believed to be a form of guidance—a way of showing you where to go and what to do next in your life as you proceed through your spiritual awakening and own life-journey.

Here are some examples of synchronicity:

- Overhearing a couple of strangers talk about something that is of great significance to your own life
- Getting the exact message you need the most at the exact right time (e.g. if you're going through a divorce, depression, betrayal, major life change, etc.)
- Meeting the exact right person at the exact right time (e.g. a partner, friend, teacher, etc.)
- Seeing the same symbols or images repeated everywhere (e.g. in magazines, on commercials, on buildings, on tattoos)
- Recurring signs that seem to lead you somewhere special (e.g. your ideal job, home, relationship)
- Strange alignments of birth dates between friends, partners, etc.

I would encourage you to do your own research on synchronicity so that you can be aware of it in your own life and learn to be guided by it. I can certainly relate to these and once I became aware of such occurrences, I could not help to notice them. I have always seen patterns in things from a young age in numbers, letters, shapes, etc. and my memory seemed to store them. I can still recall some of my dad's old car registrations from when I was about 7 or 8 years old. Somehow, my memory appears to be designed to recognise and record such things!

Here are a few examples of things I've noticed over the last couple of years that are related:

- Many, many white fluffy feathers appear where I am walking very often and I sometimes think they are just there anyway, but it seems far too frequent to be 'normal'. They sometimes fall in front of me and even onto my car windscreen whilst waiting in traffic.

Significance: It is often said that finding such feathers are a sign from a higher force that you are protected and being supported by some kind of guardian.

- Robins—it has been known to see several different ones in one walk and they seem to fly to me as if to greet me. I have two in my garden and they are playful with me when I am cutting the grass or doing something in the garden—resting on my mower or getting into a hole I am digging.

Significance: Robins have been associated as spirit animals for thousands of years and its frequent appearance can indicate new beginnings and renewal (both important for me).

- Many number sequences noticed very frequently (some daily or more)— these could be seeing 111 or numerical birth date, for example. Meeting someone really inspiring and finding they share the same birthday as you. There are many examples I could list, but the point is that you begin to notice much more of this and you need to fathom out what the meaning is like a puzzle—can make life more interesting and mystical!

Significance: Numerology is an ancient concept and it is believed that the universe is based upon a numerical system—this really intrigues me and I would encourage you to look this up for yourself and see how our entire world has numerical relationships. Seeing frequent numbers and letters often have meanings that require your decoding like a hidden language.

216

We all typically have desires in our lives which we actively chase or wait patiently for until they arrive so we can attain them. However, rather than chase our desires, we can instead attract them to us by projecting our intentions and emotions into the field—this could be health, wealth, career or anything to be honest. All you need is a good imagination, an authentic emotion and some action!

Only like or identical vibrations can co-exist, so if you are in a high vibrational state you will generally attract people who are loving, compassionate and conscious and similarly you will be a good match to abundance, prosperity and success in life. Conversely, if your vibrational state is low, then you may attract people and circumstances that are more negative, unlucky, less abundant and so forth. We are what we put out! The problem is, we have been doing this sub-consciously and are often never aware of how our thoughts, emotions and actions affect our own reality, but I can tell you that once you are aware and you are conscious of it, you will certainly consider it more and begin to notice where it is having an effect!

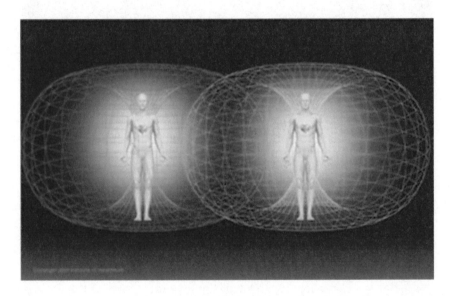

Have you ever met someone that you immediately and intuitively liked or disliked? That has everything to do with their vibes or vibration levels. People's energy, or vibe, can be either negative or positive and we can subconsciously feel these energetic frequencies if they are not a match to our own. The same can be said when you feel a positive energy boost when someone with high energy walks into a room—you literally feel it don't you? It is really going to benefit you in understanding what your energy vibration level is and work on improving it—there are only benefits in doing this, so why wouldn't you!

So, now you know that we all vibrate energetically at a particular frequency. The lower the frequency, the more dense your energy is and your problems seem heavier. At this low frequency, you may find pain or discomfort in your body and experience impacting emotions and mental confusion. It takes a good amount of effort to overcome this to achieve any goals in life and your overall life may have a negative bias to it. You know this when you find everything that you are trying to do is just not working out and it is like hitting a brick wall every time you try to move forward with something.

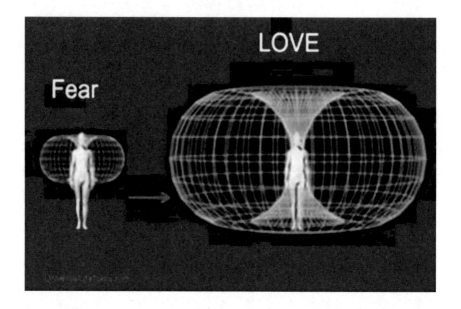

As you raise your vibrational frequency, your physical body feels lighter, emotions are less impacting and your mental state is more positive. Higher the frequency, greater the clarity, peace, love, joy and personal power. Any physical pains in your body dissipate and you can handle situations without causing yourself to become emotionally affected. You will find that your life flows much more easily and synchronicities will become more obvious to you—you can easily manifest whatever you desire! Life feels great at these higher frequencies and you are content and appreciative of the world around you.

I believe that there is also a relationship to whether you are an optimistic or pessimistic person. It is quite well documented in terms of the characteristics on either side and you may be someone who switches between these. Again, once you are more aware, you will air more towards being more of an optimist I would expect.

Here is a great diagram to highlight the differences in mindset:

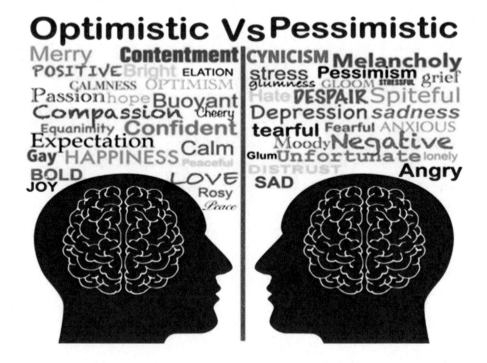

[Ref: https://4enlightenment.com/2019/01/28/optimistic-vs-pessimistic/]

You can quickly see which related characteristics reside with each mindset and those which are going to drag your vibrational state downwards. There are some great quotes that relate to this and I have shared a few below to provoke your thinking:

A pessimist sees difficulty in every situation	Winston Churchill
An optimist sees the opportunity in every difficulty	Winston Churchill
Optimism is the faith that leads achievement	Helen Keller
Nothing can be done without hope and confidence	Helen Keller
Optimism is the foundation of courage	Nicholas M Butler

I think this highlights that it is important to know who you are and how you think so that you can raise your vibration to higher states. There is a lot of synergy between higher vibrational characteristics and those exhibited by the optimist—worth thinking about!

I have put a 'vibration signs' test in the Appendix so go and check that out and see where you stand!

Heart-Brain Coherence

We have been taught that the brain controls the entire body and our heart is merely an organ that pumps blood around our body. In fact, the heart actually sends more signals to the brain than the brain sends to the heart. The signals from our heart trigger significant effects on the brain's function which can influence how we process emotional information and functions that affect memory, attention, perception and problem-solving. (Ref: HeartMath Institute)

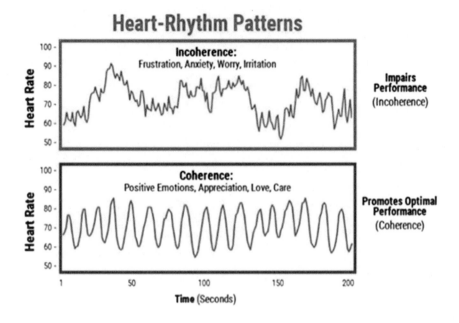

Figure 5—Heart Rhythm Patterns (Ref)

The HeartMath Institute has been researching this subject for over 29 years. It has established a significant, new understanding of our heart's role and measurable responses to underpin their theories. I have referenced and quoted them in this book, since they have pioneered this area of research and many of those who I have looked up to in my own research make specific reference to the HeartMath Institute's work.

In a state of heart coherence with the brain, it has been proven that our heart has the ability to influence the mind and body and this can help us achieve better physical health and emotional resilience. In fact, research has now proven that the heart is 100x more powerful electrically, and up to 5,000x more powerful magnetically than the brain. Yes, the heart runs the show. It actually sends more messages to the brain than the brain does to the heart (Ref: Gregg Braden). The heart's energy field projects up to 3 metres outwardly from the body. It can interact with other individual's hearts and this forms a communication link. You can literally 'feel' the energy of others and sense whether they are a low or higher energy.

Benefits of Heart Coherence:

You can see the state of harmony represented by the lower graph in Figure 5—this is when we achieve a coherent state. This is when the systems in your body are harmoniously functioning together and you will physically feel an improvement within yourself. Your immune system will improve, making you less likely to become ill and you will have more energy.

Here are a few health benefits of heart coherence (ref: www.gaiameditation.com):

- Reduces stress and anxiety (reduction in level of cortisol)
- Boosts your immune system
- Releases anti-aging hormone (DHEA)
- Enhances the functioning of your nervous and digestive systems
- Improves quality of your sleep
- Boosts your energy level

When you achieve the heart coherence state, it also means you are functioning at your peak performance. You will then see vast improvements of your cognitive functions:

- Enhancement of focus and concentration
- Improvement in learning
- Improvement in problem-solving skills

Once your heart is in coherence, you will become much more intuitive and this will influence the decisions you make—hopefully, better ones! This is that 'gut feel' you are probably more familiar with. We should be listening to our heart more—it has a lot to tell us and it can guide us in our lives if we tune into to it. You can find guided meditation can help you achieve this coherence as you begin to learn this yourself—you can noticeably feel this coherence once activated.

There are incredible accounts of patients who have received a new heart from a donor and they have memories and new likes and dislikes that were attributable to the donor themselves—this is another demonstration of what our heart really is. It is almost another brain within our body and it has a memory!

So, how do you raise your vibration? There are several methods and here are some outlined below (Ref: https://www.nexusnewsfeed.com/article/spiritual-psychic/the-top-10-ways-to-raise-your-vibration-in-earths-5d-shift/) (Ref: https://chopra.com/articles/a-complete-guide-to-raise-your-vibration):

- **Inner Inquiry**—probably the first step is to become the observer of yourself—to be committed to witnessing yourself through all events and circumstances of your life. This way, identification with the ego personality is internally challenged.

- **Gratitude and Appreciation**—this is the quickest ways to ramp up your vibration. Try it right now—stop reading and look around the room. Turn your attention to what you are thankful for in this moment. It might be support from friends, the beautiful weather, or the fact that you were blessed with another day on this earth.

- **Meditation**—after the initial soul connection it becomes essential to integrate more soul on a day by day basis. And so regular daily meditation and spiritual practice become utterly essential.

- **Positive Thoughts**—What you think about, you become, and each thought you think creates your future. If the thoughts you think are pessimistic, overtly anxious, or in any way negative, you will likely find what you are looking for. Just as gratitude draws more of the same into your life, so too does impatience, jealousy, and unworthiness.

- **Chakra Attunement**—the soul infuses through the various densities of existence through the chakras. Where these get blocked, it greatly determines your overall vibrational frequency. So, apply chakra meditations on a regular basis to free up the movement of soul into and through the various densities (see more about chakras later in this section).

- **Connection with Nature**—the natural vibrations of life resonate strongly through all the myriad of plant and animal forms around us. Simply sitting in nature and being attentive internally to the effect, can resonate reconnective soul frequencies that release attachment to lower densities and raise vibration.

- **Conscious Diet and Inner Purification**—your body becomes your temple to the divine. And so it needs to be purified through an alkaline diet. Which means the transition from dense processed foods with toxic additives, to a more plant-based diet that facilitates the free flow of soul.

- **Unleashing Creativity**—your soul consists of various frequencies of beingness, which want to come alive and create abundantly. Each of these frequencies can get supressed and lost in the density of life. Unleashing your creativity through art, music, dance, video, audio and writing, for example, can help to activate all the various frequencies in your soul.

- **Following Signs and Synchronicity**—the Universe is doing its upmost to reveal you as a multidimensional cosmic being, at one with everything. It does this through reflective signs and synchronicity. As you witness signs and synchronicities on your path, explore how each makes you feel inside. What new frequencies of being want to now come alive? What is the higher dimensional message? The purpose is to progressively raise your vibration.

- There is a lot of information on this subject nowadays, so go and find methods that work for you!

What Are Our Chakras?

This explains the seven Chakras that exist within your body and what function they represent. You can focus upon these areas during energy healing work and during your own meditation, stimulating the release of blockages or dealing with the issues that caused the blockages in the first place.

Powers   Chakra

Crown
Spirituality, knowing who you are, letting go, enlightenment, awareness.

Third Eye
Intellect, brain, open-mindedness, divine reason, bigger picture, trust.

Throat
Self expression, choice, will, follow your dream, faith, trusting life.

Heart
Love, forgiveness (does you good), compassion.

Solar Plexus
Personality, self-esteem, gut instinct.

Sacral
Creativity and sexuality. Power, control, money, relationships.

Root
Family and social belonging. Safety and security.

Figure 6—Your Body Chakras

Chakra 7—The Crown

Its colour is violet and it is located at the top of your head. It is associated with the cerebral cortex, central nervous system and the pituitary gland. It is concerned with information, understanding, acceptance and bliss. Blockage can manifest as psychological problems.

Chakra 6—The Third Eye

Its colour is indigo. It is located at the centre of your forehead at eye level or slightly above. It is the Chakra of question, perception and knowing. It is concerned with inner vision, intuition and wisdom. Your dreams for this life and recollections of other lifetimes are held in this Chakra. Blockage may manifest as problems like lack of foresight, mental rigidity, 'selective' memory and depression.

Chakra 5—The Throat

Its colour is blue and it is located within the throat. It is the Chakra of communication, creativity, self-expression and judgement. It is associated with your neck, shoulders, arms, hands, thyroid and parathyroid glands. It is concerned with the senses of inner and outer hearing, the synthesising of ideas, healing, transformation and purification. Blockage can show up as creative blocks, dishonesty or general problems in communicating ones needs to others.

Chakra 4—The Heart

Its colour is green and it is located within your heart. It is the centre of love, compassion, harmony and peace. This Chakra is associated with your lungs, heart, arms hands and thymus gland. We fall in love through our heart Chakra, then that feeling of unconditional love moves to the emotional centre commonly known as the solar plexus. When these energies move into the base Chakra, we may have the desire to marry and settle down. Blockage can show itself as immune system, lung and heart problems, or manifest as inhumanity, lack of compassion or unprincipled behaviour.

Chakra 3—The Solar Plexus

Its colour is yellow and it is located a few inches above the navel in the solar plexus area. This chakra is concerned with your digestive system, muscles, pancreas and adrenals. It is the seat of your emotional life. Feelings of personal power, laughter, joy and anger are associated with this centre. Your sensitivity, ambition and ability to achieve are stored here. Blockage may manifest as anger, frustration, lack of direction or a sense of victimisation.

Chakra 2—The Sacral

Its colour is orange and it is located between the base of your spine and your navel. It is associated with your lower abdomen, kidneys, bladder, circulatory system and your reproductive organs and glands. It is concerned with emotion. This chakra represents desire, pleasure, sexuality, procreation and creativity. Blockage may manifest as emotional problems, compulsive or obsessive behaviour and sexual guilt.

Chakra 1—The Base or Root Chakra

Its colour is red and it is located at the perineum, base of your spine. It is the Chakra closest to the earth. Its function is concerned with earthly grounding and physical survival. This Chakra is associated with your legs, feet, bones, large intestine and adrenal glands. It controls your fight or flight response. Blockage may manifest as paranoia, fear, procrastination and defensiveness.

(Ref https://www.zenlama.com/the-7-chakras-a-beginners-guide-to-your-energy-system/)

Traits of a Spiritual Person—Do They Resonate with You?

They Collect Experiences

You have realised that the accumulation of 'stuff' or material things will never truly make you happy. In fact, all it does is serve as an anchor. The more we have, the more it seems that we are physically stuck in one place, unable to leave all of these material goods behind that we have spent years working to obtain, or in most cases, have to spend years working to pay them off.

Travel, adventure, milestones and memories. These are what we should be truly accumulating throughout life and you have realised this. Your mind is constantly searching for your next experience and you are actively selling, or donating, your old 'stuff' in order to pave the way for these new experiences.7

They're Highly Positive

You are increasingly aware of both the negative people that fill your life, and of the negative behaviour you once displayed. You are drawn towards positivity, inspiration and creativity. Your soul yearns to spend time with positive people

227

who feel the same. When you hear negativity you emotionally flinch, that's just not who you are anymore.

At the same time, you do not judge those who are negative, they are not as far along the path as you are yet. Instead you marvel at the negative thought patterns and behaviours you surrounded yourself with in the past. You're eternally grateful that you have evolved from being that person and developed into the optimistic and loving individual you've turned into.

In the same breath, you are constantly exploring personal development, learning new skills and honing existing ones. You have a thirst for knowledge, especially anything to do with Nature, Spirituality, Philosophy etc. You have recognised life is learning, and you never, ever stop being the student.

They Love Immersing Themselves In Nature

You have developed a deep connection with nature and experience extreme cabin fever when you're cooped up indoors for too long. There is nothing quite like being outdoors, feeling the breeze brush across your skin and the sun heating your body. Did you even notice this before? You do now, and you yearn to explore new places and reconnect with old ones.

There is something awe-inspiring about being in the presence of mountains that have stood for thousands of years, unperturbed by the comings and goings of man. It matters not to them who lays claim to certain pieces of land and you laugh at how stupid it must seem to nature that people fight for ownership of something they will never truly own.

You recognise these thoughts and the deepness of them. Recognising that we all have our place on earth, none higher than another, is a key aspect of becoming spiritually awakened. It makes you sad that one species takes away from the planet, where everything else gives back and works in harmony. You hope that changes, and soon.

Their Lives Encompass Synchronicity

Everything falling into place? Once you make a decision that enhances your spiritual journey, the universe makes it very easy to achieve it.

Synchronicity is not a new concept, it was first described by Carl Jung, a Swiss Psychologist, in the 1920s. Synchronicity is the experience of meaningful, related events that are unlikely to be mere coincidence. It has been going on around you the entire time, but now you are clearly able to see the connectedness of everything. The reason that life seemed so hard before was because you were concentrating on the wrong things. Now you are moving forward spiritually, that friction eases and you move forward more confidently.

Synchronicity is always guiding us and it is important to tune into this and listen. Through this we know we are maintaining the correct path and are able to continue on forward.

They Actively Try To Make The World A Better Place

You are much more aware of actions and consequences. Your choices do not only affect yourself anymore, you are consciously thinking of others when you make them. Selfish desires are all but gone and your thoughts are leaning towards how you can contribute to making the world a better place.

Ego holds you back, compassion propels you forward. You witness the suffering and poverty that fills the world and experience a deep sadness. You want your existence to leave the world a little bit better than when you found it.

Making the world a better place doesn't necessarily mean being the one who can change everything. That's impossible for one person unfortunately, it would take the coming together of the majority of people for that to happen. However, knowing that even improving one person's life is in fact, changing the world for one person is a powerful knowledge and, through leading by example, we might instruct others to act in the same way.

(Ref: https://consciouspanda.com/traits-spiritual-person/)

Here are 10 reasons to raise your vibration level—take a look through them and see if they motivate you in some way (Ref: CRAIG MACLENNAN, Blissful Light).

1. Clear Negative Energies

When you raise your vibration, you create an energetic environment where low density, low vibration energies are unable to be and function. Low density and vibration energies can be negative emotions and thoughts, attachments, imprints, entities and even spells and curses. This is probably one of the most significant advantages of raising your vibration as low vibrations energies are no longer part of your reality.

2. Increase Vitality, Well-Being and Wholeness

As low vibration energies are reduced, and you increase high vibrational positive energies a consequence of this is that you feel more alert, vital and focused. You tend to find that this boosts a sense of well-being and wholeness. The things that felt missing are replaced with a stronger sense of being.

3. Experience Oneness with All

The higher your vibration, the more expansive your aura and energies become. You take up more space and feel the underlying energetic connections with all of existence more deeply and profoundly. You tend to feel a more palpable connection and knowing of the universe around you.

4. Emotional, Mental and Spiritual Balance

When lower vibrational energies are removed through the raising of your vibration your emotions, thoughts and spiritual awareness function more optimally, they are both balanced individually and in combination with each other. This is achieved through the removal of blockages and negative energies by raising your vibration.

5. Better Able to Manifest

You may notice an increase in abundance and your ability to manifest. When you are more focused, and in alignment with your desires, you are more able to manifest. Raising your vibration brings this state into balance and provides a platform to manifest more effectively.

6. Gain More Control and Direction in Life

By control, I mean not feeling like you have no say in your life. You may feel more in control of the direction of your life and not subject to events and circumstances around you. This is part of manifestation, but with the focus on being a creator of your life rather than a bystander.

7. Increase in Spiritual Gifts

The higher your vibration, the stronger your connections with the energies around you and the lower the possibilities of blockages within you. This means that your spiritual gifts tend to improve and strengthen the higher your vibration. Also, you may find new spiritual gifts coming online the more you raise your vibration (e.g. clairvoyance, clairsentience, etc).

8. Share Love and Compassion

This reason is so important in the world right now. You may find that you are happier and more loving the higher your vibration rises. These compassionate and unconditional loving energies flow from you to those around you and your environment. This is probably one of the most healing things you can do for those that are around you.

9. Spiritual Grounding

Spiritual grounding may sound like a strange reason to raise your vibration, especially as they seem contradictory. But when you raise your vibration, you strengthen your connection with mother earth. You feel more connected and more grounded the higher you raise your vibration. This may reduce over thinking and feeling separate from life.

10. Self-Empowerment and Personal Development Support

To feel fully empowered is probably one of the most life-changing experiences as you know who you are and what you want. You know just how powerful you are and also how connected you are with the world around you. Raising your vibration may boost this. It also may help with your personal development goals you may have due to the spiritual alignment and removal of negative energies.

1.5 Nutrition and Supplements—making changes to your diet

In 1964, only 1 person in 214 contracted cancer. Today it is 1 in 3 females and 1 in 2 males. The determining factor between health and disease is related to acid or alkaline levels (Ref: https://acidalkalinediet.net/cancercures.php).

I always considered that I ate a relatively healthy diet, but I quickly found elements of my diet that were likely promoting cancer. There are many facets to consider when you begin to analyse nutrition and my particular focus was obviously towards cancer related benefits. It must be highlighted that nutrition in itself forms only one aspect to the holistic approach to the cancer fight which I have endeavoured to demonstrate in this book.

I reviewed many sources of information on this subject and found some common themes in a variety of evidence from anecdotal to through to published research articles. I still feel that I have merely scratched the surface of this because there may also be synergistic, enhancing interactions to consider and how you may need to rotate and adjust the combinations of nutritional elements to keep the cancer outwitted as it learns different survival mechanisms.

I quickly and progressively became vegan as I discovered more about nutrition and its effects upon cancer and indeed your health in general. Whilst it is acknowledged that there are subtle differences between cancers, my approach was generic since I did want to narrow my method too greatly because I would rather most of my arrows to hit a larger target than many miss a small target, using this analogy. It became evident that there are many benefits in your diet becoming more alkaline and I will outline why this important in this section.

Let us first consider the circumstance in which cancer survives. In general, cancer is acidic in nature and thrives in an oxygen depleted environment. This can apply to other diseases too, so becoming more alkaline is more broadly benefitting. If we can make this environment maintain a higher alkalinity and full of oxygen, then this can cause the cancer to struggle to survive, or even manifest in the first place. The cancerous tumours will pull the body's alkalinity down as it promotes a more acidic environment, so this needs to be counteracted.

The cancer diet needs to consist of a variety of foods to address the whole cancer process from providing all the components to boost the immune system to attacking cancer cells, oxygenating them and reducing inflammation. You don't necessarily have to be vegan to meet these objectives, but I was more drawn towards the non-meat and non-dairy aspects, since it removed further possible risk in my opinion due to the pros and cons of these.

It is generally understood that the balance in your diet between approximately 80% alkaline and 20% acidic foods provide the optimal benefits, whilst acknowledging there are further considerations to apply in the combinations of foods (Ref: https://acidalkalinediet.net/acid-alkaline-diet.php).

The image below in Figure 7 shows a general comparison of foods that fall on either side of the scale of acid versus alkalinity. You are able to quickly determine those foods causing most acidity and they most likely feature in your current diet. For those who are looking at this image closely, you may have noticed that there are some non-food elements in the acidic range such as stress, worry and overworking.

These can also have the effect of promoting a more acidic environment in your body, which is the more holistic perspective I want you as a reader to better understand, as I have come to understand. If you are wondering where you are on this scale within your own body, you can test this using simple urine test kits, where your first morning pee can determine your pH level on the litmus strip.

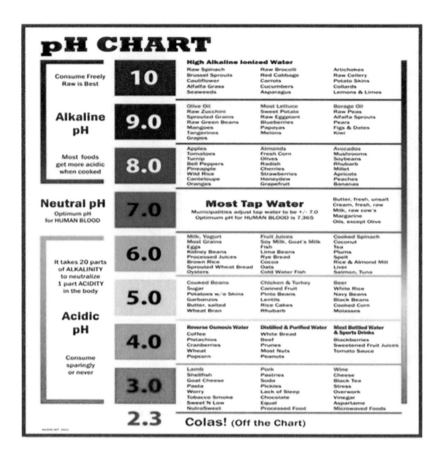

Figure 7—Acid and Alkaline Comparisons

(Image Ref: https://www.wakingtimes.com/2015/04/16/ph-chart-of-alkaline-and-acidic-foods/)

It should not be overlooked that sugar and glucose are key in providing fuel to cancerous cells and this is a controversial subject. Sugar is found in most foods—many fruits contain glucose and carbohydrates are sugars too. Sugar feeds cancer cells, but also feeds the healthy cells and our bodies need a certain amount of this fuel. If you stop the sugar intake, our bodies are clever and will find other ways of getting glucose from proteins and fats, for example. Whilst the effects of sugar on cancer are still divided, it must be noted that cancer cells use about 200 times more sugar than normal cells

(Ref: https://www.webmd.com/cancer/features/cancersugar-link#1). There is a lot of public information that suggests that high sugar intake causes obesity and it is this that can increase your cancer risk. Whilst this is true, there is also a broader consideration to be given to the way in which our bodies handle sugar intake and why it can increase risk to even healthy and non-obese individuals. Sugar is another food source that promotes acidity within the body and this depletes the cellular oxygen by creating an 'anaerobic' environment. We now know that an acidic body is one which is more at risk of developing cancer, or other chronic diseases, so it does highlight that there is benefit in cutting sugar intake where possible and allow our body to function in normal manner without putting strain on the cells attempting to survive in an anaerobic environment.

If the cells in the body become unstable or damaged from a trigger such as a virus or infection, for example, this can initiate an immune or healing response and this response may not be able to de-activate causing cell proliferation and tumour growth.

The cancer's craving for sugar is confirmed to me whenever I have had PET scans where they put a glucose solution into your blood stream—only the cancerous cells light up! This is partly down to the cancer's higher metabolic rate and the activity of the tumour can be determined as a result. So, it means that the cancerous cells love sugar and seem to consume it 'more' than the healthy cells or the concept of PET scans would not work for cancer detection. I will let you judge the role of sugar and cancerous cells for yourself, but it is a complex topic and one which warrants attention.

From Figure 7, you can soon see how the vegan diet biases the nutrition towards the highest alkalinity and this is what motivated my shift in this direction, whilst things like rice, pasta and nuts bring the balance to a healthy overall pH level. The optimal pH level for the human body is reportedly between 7.35-7.45, trending slightly higher than neutral alkalinity.

Once I had determined the higher alkaline foods, I further pursued my objective towards a cleaner diet and this then encompassed foods that were organic and free from preservatives, wherever possible. It is difficult to find organic foods consistently in supermarkets here in the UK, although even in the time I have had cancer there has been very noticeable shift in the commercial availability of both organic food and vegan products.

With my marketing hat on, this confirms to me that a general awareness is building within society and the retailers are having to respond to changing demands—I hope this continues! Organic foods are shown to contain more nutrients due to the way in which they are produced, prepared and processed without the use of chemical pesticides, fertilisers or preservatives. There are many benefits in consuming organic foods and some of these are shown below:

- **Better Overall Health**—due to absence of chemicals and more natural cultivation
- **Antioxidant Content**—free of foreign chemicals that normally react with vitamins and minerals, thus lowering the essential positive antioxidant impacts in food products
- **Better Taste**—apart from nutrition, the mineral and sugar structures are more tasty because the crops are given more time to develop and mature
- **Pesticide Elimination**—pesticide consumption linked to cancers, digestion issues, headaches and weakened immune system
- **No Genetic Modification**—organic foods are not modified and retain all of their natural nutritional benefits. GMO foods are still controversial in their effects upon the human body

(Ref: https://www.conserve-energy-future.com/15-health-benefits-eating-organic-food.php)

During the early stages of transitioning your diet, it is beneficial to conduct some detoxes to cleanse your body and reset it in many respects. There are many detoxes to consider, but chose the following which were found by others to be helpful:

1.Colon Cleanse

You can have up to 3 kg of toxic debris attached to the inside of your bowel walls. The detox will help detach this debris, hydrate and cleanse the bowels allowing them to function more effectively too. I used a magnesium oxide salt mixed in a glass of water which was consumed each morning for ten days.

2.Liver cleanse

Cleansing the liver was the second detox. This involved consumption of a third of a pineapple (incl. stem), two centimetre chunk of ginger, clove of garlic and a tablespoon of extra virgin olive oil. Filtered water was added and all blended to desired consistency. This was consumed every morning over a further ten day period before eating any food. It was advisable to refrain from caffeine three days prior to the liver cleanse.

3.Parasitic Cleanse

Parasites come in all sorts of sizes and forms, but they all comprise the body and immune system. I found an herbalist who made a tincture consisting of wormwood, black walnut hull and cloves. I added a few drops in a glass of water and built up the dosage over a three-week period.

Detoxification can make you feel unwell as your body purges, so make sure you are aware of the symptoms you are likely to experience.

With artificial preservatives, there have been many studies into links with cancer, allergies and mental health problems. Preservatives clearly have a role to play in keeping food fresher for longer, but there is again a balance needed between the persistent need for preservatives. Focusing on cancer in this instance, food additives, such as preservatives, have been shown to cause certain people to metabolise these additives differently which could become carcinogenic in some individuals, but not others.

My approach to this was to generally avoid processed foods and that eliminates the need for preservatives in many cases, since meals are prepared from fresh, organic ingredients. It is the fresh and organic elements which contribute towards a healthier nutrition because the processed and preserved foods will most likely have less nutritional value. It is obvious when you think about it, but you can easily get into habits of convenience with food and that was a notable learning I took from this experience.

(Ref: https://healthyliving.azcentral.com/pros-cons-of-rbgh12228025.html).

There were additional inclusions into my diet which supported the cancer fighting objectives. These were the following:

Additions	Cancer Related Benefits
Bitter Apricot Kernels	Rich in antimicrobial and anti-tumour properties, strengthens immunity, aids digestion, certain pain relief
Sauerkraut	Aids digestion, strengthens immunity, reduces stress, reduces cancer risk caused by DNA damage and cell mutations, strengthens bones
Nutritional Yeast	Preserves immune system, anti-viral and anti-bacterial properties, improves digestion, high protein (for vegans), promotes healthy hair, skin, nails
Chia Seeds	High nutritional content, antioxidants, high protein (for vegans), high Omega-3 fatty acids (for vegans), high calcium (for vegans)

Figure 8—Cancer benefitting additions

You may be surprised that mental and emotional stress can also cause the body to become more acidic due to the production of cortisol, so addressing any stressors in your life is really important for you to maintain a healthy balance in your body. I believe that stress was a major contributing factor in my life in contracting cancer, since there was little else that I could see creating this risk. Have a look at the 'Stress Management' section in this book to learn more about this because so much of all of this is connected.

I was never a regular consumer of alcohol, but contracting cancer made me review all of drinks I consume in general. I removed alcohol consumption entirely because many studies showed that it increased your risk to cancer by significant amounts. One article indicated that the risk of contracting my type of cancer was almost five times more likely for heavy drinkers and still twice as likely for moderate drinkers (Ref: https://www.healthline.com/health-news/how-alcohol-can-increase-cancer-risk#2).

Whilst I wasn't much of a beer drinker, I was a bit of a coffee addict and found that this was more habitual than anything else, but since I was resetting all of my diet, I decided that it would be a good time to ditch the coffee too! During my research, there had been concerns that coffee was possibly carcinogenic, yet more recent studies suggest that it may even be beneficial. However, having noted that my 'higher than average' coffee consumption had not stopped my cancer from developing, it was off my list! I won't forget the headaches though as I was detoxing from the caffeine!

I switched my coffee for green tea and I must admit I didn't like the taste of it at all at first. I was very determined to consume green tea as an alternative to coffee, albeit not the same quantities. Green tea has many benefits which I was keen to leverage, so I persevered until, eventually, I loved the stuff! I later discovered the benefits of essiac tea too and added this to the mix, although I am still not a fan of the taste of it! Fizzy drinks and artificial sweeteners were avoided all together due to the risks outlined in various studies, including cancer. I would encourage your own research in these areas so you can judge these associated risks for yourselves.

Here were my main sources of fluid intake:

My Beverages	Cancer Related Benefits
Green Tea	Antioxidants—improved brain function, cancer protection, heart health Reduces inflammation, boosts immune system
Essiac Tea	Enhances immune system, boosts cardiovascular health, aids digestion, skin health, combats free radicals (cause cell damage), detoxifier
Filtered Water	Removes toxins, lowers cancer risk from chlorine, retention of healthy minerals, removes bacteria, removes fluoride
Juicing	Higher nutrient absorption, good gut bacteria, cancer fighting, lowers cholesterol, helps detox your body

Figure 9—Cancer benefitting beverages

Filtered Water

We purchased an 'Epic' water jug filter that removed almost all of the harmful elements in the tap water, including fluoride. Fluoride in tap water benefits tooth enamel, but eating less sugar and cutting out sweets will naturally benefit teeth. I have not been to dentist in four years and have had no problems despite having teeth susceptible to cavities. Fluoride has been seen to be linked to an array of conditions including cancer, bone problems and certain organ functioning so these outweigh any of the benefits in my mind. The water tastes much better too!

Juicing

There are so many combinations of food products you can use in juicing and my juicing was primarily focused upon raw cancer fighting foods that were packed into a juice which was consumed daily. I have described this basic juice already in this book, but I will include it here for those who are page jumping:

- Fresh lemon (quarters cut and frozen in ice cube tray):Cancer preventing
- Reduces infections—vitamin C
- Improves liver function
- Strengthens nails—mine had become brittle and weak
- Helps balance PH levels—I was on plant-based diet and the more alkaline, the better for cancer

Spinach/Kale:

- Packed with vitamins A, C and K
- Spinach helps as an antacid, which was beneficial for my cancer and its location

Beetroot:

- Improves blood flow—this means more oxygen distribution which cancer doesn't like
- Boosts stamina—I needed this with the chemotherapy impacts
- Detoxifies the liver
- Helps reduce risk of cancer—vitamin C and red cell regeneration to help prevent anaemia

I often included kiwi too to mix it up a little and added filtered water to desired consistency. The kiwi was chosen for its antioxidants and immune health benefits and is also packed with vitamin C!

Supplements

Vitamins and minerals are essential nutrients required for functioning and healing of the body. Insufficient nutrients can result in vitamin and mineral deficiencies and disease can occur. In a perfect world, there wouldn't be a need for supplements if everyone was getting enough of their nutritional needs from their food. However, our diets in general are not consistently high in nutrition and we often need to boost certain areas with the use of supplements. Supplements can also be beneficial for non-nutritional reasons, such as needing help with sleeping better, for example. I ensured that the supplements I took were as natural as possible, meaning not a chemical replication of something.

My reasons for taking supplements were to boost certain areas where I was deficient because of the cancer and to include targeted additions to help fight the cancer and my body's overall resilience to the attack. I progressively found which supplements to include and added them to my regimen. There may well be more to consider, but I was conscious of taking too many without knowing more about the interactions or load it would put upon my body with multiple interactions. Each supplement was chosen for its stated benefit and I have shown these in the table in Figure 10. I tried to take capsule forms of supplements wherever possible because the product would be less processed:

Supplement	Key Cancer Benefits
Fermented cod liver oil	Chronic inflammation, prevent rickets, boost bone health, aid in digestion, and feed the brain
Concentrated butter oil	Organic source of Vitamin A, Vitamin E, & Vitamin K, natural CoQ enzymes, relieve constipation, antioxidant, strengthens teeth and bones, enhances absorption of digestive nutrients
Graviola	Antioxidant, digestive support, found to kill cancer cells and leave healthy cells unharmed, slowing cancer cell growth, boost the immune system
Turmeric	Prevents metastasis, helps kill cancer cells and leave healthy cells unharmed, prevents growth of cancer cells
Natural vitamin C	Antioxidant, immune system boost, targets cancer-causing free radicals responsible for cell damage
Astragalus root	Stress reducer, immune system boost, protects cardiovascular system, detox and protect liver, anti-inflammatory, antioxidants, aids wound healing
Thyme leaf	Reduces blood pressure, cough remedy, immune system boost
Vitamin B12	Helps red blood cell formation, anaemia prevention, promotes bone health, improves mood, energy boost, improve heart health, supports healthy hair, skin, nails
Acidophilus Digestizyme	Balance gut flora, balance immune system, ease diarrhoea
CBD oil	Pain relief, anxiety and depression relief, alleviate cancer symptoms, support heart health, prevents spread of some cancers
THC oil	Promotes cancer cell apoptosis and impairs cancer growth, relief from nausea, pain and inflammation
Mistletoe	Anti-cancer properties where immune system stimulated to kill cancer cells and help reduce tumour size
Vitamin D3 with K2	Regulates immune system, lower blood pressure, maintain healthy lungs and brain function, blood clotting regulation, bone protection, cancer risk reduction

Berberine	Inhibitory effects for some cancers and disrupts the cancer progression process, antioxidant and anti-inflammatory, infection prevention
Selenium	Antioxidant, reduce risk of certain cancers, immune system boost
Zinc	Immune system boost, wound healing, inflammation reduction
Serrapeptase	Inflammation reduction, pain relief, infection prevention, dissolve blood clots
CoQ-10	Cancer prevention via protection of cell DNA and cell survival
Vitamin E	Antioxidant, immune system boost, wound healing, blood clot prevention, slows ageing of cells
Spirulina	Antioxidant and anti-inflammatory, lower cholesterol, anti-cancer properties, reduce anaemia
Oregano oil	Natural antibiotic, lower cholesterol, antioxidant, fight yeast-based infections, anti-inflammatory, relieve pain, anti-cancer properties

Figure 10 —Supplements and benefits

You can see from the benefits that there are some clear themes that relate to the following:

- Inflammation reducing—broadly providing a protective response to harmful attack
- Immune system boosting—helps fight against infections
- Cancer fighting attributes—typically killing cancer cells, preventing or disrupting them
- Healing support—additional assistance to help heal affected areas of your body quickly
- Antioxidants—inhibiting oxidation that may lead to cell damage
- I felt that I was providing my body with another shield of protection in addition to my improved nutritional intake in food and beverages.
- I have included some recommended reading in the Appendix that would help with your own understanding.

1.6 Learning Focus: Nutrition—Part 2

I would never have thought that 'what' you consume has such an effect upon your digestive system until I experienced this for myself. I had always been able to eat or drink practically anything, so had not believed that the cramps and nausea I was feeling was attributable to this. Having learnt what I had from this, I wanted to share this information which may help you, or others you know, with such symptoms.

Food is a common trigger of digestive symptoms. Interestingly, restricting certain foods can dramatically improve these symptoms in sensitive people. In particular, a diet low in fermentable carbohydrates known as FODMAPS is clinically recommended for the management of irritable bowel syndrome (IBS) and other similar conditions.

Let me introduce the FODMAP diet! What is FODMAP anyway?

FODMAP stands for fermentable oligo-, di-, mono-saccharides and polyols. These are the scientific terms used to classify groups of carbohydrates that are notorious for triggering digestive symptoms like bloating, gas and cramps.

FODMAPs are found in a wide range of foods in varying amounts. Some foods contain just one type, while others contain several.

The main dietary sources of the four groups of FODMAPs include:

+ **Oligosaccharides**: Wheat, rye, legumes and various fruits and vegetables, such as garlic and onions.
+ **Disaccharides**: Milk, yogurt and soft cheese. Lactose is the main carbohydrate.
+ **Monosaccharides**: Various fruit including figs, mangoes and sweeteners such as honey and agave nectar. Fructose is the main carbohydrate.
+ **Polyols**: Certain fruits and vegetables including blackberries and lychee, as well as some low-calorie sweeteners like those in sugar-free gum.

If you are like me, then you may have never heard of this breakdown before yet can relate to the foods within each group.

Let's start by looking at the 'GO' and 'NO GO' foods and drinks in the following tables before we talk about the strategy. The following pages quickly show the low and high FODMAP food and drinks, which a very useful reference aid when you are re-evaluating your diet. You may spot things on these tables straightaway which you believe may be causing you issues, but we will review the process later in this section.

Vegetables and Legumes

Low FODMAP	High FODMAP
Bamboo shoots	Garlic
Bean sprouts	Onions
Broccoli (3/4 cup)	Asparagus
Cabbage, common and red (3/4 cup)	Beans e.g. black, broad, kidney,
Carrots	lima, soya
Celery (less than 5cm stalk)	Cauliflower
Chick peas (1/4 cup max)	Cabbage, savoy
Corn (1/2 cob max)	Mange tout
Courgette / Zucchini (65g)	Mushrooms
Cucumber	Peas
Eggplant (1 cup)	Scallions / spring onions (white
Green beans	part)
Green pepper (1/2 cup)	
Kale	
Lettuce e.g. Butter, iceberg, rocket	
Parsnip	
Potato	
Pumpkin	
Red peppers	
Scallions / spring onions (green part)	
Squash	
Sweet potato (1/2 cup)	
Tomatoes (1 small)	
Turnip (1/2 turnip)	

Fruits

Bananas, unripe (1 medium)	Apples
Blueberries (1/4 cup)	Apricot
Cantaloupe (3/4 cup)	Avocado
Cranberry	Bananas, ripe Blackberries

Clementine	Grapefruit
Grapes	Mango
Melons e.g. Honeydew, Galia (1/2 cup)	Peaches
	Pears
Kiwi fruit (2 small)	Plums
Lemon	Raisins
Orange	Sultanas
Pineapple	Watermelon
Raspberry (30 berries)	
Rhubarb	
Strawberry	

Meats and Substitutes

Beef	Sausages (check ingredients)
Chicken	Processed meat (check ingredients)
Lamb	
Pork	
Quorn mince	
Cold cuts e.g. Ham and turkey breast	

Breads, Cereals, Grains and Pasta

Oats	Barley
Quinoa	Bran
Gluten free foods e.g. breads, pasta	Couscous
Savoury biscuits	Gnocchi
Buckwheat	Granola
Chips / crisps (plain)	Muesli
Cornflour	Muffins
Oatmeal (1/2 cup max)	Rye
Popcorn	Semolina
Pretzels	Spelt
Rice e.g. Basmati, brown,	Wheat foods e.g. Bread, cereal, pasta

Nuts and Seeds

Almonds (max of 10)	Cashews
Chestnuts	Pistachio
Hazelnuts	
Macadamia nuts	
Peanuts	
Pecans (10 halves)	
Poppy seeds	
Pumpkin seeds	
Sesame seeds	
Sunflower seeds	
Walnuts	

Milk

Almond milk	Cow milk
Coconut milk (125ml)	Goat milk
Hemp milk (125ml)	Sheep's milk
Lactose free milk	Soy milk made with soy beans
Oat milk (30ml max)	
Rice milk	
Soya milk made with soy protein	

Dairy and Eggs

Butter	Buttermilk
Dark chocolate (5 squares)	Cream
Eggs	Custard
Milk chocolate (4 squares max)	Greek yoghurt
White chocolate (3 squares max)	Ice cream
	Sour cream (over 2 tbsp)
	Yoghurt

Cheese

Brie	Cream cheese (over 2 tbsp)
Camembert	Ricotta cheese
Cheddar	
Cottage cheese	
Feta	
Mozzarella	
Parmesan	
Swiss	

Condiments

Barbeque sauce (check ingredients)	Hummus dip
Chutney (1 tbsp max)	Jam (mixed berries)
Garlic infused oil	Pasta sauce (cream based)
Golden syrup (1 tsp)	Relish
Strawberry and raspberry Jam / jelly	Tzatziki dip
Mayonnaise	
Mustard	
Soy sauce	
Tomato sauce	

Sweeteners

Aspartame	Agave
Acesulfame K	High Fructose Corn Syrup (HFCS)
Glucose	Honey
Saccharine	Inulin
Stevia	Isomalt
Sucralose	Maltitol
Sugar / sucrose	Mannitol
	Sorbitol
	Xylitol

Beer (one max)	Apple juice
Coffee, black	Pear juice
Drinking chocolate powder	Mango juice
Herbal tea (weak)	Sodas with HFCS
Orange juice (125ml max)	Fennel tea
Peppermint tea	Herbal tea (strong)
Water	
Wine (one max)	

Fish, including shellfish, are all considered low FODMAP so can be enjoyed without causing concern. Just make sure that none of them have any garlic or onion associated with them.

There are three main stages to adopting the diet and then evaluating those areas that you may or may not tolerate well. You may still find that some of the low FODMAP food or drinks still cause you problems, so it is really a trial-and-error approach which is very personal to you.

Stage 1: Restriction

This stage involves strict avoidance of all high-FODMAP foods. Please see the preceding tables for your reference—this is a quick step change starting point.

People who follow this diet often think they should avoid all FODMAPs long-term, but this stage should only last about 3–8 weeks. This is because it's important to include FODMAPs in the diet for gut health.

Some people notice an improvement in symptoms in the first week, while others take the full eight weeks. Once you have adequate relief of your digestive symptoms, you can progress to the second stage.

If by eight weeks your gut symptoms have not resolved, this may be because your body may not respond to such changes—it is reported that 30% of people do not respond to the dietary changes. Stress can be a major contributor to triggering these symptoms too, so you may need to look more broadly at your lifestyle to determine the root causes.

Stage 2: Reintroduction

This stage involves systematically reintroducing high-FODMAP foods back into your diet.

The purpose of this is twofold:

+ To identify which types of FODMAPs you tolerate. Few people are sensitive to all of them.
+ To establish the amount of FODMAPs you can tolerate. This is known as your 'threshold level'.

In this step, you test specific foods one by one for three days each.

It is worth noting that you need to continue a low-FODMAP diet throughout this stage. This means even if you can tolerate a certain high-FODMAP food, you must continue to restrict it until stage 3.

It is also important to remember that, unlike people with most food allergies, people with IBS type symptoms can tolerate small amounts of FODMAPs. Although digestive symptoms can be debilitating, they will not cause long-term damage to your body.

Stage 3: Personalisation

This stage is also known as the 'modified low-FODMAP diet'. In other words, you still restrict some FODMAPs. However, the amount and type are tailored to your personal tolerance, identified in stage 2.

It is important to progress to this final stage in order to increase diet variety and flexibility. These qualities are linked with improved long-term compliance, quality of life and gut health.

(Ref: www.ibsdiets.org)

(Ref:www.healthline.com/nutrition/low-fodmap-diet#Benefits-of-a-Low-FODMAP-Diet)

2.Levels of Consciousness

Shame

According to Hawkins, this is one step above death. At this level, the primary emotion one feels is humiliation. It's not surprising that this level, being so close to death, is where most thoughts of suicide are found. Those who suffer from sexual abuse are often found here, and without therapy they tend to remain here.

Guilt

Not too far from shame is the level of guilt. When one is stuck in this level, feelings of worthlessness and an inability to forgive oneself are common.

Apathy

The level of hopelessness and despair; this is the common consciousness found among those who are homeless or living in poverty. At this level, one has abdicated themselves to their current situation and feels numb to life around them.

Grief

Many of us have felt this at times of tragedy in our lives. However, having this as your primary level of consciousness, you live a life of constant regret and remorse. This is the level where you feel all your opportunities have passed you by. You ultimately feel you are a failure.

Fear

People living under dictatorship rule or those involved in an abusive relationship find themselves at this level. There is a sense of paranoia here, where you think everyone is out to get you. Suspicion and defensiveness are common.

Desire

Desire is a major motivator for much of our society. Although desire can be an impetus for change, the downside is that it leads to enslavement to ones appetites. This is the level of addiction to such things as sex, money, prestige or power.

Anger

As one moves out of Apathy to Grief and then out of Fear, they begin to want. Desire which is not fulfilled leads to frustration which brings us to Anger. This anger can cause us to move out of this level or keep us here.

Pride

According to Hawkins, since the majority of people are below this point, this is the level that most people aspire to. It makes up a good deal of Hollywood. In comparison to Shame and Guilt, one begins to feel positive here. However, it's a false positive. It's dependent upon external conditions such as wealth, position or power. It is also the source of racism, nationalism and religious fanaticism.

Courage

This is the level of empowerment. It is the first level where you are not taking life energy from those around you. Courage is where you see that you don't need to be tossed to and fro by your external conditions. This empowerment leads you to the realisation that you are a steward unto yourself, and that you alone are in charge of your own growth and success. This is what makes you inherently human: the realisation that there is a gap between stimulus and response and that you have the potential to choose how to respond.

Neutrality

Neutrality is the level of flexibility. To be neutral, you are, for the most part, unattached to outcomes. At this level, you are satisfied with your current life situation and tend not to have a lot of motivation towards self-improvement or excellence in your career. You realise the possibilities, but don't make the sacrifices required to reach a higher level.

Willingness

Those people around you that are perpetual optimists—this is their level of consciousness. Seeing life as one big possibility is the cornerstone of those operating here. No longer are you satisfied with complacency—you strive to do your best at whatever task you've undertaken. You begin to develop self-discipline and willpower and learn the importance of sticking to a task till the end.

Acceptance

If Courage is the realisation that you are the source of your life's experiences, then it is here where you become the creator of them. Combined with the skills learned in the Willingness phase, you begin to awaken your potential through action. Here's where you begin to set and achieve goals and to actively push yourself beyond your previous limitations. Up to this point you've been generally reactive to what life throws at you. Here's where you turn that around, take control, and become proactive.

Reason

The level of science, medicine, and a desire for knowledge. Your thirst for knowledge becomes insatiable. You don't waste time in activities that do not provide educational value. You begin to categorise all of life and its experiences into proofs, postulates, and theories. The failure of this level is you cannot seem to separate the subjective from the objective, and because of that, you tend to miss the point. You fail to see the forest because you're tunnel-visioned on the trees. Paradoxically, Reason can become a stumbling block for further progressions of consciousness.

Love

Only if, in the level of Reason, you start to see yourself as a potential for the greater good of mankind, will you have enough power to enter here. Here is where you start applying what was learned in your reasoning and you let the heart take over rather than the mind—you live by intuition. This is the level of charity—a selfless love that has no desire except for the welfare of those around them. Gandhi and Mother Theresa are examples of people who were living at this level. Only 0.4 percent of the world will ever reach it.

Joy

This is the level of saints and advanced spiritual people. As love becomes more unconditional, there follows a constant accompaniment of true happiness. No personal tragedy or world event could ever shake someone living at this level of consciousness. They seem to inspire and lift all those who come in contact with them. Your life is now in complete harmony with the will of Divinity and the fruits of that harmony are expressed in your joy.

Peace

Peace is achieved after a life of complete surrender to the Creator. It is where you have transcended all and have entered that place that Hawkins calls illumination. Here, a stillness and silence of mind is achieved, allowing for constant revelation. Only 1 in 10 million (that's .00001 percent) people will arrive at this level.

Enlightenment

This is the highest level of human consciousness where one has become like God. Many see this as Christ, Buddha or Krishna. These are those who have influenced all of mankind.

Ref: https://www.thehealersjournal.com/2013/07/26/hawkins-scale-consciousness-how-to-raise-your-number/

3.Your Vibration Signs Test

(With thanks to https://in5d.com/76-signs-take-the-spiritual-vibration-test/ for this information)

Here is a basic test so that you can identify whether your overall spiritual vibrations are positive or negative. It could highlight some areas of your life that you may need to work on—give it a go:

Low Spiritual Vibration Signs Give yourself A-1 for each one	High Spiritual Vibration Signs Give yourself a +1 for each one
You live in perpetual fear	You live in the vibration of love as much as possible
You lack patience	You're patient
You are a pessimist	You're forgiving
You are narcissistic	You express gratitude
You are self-centred	You often find yourself grounding in nature
You rarely connect to nature	Your gut feelings are ruled by ego
You have no connection to a higher power	You have a strong connection to a higher power
You watch a lot of TV	You are more service to others thank service to self
Your gut feelings are ruled by ego	You rarely watch TV
You listen to dissonant music	You are highly intuitive
You curse and swear often	You listen to uplifting music
You drink alcohol to get drunk	Rarely, if ever, do you swear or curse
You're stuck in the past	Rarely, if ever, do you drink alcohol
The same lessons keep repeating themselves to you	You live in the NOW
You are highly competitive	You learn from your past
You talk badly about others behind their backs	You work well with others

You lack empathy	You are empathic
You feel your life has no purpose	You feel your life has a greater purpose
You are emotionally unbalanced	You are emotionally balanced or working on attaining balance
You criticise more than you laugh	You laugh a lot
You take life too seriously	You enjoy life and appreciate the lesson from good, the bad and the ugly experiences
You ridicule others for being different	You appreciate everyone's contributions to making this world a better place for all of us
You're unable to connect synchronicities	Synchronicity is an everyday awareness
You have an unhealthy diet	You have a healthy diet
You're unwilling to question everything	You question everything
You value money more than love	You value love more than anything
You attract negative people	You attract positive people
You talk about politics more than spirituality	You talk about spirituality topics every day
Children fear you	You're a child magnet, as if they can see your aura
You enjoy low vibrational movies such as horror flicks	You enjoy high vibrational movies such as time travel and friendly extra-terrestrial contact
You look to others to solve your problems	You look within to resolve issues
You look for love from others that you can't find within yourself	You love yourself just as you are
You often ridicule others	You love others, just as they are.

You live a stagnant lifestyle of repetitiveness	You're always looking to grow spiritually and intellectually
You lack personal hygiene	You maintain personal hygiene
You abuse animals	You love animals
You're connected to physical 'things'	You have a cosmic connection
You can't see how everything is connected	You realise everything is connected

SCORING—Add both scores together for an overall score:

<10: Below average, Low Vibration. You have a lot of work to do but you can do it!

11-20: Average High/Low Vibration. You have some work to do, but you're also doing a lot of good things, too!

21-30: Above average, High Vibration. Keep up the good work!

31-38: Stellar, High Vibration. Congratulations! You'll be a light body before you know it!

If your score is 31 or higher, you have very high vibrations and are reaching for the stars with your forming Lightbody!

4. Recommended Reading

Book Title	Genre	Author
Becoming Supernatural	Mind and Body	J. Dispenza
How Not to Die	Nutrition	M. Greger
How to Starve Cancer	Nutrition	J. McLelland
Reiki for Life	Healing	P. Quest
The 4 Pillar Plan	Nutrition and Lifestyle	Dr. R. Chatterjee
The Biology of Belief	Spirituality and The Universe	B. Lipton
The Cancer Revolution	Nutrition, Lifestyle, Cancer	P. Peat
The China Study	Nutrition and Cancer	T. Colin Campbell
The Divine Matrix	Spirituality and The Universe	G. Braden
The Power of Now	Spirituality and The Universe	E. Tolle
The Power of your Subconscious Mind	Spirituality and The Universe	Dr. J. Murphy
The Rainbow Diet	Nutrition	C. Woollams
The Secret	Spirituality and The Universe	R. Byrne
The Seven Spiritual Laws	Spirituality	D. Chopra
What we did to Beat Cancer	Nutrition and Cancer	R. Olifent

This will provide you with a good start. There is a great amount of material online, which has also been immensely helpful and insightful.